Sexual Assault on Campus

The Problem and the Solution

Carol Bohmer • Andrea Parrot

LEXINGTON BOOKS
An Imprint of Macmillan, Inc.
NEW YORK

Maxwell Macmillan Canada
TORONTO

Maxwell Macmillan International
NEW YORK   OXFORD   SINGAPORE   SYDNEY

Library of Congress Cataloging-in-Publication Data

Bohmer, Carol.
    Sexual assault on campus : the problem and the solution / Carol
Bohmer and Andrea Parrot.
      p.   cm.
    Includes bibliographical references and index.
    ISBN 0-02-903715-8
    1. Rape—United States.   2. Women college students—United States—
Crimes against. I. Parrot, Andrea. II. Title.
    HV6561.B65   1993
    364.1'532'0973—dc20   93-22067
                                           CIP

Copyright © 1993 by Lexington Books
An Imprint of Macmillan, Inc.

Lexington Books
An Imprint of Macmillan, Inc.
866 Third Avenue, New York, N.Y. 10022

Maxwell Macmillan Canada, Inc.
1200 Eglinton Avenue East
Suite 200
Don Mills, Ontario M3C 3N1

Macmillan, Inc. is part of the Maxwell Communication Group of Companies.

Printed in the United States of America

printing number
1 2 3 4 5 6 7 8 9 10

*To all the survivors of sexual assault
who became crusaders to make this problem
less severe for those who will follow them,
and to all the sexual assault victims
who died as a result of their assaults.*

*We also dedicate this book to Frank Carrington,
the father of the Victim's Rights Movement.*

Contents

Foreword

Quite simply, this is a book campus administrators and law enforcement officials cannot afford to leave unread. Sexual assaults are occurring on college and university campuses in larger numbers than even they might imagine. Recent statistics show one-fourth of all college women will experience some form of sexual assault by the time they graduate, and campus rapes are notoriously underreported.

To address this serious problem, and countless reports that certain college and university officials were mishandling rape allegations, I co-authored and introduced in Congress the "Campus Sexual Assault Victim's Bill of Rights Act of 1991." This legislation was modified and passed by Congress and signed by the President in 1992, as this important book explains.

Professors Bohmer and Parrot deserve high praise for their joint effort which should inspire others concerned with the well-being of students on campus—parents and other family members, rape crisis counselors, and yes, even my fellow lawyers! The book's numerous case studies put a face on the statistics and graphically illustrate appropriate and inappropriate institutional responses to campus rape allegations.

Like other crimes too prevalent today, we will never be able to completely eliminate sexual assaults on our college and university campuses. However, effective steps can be taken to significantly reduce their incidence. Education and prevention programs and swift and certain punishment for this heinous crime can be effective deterrents. The "boys will be boys" mentality must be removed from society's mindset and be replaced by the conviction that acquaintance rape is rape, and rape is a serious crime.

In addition to rape prevention and awareness efforts on campus, there is much room for improvement in the way college officials respond to the needs of individual rape victims. As hearings on my legislation revealed, many campus rape victims suffer worse trauma from the mishandling of their rape allegations than from the actual assaults.

Professors Bohmer and Parrot have collaborated on a truly unique book that should be of invaluable assistance to those responsible for implementing the Campus Sexual Assault Victim's Bill of Rights Act. Obviously, this law will only be effective if properly implemented, which is why I strongly encourage colleges and universities to follow both the letter and spirit of the law as they adopt policies to address campus rape.

In closing, I want to commend Professor Andrea Parrot and Professor Carol Bohmer for writing this important book, and Dr. Parrot for her testimony and counsel on the recent landmark legislation. A safe and trusting learning environment for all students—male and female alike—is a prerequisite for maximizing educational opportunity and growth during the formative years in a young person's life. This book helps secure such an environment.

Representative Jim Ramstad (R—MN)

1

Introduction

"Bard Coed: Fellow Student Raped Me and Confessed in Letter" (*New York Post,* 8/28/91)

"Colleges Degrade Rape Victims" (*USA Today,* 6/11/91)

"University, Blamed in Rape, Is Told to Pay Victim" (*New York Times,* 3/29/92)

"Parental Emotions Are Also on Trial in Lurid St. John's Sex Abuse Trial" (*New York Times,* 6/24/91)

"College-Rape Risk Linked to Earlier Assaults" (*Palm Beach Post,* 8/17/92)

"Campus Justice on Trial" (*Dallas Morning Post,* 8/25/91)

These recent headlines highlight the fact that sexual assault on college campuses is a major problem. The public is now beginning to recognize what some have known for a while: that women can no longer feel safe on college campuses.

The largest study of sexual assault on the college campus suggests that a female student's risk of being sexually assaulted is 25 percent. This is probably an underestimate, as many women who are assaulted drop out of school.[1] Very few cases are reported to school or other authorities; fewer still are pursued through campus judicial procedures; a minuscule proportion are reported to the police; and only a fraction of those result in conviction. When a case is reported, campus authorities often mishandle the case, causing further trauma to the victim. In many cases, the mishandling leads to the polarization and alienation of many members of the campus community and can even result in civil lawsuits and subsequent media attention.

Schools where recent cases have been in headlines in major newspapers include St. John's University, Carleton College, the University of Southern California, and the College of William and Mary.

This concern about campus sexual assault is part of a growing awareness of many aspects of sexual behavior that have previously been ignored by the public. *Acquaintance rape, date rape, sexual assault,* and *sexual harassment* have all become household terms for Americans in the 1990s. Many people first began hearing about these issues with the convictions of Nigel Clay and Mossy Cade, University of Oklahoma football players. Then there was the highly publicized conviction in the gang rape case of a mentally retarded high school girl in Glen Ridge, New Jersey in which she was raped by members of that town's high school football team. The gang rape trial of the St. John's University lacrosse team received extensive media coverage in the summer of 1991. Then, in the fall of that year, Supreme Court nominee Clarence Thomas was accused of sexually harassing law professor Anita Hill when he was her work supervisor. Even the United States Navy was implicated in sexual assault and harassment charges with the Tailhook scandal, which eventually led to the firing of three admirals for their reluctance to investigate the event properly. In 1992, the media had a field day with the acquaintance rape trials of William Kennedy Smith and Mike Tyson. In the same year, a woman filed a civil suit against twenty current and former members of the Cincinnati Bengals football team for participating in a gang rape against her or standing by and watching while she was assaulted.

Several other campus cases were also highlighted in the media, including articles in the *New York Times* and *Time, Newsweek,* and *People* magazines, not to mention on numerous talk shows. For example, Kristen Buxton went public with her case against Colgate University. Katie Koestner was on the front cover of the issue of *Time* in which she told the story of her rape at William and Mary. Carleton College was sued by four women for failure to act responsibly following rapes reported to the college; the suit was settled out of court in the fall of 1991.

Sexual assault committed by college athletes has been receiving a great deal of media coverage. In response to a charge of rape in which the assailant was an athlete, a coach at a Big Ten college phoned the victim and pressured her to drop the charges so she wouldn't hurt the player's reputation and the team's ability to win. Another coach expressed his priorities when he told a television reporter, "I think that if rape is inevitable, [the woman should] relax and enjoy it."[2]

Between 1990 and 1992, these behaviors have occupied the headlines of the national media. People have been exposed to allegation after allegation of sexual assault. Frequently, both the men accused and their victims are in college at the time of the assault. This exposure has heightened the public's awareness of the problems of sexual violence in our society in general, and on the college campus in particular.

One of the most widely publicized cases of acquaintance gang rape on a campus was the alleged assault, mentioned above, by members of the St. John's University lacrosse team. In that case, three of the men were acquitted by the court, but the university subsequently expelled them. Even though they were not convicted in criminal court, university officials did believe that they had behaved immorally and in violation of the St. John's code of conduct. Such actions on the part of the St. John's administration illustrate one of the major arguments of this book: while the offensive behavior may be the same, the standards for dealing with it (and the goals for such treatment) are very different in criminal court and on the campus. This book will discuss these differences and their implications. It will also consider why, even with all the recent media publicity, few people on college campuses seem to have a clear idea about how to handle the problem of campus sexual assault. That is not to say that the problem has gone unnoticed by the college community; many administrators are struggling to develop policy and procedures to handle such cases when they occur, as well as trying to prevent them from occurring.

Terms

The terms *sexual assault, acquaintance rape,* and *date rape* are often used interchangeably and incorrectly. *Sexual assault* is a general term that describes all forms of unwanted sexual activity. It includes, but is not limited to, rape. Other forced sexual experiences, such as forced oral or anal intercourse or sexual experiences not involving intercourse, are all included in the definition. *Acquaintance rape* describes a rape in which the victim and the assailant know each other, whether they are friends, spouses, lovers, or people who just know each other slightly. *Date rape* is included in the definition of acquaintance rape and describes a rape that occurs while the victim and the assailant are on a date. In both criminal court and campus judicial hearings, cases of acquaintance rape and date rape either are not prosecuted at all or are treated very leniently, despite the fact that both fit into the legal definition of rape.

Traditional rape law only applied to male-female forced vaginal intercourse. In the 1970s, as part of the women's movement, there was an effort to have rape laws revised so that they would be more sensitive to what really happened, more gender neutral, and less punitive toward women. It was believed that such changes would help rectify the situation in which rape had the lowest conviction rate of any major felony. To achieve this goal, some states changed their statutes so that the term *rape* was replaced by the term *sexual assault*, usually separated into several degrees of seriousness. Other states kept the term *rape* but applied it more broadly, for example, when men were victims. Still others continued to use such terms as *deviate sexual intercourse* for anal and oral sex.

For these reasons, it is impossible to give an exact legal definition of rape. The definition of rape, however, generally covers sexual intercourse against a victim's will and without the victim's consent. In other words, if a victim is forced to have sexual intercourse after she or he says no and means it, that is rape. The victim does not even have to *say* no, however, if she or he is mentally incapacitated and therefore unable to consent (whether through retardation, drugs, or alcohol), or fearful for her or his safety or life.

People sometimes confuse *sexual assault* and *sexual harassment*, or use the terms interchangeably. They are, however, different. Sexual harassment is related more to the abuse of power, whereas sexual assault is related to force. Sexual assault is a criminal offense as well as a behavior for which there is a civil remedy. Sexual harassment, on the other hand, is *only* actionable in civil law, usually under Title VII of the Civil Rights Act of 1964 (relating to employment) or Title IX of the Education Act of 1972 (in the educational context). Sexual harassment that takes place outside an employment or educational context is not usually actionable in law except under general harassment laws.

Elements necessary for a situation to be sexual harassment are as follows: (1) there is unwanted sexual attention or touching that causes emotional discomfort which interferes with a person's work or academic performance or creates a hostile, offensive or intimidating environment, (2) the violation is related to gender, and (3) the assailant exercises power over the victim (however, assailants can also be co-workers). Behaviors that may constitute sexual harassment include sexual comments & jokes, invading another's personal space boundaries, unwanted verbal sexual advances, unwelcome personal invitations, unwelcome physical advances, unwelcome explicit sexual propositions, and sexual coercion or bribery.

Sexual harassment is usually actionable only if the victim makes it clear to the harasser directly or indirectly that the behavior is offensive, or if the behavior violates the "reasonable woman standard" (now beginning to replace the "reasonable man standard" that was traditionally used) of what most reasonable women would consider to be sexual harassment. Even if the case is not actionable, the college still should make it clear to the harasser which behaviors are unacceptable. Despite the differences between sexual harassment and sexual assault, many college policies use the terms interchangeably. We believe that this policy is inappropriate and will discuss the reasons for this in Chapter 5. We will not address sexual harassment directly in this book, except to allude to cases in which lessons may be learned that also apply to sexual assault.

In this book we will be using the term *victim* to refer to people who claim to have been sexually assaulted. Even if the alleged perpetrator was not found guilty, that does not mean that the person assaulted does not still feel like a victim. In fact, the victim may suffer from a more severe case of rape trauma syndrome if the defendant is acquitted, because she is likely to feel more traumatized and alone if she thinks that no one believes her. In addition, the victim may be afraid because the defendant is free to violate her again.

The term *defendant* will be used to refer to those who are accused of sexual assault, unless they have been found guilty, or unless we are discussing a hypothetical case where we presume the man to have sexually assaulted the victim. In those cases we will use the terms *perpetrator, assailant,* or *rapist.* Where necessary, we will use the word *alleged* to emphasize that there has been no finding of guilt. We have chosen the word *defendant* for general use because it does not mean that the man has committed the crime, only that he has been charged with the crime.

Incidence

Most of what we know about acquaintance sexual assault comes from studies conducted using college populations and from cases that have occurred on college campuses. Acquaintance sexual assault is not a new phenomenon. The first study looking at the issue of acquaintance rape was done in 1957 by Clifford Kirpatrick and Eugene Kanin at Purdue University.[3] They did not, however, use the term *date rape* to refer to sexual aggression in relationships and dating. Instead, they referred to the victims as "offended girls," and to sexual assault as "a progressive pattern of exploitation." Despite the absence of discussion in the literature before Kirpatrick and Kanin, we are sure that the problem existed before then. Because of different social mores, however, sexual assault probably did not often happen on the first or second encounter; rather, it was more likely to happen later in the relationship. Many victims of date rape from decades ago have shared their stories with us to testify that acquaintance rape has a long history.

Most of the empirical research on date rape, however, has been done in the last decade, starting with a 1982 study by Koss and Oros published in *Ms.* magazine.[4] Data from recent studies done nationally reveal that between 20 and 25 percent of college women have experienced forced sex (including rape, oral sex, anal sex, and other forms of penetration) at some time during their college careers,[5] and approximately one-third of those women had experienced it prior to college.[6] As many as 15 percent of men also indicate that they were forced to have sex when they did not want to.[7] Only about 5 percent of male college students commit rape knowing it is wrong, but continue to do so; however, 10 to 15 percent commit acquaintance rape and date rape without knowing that what they are doing is wrong.[8]

The number of sexual assaults against women on college campuses is alarmingly high. The reasons for this include societal socialization of males; females and males having almost unlimited access to each other as a result of coeducational residence halls and the abolition of curfews; and students advertising for rides on unmonitored "ride boards."[9] Sexual assault on campus usually happens to women early in their college careers. It frequently takes place after a party, especially one held in a fraternity house and where alcohol is served.

Peer pressure, alcohol, and all-male groups are important elements that combine to increase the likelihood of campus sexual assault.

The time line in Table 1–1 chronicles the patterns of identification and increased awareness of sexual assault since the 1950s. Although it is not a new phenomenon, as the reader has seen, it has only recently been named and recognized as a serious social problem.

College Response

The problem of sexual assault on campus is one with which all colleges must deal. It happens at large, small, urban, rural, public, private, religious, secular, single-sex, and coed colleges. It even happens at those schools where no cases are reported. What is less clear than the existence of sexual assault at all campuses is its incidence on a particular campus. Because so few cases are reported, it is very difficult for an individual school to know the extent of the problem without the kind of monitoring that few have so far undertaken. Those that do often find that the incidence is fairly similar to that reported in the nationwide research.

There are a variety of ways in which college and university administrations view and respond to acquaintance rape and sexual assault. Each approach is accompanied by implicit messages that reflect the administration's attitude toward acceptable male and female behavior. The way in which administrations deal with acquaintance rape cases that are brought to their attention will in some part determine the extent to which future cases will be reported. A 1986 example illustrates this point.

A junior football player at a large northeastern university was charged in criminal court with two counts of first degree rape for forcing a first-year female student to have sex. The district attorney refused to present the case to the grand jury. The athlete pleaded guilty to the misdemeanor of sexual misconduct and the judge sentenced him to three years probation and three hundred hours of community service. In a campus judicial hearing an administrative tribunal from the university advised no sanctions; the student could continue to attend the university, play football, and retain his scholarship. The university chancellor overruled the decision of the tribunal and placed him on probation and prohibited him from playing his first five games.[10]

TABLE 1-1

Landmark Events in Acquaintance/Date Rape History

1957	First documentation (by Kanin) in the scholarly literature of sexual aggression between dating couples.
1975	Rape laws began to change to allow for easier prosecution.
1976	*Against Our Will,* Susan Brownmiller's historical treatise on rape, published (coined the term *date rape*).
1978	*Rideout* case in Oregon; first husband still effectively living with his wife tried for marital rape.
1979	Landmark two-part study by Giarrusso, Goodchilds, Johnson, and Zellman revealed significant percentage of teenagers believed forced sex on dates was sometimes acceptable (Giarrusso et al., 1979; Goodchilds et al., 1979; *see also* Goodchilds et al., 1988).
1979	Irresponsible portrayal of date rape on the soap opera "General Hospital": Luke raped Laura, and she left her husband to marry him.
1981	Study by Neil Malamuth in which 35% of college men indicated some likelihood that they would rape if they could be assured of getting away with it.
1982	First use of the term *date rape* in widely read national magazine (*Ms.* magazine article based on Koss's research).
1984	First syndicated talk show ("Donahue") on date rape.
1985	Cathleen Crowell Webb admitted to falsely accusing Gary Dotson of rape after he spent eight years in prison for the alleged crime, thereby reinforcing the myth that women frequently charge rape falsely.
1985	Nationwide survey of rape by Dr. Mary Koss, including more than 6,100 college students and 30 college campuses, documented that one in four college women have experienced rape or attempted rape.
1986	National television commercial condemning date rape (from a male perspective) produced by the Santa Monica rape treatment center.
1986	Syracuse University football player earned national recognition for pleading guilty to sexual misconduct after being charged with rape and sexual assault. Syracuse University found him innocent of any wrongdoing.
1987	Harvard Law School professor Susan Estrich's *Real Rape* published (a book about how acquaintance rape is treated by the legal system).
1987	Soap opera "All My Children" ran segment on date rape in which rapist was convicted and sent to prison.
1988	Robin Warshaw's book, *I Never Called It Rape* (based on Koss's nationwide survey of college campuses) published; first book on acquaintance rape written for general audience.

TABLE 1-1 (*continued*)
Landmark Events in Acquaintance/Date Rape History

1988	*The Accused*, a film about acquaintance gang rape, released. Jodie Foster won Academy Award for role as rape victim.
1989	Made-for-television documentary, "Against Her Will," focusing on date rape on college campuses, narrated by Kelly McGillis on Lifetime Cable Network.
1989	Jury in *State of Florida* v. *Lloyd* acquitted defendant on rape charges because victim was wearing lace "short shorts" and no underwear.
1989	Made-for-television, prime-time movie, "When He's Not a Stranger," portrayed date rape on a college campus.
1990	Glen Ridge High School football players charged with gang rape.
1991	St. John's University lacrosse players charged with gang rape were acquitted.
1991	Carleton College settled a civil suit with four students who claimed to have been raped while at Carleton.
1991	Justice Clarence Thomas was accused of sexual harassment by law professor Anita Hill during his Supreme Court confirmation hearings.
1991	William Kennedy Smith was tried and acquitted for date rape in Florida.
1992	Mike Tyson was tried and convicted for date rape of a Miss Black America beauty pageant contestant.
1992	Tailhook Navy sexual harassment scandal occurred; several high-ranking naval officials were fired as a consequence of their mishandling of the events.
1992	20 current and former members of the Cincinnati Bengals were named in a civil suit for either participating in or watching a gang rape.

Source: Adapted from Parrot & Bechhofer (1991).

Subsequent victims at that institution were probably more reluctant than usual to report cases to the administration, when they realized that an assailant would be treated so leniently.

Until very recently, colleges had no obligation to publicize statistics of the number of reported sexual assaults on their campuses; thus, we know very little about the actual number of cases reported. We do know that the way in which authorities handle these cases can vary considerably from one college to another. In some instances the college administrators view a charge seriously and, after careful consideration of the facts, take formal action. This may include referring the case to the district attorney for criminal prosecution and/or adjudicating the case in the campus judicial system. These administrators make it clear on campus that they do not tolerate sexual assault; when someone is found guilty of the offense, he is routinely expelled from the school. In other instances the administrators do not believe that acquaintance rape exists, and therefore do not view any charge as truthful. This is especially true in those cases where both parties agree that sexual intercourse occurred, but disagree about whether there was consent.

In yet other situations, the administration may view the case as a serious university matter and worry that such a charge may reflect poorly on the institution. They fear that the case may have a negative impact on future admissions, that the institution will receive fewer gifts from alumni, or that it may become a third-party defendant in the case. The administration may attempt to silence a victim by bringing charges against her for having been drinking alcohol while under the age of twenty-one. Such administrative action will most likely keep other women from reporting acquaintance rapes on that campus. In one case, the administration tried to silence the resident assistant to whom rapes had been reported: he was ordered to keep quiet about the alleged rapes, or else "jobs would be at stake."[11]

A fear of lawsuits, however, may become self-fulfilling. To the extent that the authorities refuse to take action on complaints, they may be increasing the likelihood that a frustrated victim will turn to civil law to file a suit against the institution. In addition, with the new student right-to-know legislation (see Chapter 9), if an assailant is found guilty at a judicial hearing, information about that sexual assault must be made public in admissions materials upon request.

In some instances of campus sexual assault, the victim is assaulted because of the negligence of the institution or some member of the campus community. Many campuses have not been able or willing to deal ethically and appropriately with the causes of the problem, the offenders, or the victims, and the result is increasing numbers of civil suits against the colleges. There have already been cases in which an institution has been named as a third-party defendant in rape cases, several of which are detailed below.

Four women from Carleton College in Minnesota alleged that Carleton had knowledge that two men were rapists on that campus, and that it did not act in a responsible way to protect other women at Carleton from those men. The women, who were sexually assaulted by the assailants after the college knew them to be rapists, sued the college. In 1991 the college settled for an undisclosed sum after a protracted legal battle.

In a case at a large northeastern university, several fraternity brothers had been found guilty of sexually assaulting women in their fraternity house. The fraternity house contained a room with locks on the outside for the purpose of having sex with reluctant women. As a result of the finding of guilt, the fraternity's charter was rescinded for four years. The dean of students and the university were sued by the fraternity and its alumni for improper actions because the revocation of the charter should have been decided by a different hearing board on campus. The lawsuit was eventually dropped.

At another large northeastern university, after an alleged gang rape in a fraternity that resulted in the suspension of the fraternity from campus for six months, the university was sued by the fraternity. No action was taken against the individuals involved. The victim was paid a substantial sum of money by the university on the understanding that she would not take the matter further.

"The identity of this fraternity is confidential and further details about the case are not available. Whether buying off a victim who might have brought a civil suit against the university is a proper use of tax-exempt institutional funds was never publicly discussed. The university was satisfied with the resolution because the adverse publicity ceased. The alumni who are substantial contributors were mollified. The fraternity brothers were relieved that they would not be tried or punished. The women's groups were outraged but impotent. And so the matter was closed.[12]

Many colleges are discovering, too late, that their existing policies and procedures are woefully inadequate to address the special needs posed by campus sexual assault. For example, they often have no way of holding closed hearings, no way of separating the victim from the defendant before the case is heard, and no real definition of the behavior that is to be considered unacceptable. In addition, they do not train the judicial board about rape myths, or disabuse board members of their beliefs in the sexual double standard (we will discuss these issues in detail in Chapter 5). Below are two actual acquaintance rape cases that illustrate the inadequacy of many existing college policies and the ineffective way college administrators are dealing with cases.

> During spring semester Eric, a college senior, was charged with raping a woman while she was drunk at a fraternity party. There was strong evidence to support the charges, and the case was to be heard by the Judicial Board on the campus. Eric's attorney kept applying for continuances until the semester was over. By that time, Eric was about to graduate, and he hoped that a guilty charge against him after he graduated would amount to no more than a "slap on the hand." If Eric were to be found guilty while he was a still a student he could have been suspended, expelled, given mandatory counseling, put on social probation, etc. However, once he graduated, the university would be powerless to punish him."[13]

> Katie Koestner was raped at the College of William and Mary by another student, who was found guilty by the college administrator hearing the case. He subsequently told Katie, "I did find him guilty but I talked to him for a couple of hours this morning and I think he is a good guy. . . . You two should work through this little tiff and get back together next semester."[14] This response indicates how little administrators can understand about the impact of rape on the victim.

As Peggy Sanday, the author of a book about a fraternity gang rape, puts it, "The strongest signal a university can send to its students that unethical and illegal conduct will not be tolerated is to take two simple measures: file criminal complaints and suspend or expel all members of the college community who violate the law or basic norms of decent behavior. This applies to groups such as fraternities as well as to individual students."[15]

Why Victims Rarely Report

Even though sexual assault is relatively common on college campuses, few cases are reported to the authorities, and even fewer of those cases are referred to the criminal justice system or for campus judicial action. Campus authorities often do not take any action on cases that come to their attention. Victims usually do not report cases to anyone, especially the authorities, because they often believe that they are at fault for drinking and for going out voluntarily with the men who raped them. They often worry that the authorities will blame them for the rape. The assailant, and some authorities, often also believe that the woman brought the assault on herself and was "asking for it," and that therefore it was not a rape.

Many women do not report because they know that the college does not take complaints seriously. They decide that it is not worth the trauma of going through a judicial proceeding when the chances are high that nothing will happen to the defendant. In a well-publicized case at Brown University, women took matters into their own hands and made a list on the bathroom walls of the male students whom they said had raped them.[16] This served as a warning to other women to beware of these men, given that the administration did not seem to be protecting the women students. It also caught the attention of the administration, which has since begun to take these cases much more seriously.[17]

Swanson, Chamelin, and Territo have suggested several reasons for victims' failure to report sexual assault to authorities: lack of belief in the police ability to apprehend the subject; concern that the victim would receive unsympathetic treatment from the police and would have to go through discomforting medical procedures; interrogation by the police and attorneys, embarrassment from the publicity; and fear of reprisal by the rapist.[18] Others have pointed out that the victim fears that she would be further victimized by the court proceedings.[19] If victims do report an assault to the authorities, they often fear, among other things, that their names will be made public. The media have struggled visibly with the decision about maintaining the anonymity of the alleged victim in a sexual assault case. In May 1991 a revision to NYS Law Section 50-b of the civil right law protects the identity of victims of a sexual offense. Some people argue that because the accused's reputation is called into question—and may even be ruined during a rape trial—the victim should be held accountable for her allegations, especially if a defendant is found to be not guilty. Logic applied by the media suggests that according to the law, if the defendant is found not guilty, he did not commit that crime, and so the plaintiff is no longer a victim. Therefore, many newspapers have decided to report the alleged victim's name in the event of an acquittal.

Our Research

The research that forms the basis of this book has included interviews with a wide range of people who are involved with the problem of campus sexual assault. We have talked to campus administrators at all levels of college administration. We have interviewed many campus sexual assault victims, ranging from those who did not report the assault at all to those who reported to the campus authorities, the police, or both. Several victims had decided to sue their assailant, the college, or both; some of the women we have talked to contemplated suing in civil court but then decided against it. We have also interviewed the parents and the attorneys of those victims for whom a lawsuit was contemplated or filed. In addition, we have examined the campus codes of approximately fifty colleges of all types, in all regions of the country.

We believe that interviews with as wide a range of victims and administrators as possible is very important for our understanding of the problems of campus sexual assault. Through these interviews, we have hoped to understand better how victims feel about their assault and the handling of it by the college. Finding victims has not been easy because, as has been mentioned, many do not report their assault. We know that many of them drop out of school or transfer, usually without notifying the school of the reason. Therefore, it is difficult to obtain general information about the responses of victims of campus sexual assault. By studying in detail as wide a range of victims as possible, as well as others involved in the problem and the procedures undertaken to handle campus sexual assault, we have been able to piece together a picture of what happens both to victims and to their assailants.

We have also focused on those victims who take the process through to a court case. Through them, we have been able to learn a great deal about what happens in the worst cases. These victims are among those who are most critical of the circumstances leading to their assault, as well as of the way it was handled by the institution. Their experiences provide many lessons as to how colleges can handle these cases well and thereby minimize the risk of being sued.

As part of our research, we have also been following all the cases on campus sexual assault that have been or are presently in the courts. This has provided us with additional information about which cases do end up in court. From this material, we can determine exactly what behavior places a college at the greatest risk for a lawsuit.

Finding these cases, like finding victims, is not an easy matter. There is no central nationwide register of all the cases in which campus sexual assault victims have sued their institutions. Only cases that are reported can be obtained through the traditional law library sources; most of the cases we have been following have not reached (and probably never will reach) the stage where there is a full hearing, let alone an appellate decision or even a report of the trial. For this reason, in attempting to collect a list of these cases, we have had to rely on word of mouth to obtain information. Although we have developed a network of sources through lawyers, conferences, and personal contacts, we have no way of knowing the extent to which this collection represents the universe, an unbiased sample, or the direction of any possible bias.

It is clear, however, that the group of young women who sue their institutions after having been raped is very small, especially given what we know about the extent of the problem of campus sexual assault. We have interviewed the victims, their lawyers, and family members in only about a dozen cases in which court action is pending; there are a number of other cases about which we have obtained information from court reports. Despite what may look like long odds, however, from the perspective of the college the damage done by such a lawsuit is so great that a school would want to avoid it at all costs.

Conclusion

Concern for the problem of campus sexual assault has been increasing among members of the college community as well as the public. It has been the subject of national debate on major television shows, and even in congressional hearings. Several pieces of state and national legislation have recently been passed. The most important of these was the Campus Sexual Assault Victim's Bill of Rights, introduced by Congressman Jim Ramstad of Minnesota in 1991 and signed into law in 1992. This statute will ensure that campus authorities conduct appropriate disciplinary hearings, treat sexual assault victims and defendant with respect, make their rights and legal options clear, and cooperate with them in fully exercising those rights. This legislation is discussed in detail in Chapter 9. In addition, Senator Joseph Biden of Delaware has introduced a bill to make rape a hate crime, to increase penalties for rape, and to establish educational funds for rape education on college campuses. All this legislation will be discussed in a later chapter so that the reader can understand its impact and its requirements.

As this issue gains more attention, more victims are able to label their experiences as rape; an increasing number of them want some retribution or redress in the criminal or civil courts, or on the campus judicial processes. This book will address how sexual assault, date rape, and acquaintance rape cases that occur on college campuses are currently being handled, and how we believe they should be handled.

In this book, we examine a number of questions about the issue of campus sexual assault. They include such questions as the following: What is the nature and severity of pressures on college administrators regarding the handling of reported acquaintance rape cases? How are acquaintance rape and sexual assault cases that are reported to the authorities handled on campus? What is the relationship between the campus and the legal system in such cases? What are the outcomes of these cases? Who sues the college or the defendant, and why? What are the appropriate lessons to be learned by colleges in this area? Why are some of the lessons being learned the wrong ones, and from whose point of view are these lessons wrong? Whose interests do these lessons serve?

Because acquaintance rape is the most common form of sexual assault on college campuses, the majority of the book will focus on it, although we will discuss stranger rape where it is relevant. Most of the cases include only sexual assault, though in some cases the victim was also robbed, stabbed, or even murdered. Because most of the victims are female students we will focus most on them, though we will discuss cases involving male victims and victims who are faculty or staff members where it is appropriate.

This is a study based on U.S. material. Our experience has shown that many of the issues are relevant to campuses abroad, although we do not profess to be experts on the subject outside the United States.

In this book, we use a number of case studies to illustrate elements of the problems of campus sexual assault. In many cases, the information is already public knowledge. To protect the confidentiality of our informants, however, we have, where appropriate, altered some of the details of the cases.

We believe this book will be helpful for those who have been the victims of sexual assault on college campuses and want to know what their options are. In addition, anyone working with those victims as counselors, support people, or advisors (such as therapists, and counselors from rape crisis centers) should know how to advise victims regarding their options and rights. Professionals working on college campuses who may be involved in the process of advising students, or who are involved in the handling of these cases through a judicial process, will also find the book useful; this would include representatives of the women's center, college administrators, deans of students, and judicial administrators and advisors, among others. Those who teach courses related to sexual assault, the proper handling of cases, and the impact of acquaintance rape or sexual assault on the victim (such as law schools, counseling and social work programs, women's studies programs, and sociology, psychology, social work, or human service studies departments) should also read this book.

The area of campus sexual assault is an important one; the lives of many young men and women in our colleges are significantly affected by it. We owe it to them to recognize it as a problem, to make every effort to reduce its incidence, and to handle it in the best possible way when it occurs.

Scope of the Problem

Most people, including those who have experienced it, have trouble understanding sexual assault. This is especially true if the victim and assailant are acquainted, are friends, or are dating. Many of the common questions about sexual assault on a college campus will be addressed in this chapter.

Who Are the Victims of Campus Sexual Assault?

The case that follows includes many of the elements common to cases of sexual assault on campus. In this case the victim did report the sexual assault to the campus authorities, but she was manipulated into not pursuing legal or judicial authorities.

> Ellen, a first-year student, went to several parties the first Saturday of the fall semester. She had a lot to drink over the course of the evening. She was then taken by one of the men she had met at one of the parties to his residence hall, where there was a toga party under way. They both dressed in sheets and drank more alcohol at the residence hall party. Ellen passed out, and when she gained consciousness, she discovered his penis in her mouth.

Ellen was a typical victim of campus sexual assault in that she was female, a freshman in college, and had been drinking alcohol. Victims of rape may be men or women of any age; however, they are usually females between the ages of fifteen and twenty-four. Most of them are of college age, an age when they are dating most frequently.[1]

Most sexual assaults occur between acquaintances, frequently on dates. The sexual assault victims we will be discussing in this book are most often college women between seventeen and twenty-one. It is possible for men to be raped by male assailants—or, more rarely, by female assailants—but because the vast majority of acquaintance rapes involve male assailants and female victims, this book will primarily focus on this type of sexual assault.

The two most important determining factors regarding whether a date rape will occur are the number of men a woman dates,[2] and the degree of intoxication of those men.[3] The first factor is based on probability of exposure, in part because it is impossible to tell a date rapist by the way he looks, and in part because women are socialized to ignore cues that may indicate that some men are a threat. For example, if a man calls a woman a derogatory name (such as "bitch") or continues to tease her when she asks him to stop, he is harassing her and is likely to exploit her. If he harasses, exploits, and/or objectifies her in a nonsexual situation, he is likely to do so in a sexual situation as well. Most women are socialized to put up with harassment, however, because saying something assertive is considered contrary to proper feminine behavior. The more times a woman experiences harassing kinds of behaviors, the more they become part of her social environment, and the more she learns to "grin and bear it."

Some sexual assault victims have such low self-esteem that they feel that they are worthless without a relationship, and that it is better to be associated with any man than no man at all. This attitude is also enforced in American culture. The victim may say, "As soon as he gets to know the real me, he will fall in love with me, and will stop doing that. He will change for me." Or she may say, "I know he did something to me that I didn't like, but that is all I deserve." The victim may have watched her father harass or assault her mother, making her believe that this is the way adult sexual relationships are supposed to be. She may even have been sexually assaulted as a child; forced sexual experiences may be the only kind of sexual relationships she knows. Some victims may not want to believe that someone they love could do anything as terrible as rape them, so these victims may define the sexual assault as their own fault rather than believe that their boyfriends are rapists. For example, a victim may say, "I got him so excited that he couldn't stop himself."

With regard to the second factor, the more intoxicated a man is, the greater the likelihood that he will ignore a woman's protests or be unable to interpret her words and actions as she intended them. This is especially true if she does not want to have sex but he does, which is a common pattern in acquaintance sexual assaults.

> While visiting from another institution, John got drunk at a fraternity party and raped a woman at the party. His friends, who were fraternity brothers, helped to get her drunk and then encouraged the assault by cheering him on. After the party the woman filed a complaint with the college administration, but because the alleged rapist was not a student at the college, the administration was not able to do anything to him.

Studies have not consistently indicated any female personality traits that make a woman more likely to become a date or acquaintance rape victim. Our research indicates that the typical scenario of sexual assault on college campus includes the woman's drinking at a party (especially a fraternity party) and playing drinking games, a situation where she has been given a drink in which the alcohol has been disguised as punch. First-year college students are most likely to become the victims of sexual assault while in college.[4] Sexual assault, however, can and does also happen in other circumstances.

Sexual assault victims sometimes have sex again with their assailant. In many cases in which the victim has sex with the assailant again, the latter was the boyfriend of the victim. The victim may believe that, although he did force her to have sex, he will treat her better and not rape her once he really gets to know what a wonderful person she is (and, presumably, falls in love with her). Only after repeated sexual assaults over time does she realize that he will not change, and so she ends the relationship.

Neil Gilbert, a professor of social work at Stanford University, believes that if a woman does not know that what has happened to her is rape, then it is not rape.[5] This type of attitude is probably pervasive among the administrations of some colleges. Gilbert cites FBI statistics, which consist disproportionately of reports of stranger rape, to prove that the 20 to 25 percent estimate of sexual assaults on female college students is inflated. The FBI estimates that fewer than one in ten stranger rapes are actually reported to them, however, and data from national studies suggest that fewer than one in one hundred acquaintance rapes are reported to the police.[6] Because most rapes and sexual assaults that occur in college are between acquaintances, they are not likely to be reported to the police or even the college administration. This is especially true if administrators have made it clear to victims that they don't believe sexual assault happens on their campus.

Who Are the Assailants?

Approximately 5 to 8 percent of college men know that raping acquaintances is wrong, but choose to do it because they know the odds of their being caught and convicted are very low.[7] There is a larger group of men who rape acquaintances but do not believe it is rape. They often believe they are acting in the way men are "supposed to act"—that no really means maybe, and maybe really means yes. Once a case becomes public, several other women often come forth who are willing to testify that the assailant sexually assaults them as well, even though the other women had not pressed charges themselves. This was the case in the William Kennedy Smith trial, although the three women who also claimed to have been raped by him were not permitted to testify.

Some studies have compared the incidence of sexual assault among various groups of men. One study indicated that 35 percent of fraternity men reported having forced someone to have sexual intercourse. This figure was significantly higher than for members of student government (9 percent) or men not affiliated with other organizations (11 percent).[8] Based on an FBI survey, basketball and football players from NCAA colleges were reported to the police for committing sexual assault 38 percent more often than the average for males on college campuses.[9]

The men who are most likely to rape in college are fraternity pledges.[10] It is unclear whether this is because either forced sexual intercourse or sexual intercourse under any circumstances is a condition of pledging, or because the pledges are trying to act in a way that they believe the brothers will admire. The process of pledging a fraternity often desensitizes men to behaviors that objectify women, and it also creates a "groupthink" mentality.[11] As a result, once men become pledges or fraternity members, some of them may commit a sexual assault to be "one of the brothers." All of these factors, plus the heavy alcohol consumption that occurs in fraternities, contribute to the likelihood that a sexual assault will occur on campus. Not all fraternity pledges who abuse alcohol, however, actually commit sexual assault. Conversely, women should not automatically feel safe with a man who is not in a fraternity and who is a teetotaler.

> Tom sexually assaulted Carol, the girlfriend of one of his fraternity brothers. Carol passed out from drinking too much at a fraternity party, and Tom had sex with her while she was unconscious in her boyfriend's bedroom. When she started moaning her boyfriend's name during the rape, Tom panicked and went to get the boyfriend, encouraging him to have sex with her so that if she regained consciousness, she would see him instead of Tom. Friends of Carol saw Tom leave the room and then reappear with her boyfriend, who he pushed into the room. Tom, however, had inadvertently left his tie in the bed, which was seen as evidence that he had been there with Carol. Tom was subsequently convicted of sexual assault by the campus judicial board.

The likelihood to commit a sexual assault also increases if men choose to live in all-male living units when coeducational units are also available. In fact, men who elect to live in all-male residences often do so in order to be able to behave in a violent or antisocial way, such as punching walls or getting drunk and vomiting in the hallways. There is significantly more damage done in all-male living units than on male floors of coeducational residences for this reason.[12]

Another group at risk for committing rape in college are athletes competing in such aggressive team sports as football, lacrosse, and hockey. Athletes are most likely to sexually assault after a game, when they are out either celebrating a win or drowning their sorrows after a loss. Drinking parties are frequently part of the post-game ritual, with female fans helping the athletes celebrate or commiserating with them. The likelihood of a sexual assault is greatest at this point if a female "groupie" appears to be "throwing herself" at an athlete with the intent of being seen with him or because she wants to be his friend. The athlete may be unable to distinguish between her desire for friendship and his perception that she is throwing herself at him because she wants sex. Further, he may believe that this is what he deserves as a result of his "star" status. There have been many celebrated cases of high school, college, and professional athletes who were successfully charged with rape or sexual assault by college and civil authorities.

Assailants are not limited to fraternity members and athletes, however, and the vast majority of fraternity men and athletes do not rape. The rate is higher among these two groups because of their position of privilege on campus, and because of their involvement with alcohol. The characteristics that are most important in determining if a man will become an acquaintance rapist are macho attitudes, antisocial behavior, and abuse of alcohol (either on a regular basis, or through binge experiences).[13] Athletes and fraternity men may exhibit some or all of these traits.

> Bill, a fraternity pledge, was a virgin at the time he was pledging. He was told by the brothers that they did not accept virgins into their house, and so he would have to do something about his virginity status. When he protested that he did not have a girlfriend, he was told that he should bring a girl to their fraternity formal, and the brothers would do the rest. He invited a very naive first-year student, Lori, to the party. Once there, she was given punch spiked with grain alcohol. When Lori blacked out, Bill took her to the bedroom of one of the brothers, put a condom on, and forced her to have sex over her feeble protests. She was also a virgin at the time, and she became pregnant because the condom broke during the rape.

Different Types of Campus Sexual Assault and Rape

Each different type of sexual assault has specific characteristics and problems associated with it. Campus sexual assaults vary by the status of the victim (student, faculty, staff, visitor, and so on), the status of the assailant, the number of assailants involved, and the degree of acquaintanceship between those involved. Rape or sexual assault on college campuses may be committed by an acquaintance or a stranger; most typically, the assailant is someone the victim knows. For the purposes of this book we have defined *campus sexual assault* as assault cases in which at least one of the people involved is associated with the institution.

Sexual Assault of a Member of the College Community by a Stranger from Outside the Campus Community

We probably hear about this type of sexual assault more often than any other. Women are much more likely to report a sexual assault in which they are seen as having little or no culpability. Therefore, victims are more likely to report a sexual assault to the police or campus authorities if they do not know the assailant, do not share the same friends, and consequently do not receive any pressure from friends or acquaintances to keep quiet so the assailant's life will not be "ruined." Stranger rape usually occurs more in urban than rural areas because of higher crime rates in urban areas.

> On the night of January 2, 1989, a female employee of the University of Southern California was attacked near the school's credit union building by an unknown man who dragged her into some bushes, where she was beaten, stabbed, robbed, and raped. The attack lasted forty minutes, during which time no one came to the woman's aid. She was rescued by two passersby, who scared off the assailant and then helped her to walk to the security office about a block away. It turned out that only one security officer was in the field at the time of the attack. Six months before the attack, there was a report that identified the building as a security risk, but no one had ever followed up on the report's recommendations, which included increasing the lighting and cutting back the bushes.

> A young woman at Clarkson University was assaulted while walking home through an isolated area behind the field house. A fire watchman who was inside the field house reported it to another fire watchman who was on patrol on another part of campus. The watchman in the car came to the building to investigate. He came upon two people having what he believed to be consensual sex. He called the other fire watchman and they were unsure of how to respond. When they went to check the scene again, they found the woman alone, bloody, and unconscious. They then called the village police, who responded and apprehended the man after he had raped and beaten the woman. She later died in the hospital. Clarkson College was sued and settled out of court. The college has subsequently hired a director of campus safety with a law enforcement background and has dramatically upgraded the training for its campus safety personnel.[14]

Sexual assault by a stranger (other than a student) from within the campus community is more likely in large campus communities than on smaller campuses, where most people tend to know each other. These rapes may be between students and faculty, administrators, or college staff members or visitors to the campus community.

Rape by a Student Unknown to the Victim

This type of sexual assault is also more common in larger schools, and may happen in circumstances such as after the assailant notices the victim in a bar or at a large party. It may also occur if a woman has a "bad" reputation, passes out at a party after drinking alcohol, and is used sexually by male students who are strangers to the victim. In some instances, the victim is in a presumably safe place but is attacked by a stranger who has gained access based on false pretenses (for example, posing as a student or pizza delivery person). It is typical in gang rape that at least some of the assailants are strangers to the victim.

> In 1986, Lehigh freshman Jeannie Clery was raped, sodomized, and murdered while sleeping in her bed at 6:00 A.M. That night another student, who had been drinking and who did not know her, entered her residence hall through three automatically locking doors that were propped open, entered her room, and sexually assaulted and strangled her. Her parents sued the university for failing to provide a safe environment for their daughter and for violation of "foreseeable action." They settled for an undisclosed sum, and in addition, they committed Lehigh to extensive improvements in dormitory security.

Acquaintance Rape and Sexual Assault

Acquaintance rape and date rape are not legal categories; the term *rape* usually applies to any forced intercourse, regardless of the degree of acquaintance. We are using the terms *acquaintance rape* and *date rape* for clarity of understanding in a sociological rather than a legal sense.

> Amy, a senior in high school, was visiting her sister, Jill (a first-year student), for the weekend at a small liberal arts college. They went to a lacrosse game, and Jill had a party in her room afterward. One of the lacrosse players, Adam, attended the party after the game, and Amy spent over an hour with him there. Amy and Adam both got drunk and went into an adjoining room during the party for about an

hour. When they emerged, he went home, and Amy told Jill that Adam had raped her. Amy and Jill reported the event to the authorities, and Adam was suspended. Adam sued the college on the grounds that the campus policy explicitly stated that the college community would protect its students, but it said nothing about protecting visitors.[15]

Acquaintance sexual assaults are by far the most common type of rape both on and off the campus; however, they are rarely reported to authorities. Date rape (the most common type on college campuses) and acquaintance rape are estimated to happen to one-fifth of college women, whereas one-quarter of college women will experience either attempted or completed forced sex.[16] These sexual assaults happen most often during the woman's first year, although a victim may also experience further episodes later on. Sexual assaults often happen to victims in the first week of college, before they know the social "rules." At colleges where first-year students live on campus and then must move off campus during their sophomore year, however, the incidence increases when students no longer have the protection of the structured college living environment.[17]

Gang Rape and Sexual Assault

Although gang rape occurs on college campuses, it is not unique to them. It usually occurs in all-male living units where alcohol and peer pressure are abundant. Fraternity gang rape is especially difficult to prove, because an accused's fraternity brothers are usually unwilling to provide evidence to the local or campus police. In fact, of the documented cases of alleged gang rape by college students from 1980 to 1990, 55 percent were committed by fraternity members, 40 percent were committed by members of team sports (football, basketball, and lacrosse), and only 5 percent were committed by men who were not affiliated with formal organizations.[18] Other studies also show that a majority of gang rapes committed on college campuses occur in fraternity houses.[19]

Many of the people who are involved in gang rape are "followers" rather than initiators.[20] One of five Kentucky State University defendants charged with sodomizing a fellow student told police that at first he left the woman alone when he found her partially undressed in his room, because she was unwilling to have sex with him. When he later returned and found his friends assaulting her, he joined them.[21]

Tanja was raped in her dormitory in September of her first year of college at the University of California at Berkeley. An unsupervised party had been held in the dorm during which alcohol was consumed, despite the agreement between students and the university that there would be no drinking in the dorms. After the party, Tanja went to the room of an acquaintance, Donald, to borrow a cassette tape. There she met Donald's twin brother Ronald, who forced her down the interior stairs of the building to a dark landing where a light bulb had been shattered. He forced Tanja to have intercourse and oral sex with him. Ronald then took Tanja to a room occupied by John and Christian, where Donald soon joined them. Donald suggested that they all go to his room, where he encouraged the other three men to have oral sex with Tanja against her wishes. When she protested forcefully, Donald told the others to leave, but told her that if she didn't stop yelling, he would beat her. Donald then forced Tanja to have intercourse with him, while the other three friends watched, laughing. Tanja was finally permitted to leave. All four men were members of the university football team.

Like other acquaintance rape victims, the victim in a gang rape may be drunk or passed out at the time and therefore may have no memory of the rape; if she does remember it, her memory may be incomplete. She may have voluntarily gone to the location of the rape and may have consented to have sex with one of the men, but not with all of them. If she has a reputation for sleeping around, she may fear that she will not be believed if she reports the event to the police or the campus authorities. In fact, regardless of her reputation, when a woman is being gang raped, the last men are likely to feel more justified in forcing her because they feel that she deserves it for being so "loose." Gang rape may occur when women who are believed to be "easy" are imported from off campus for this purpose.[22]

In the event of a fraternity gang rape, powerful alumni and current brothers may put pressure on the institution to squelch the case. Information is often covered up in these cases to protect the assailant or to prevent the charter of the fraternity from being revoked. Members of the group that raped the victim, as well as the rapists themselves, may also harass her or put pressure on her not to report the assault, or to drop the charges. For all of these reasons, charges are rarely filed in gang rape cases, whether they occur on or off campus. If they are filed and the case goes to trial, the result is often an acquittal. In such cases, it is usually the word of the victim against that of the assailants, and the assailants' stories usually agree with each other. In addition, the assailants are often "nice boys" from "good families," in contrast with the victim's frequently "bad" reputation. In such cases it is difficult to convince the entire jury beyond a reasonable doubt that she was not a willing participant.

Peggy Sanday suggests that gang rape is often the means by which homophobic men who want to share a sexual experience with other men are able to do so through a woman.[23] Sanday believes that these men want to have sex with each other, but will not do so because of the societal taboo against homosexual behavior. Therefore they select a woman whom they do not know and have sex with her in the presence of their male friends as a means of sharing a sexual experience in a "socially acceptable" heterosexual way. This process is unspoken, and perhaps unconscious, because these men would never admit wanting to have sex with another man. They are also misogynistic if they are able to abuse a woman in this manner to fulfill their own desires.

Judge Lois Forer believes that gang rape is becoming less acceptable off campus, but is viewed much less negatively on campus.[24] In gang rape, as in acquaintance rape, if we hear of only a small number of cases being reported to the police or campus judicial authorities, it probably means that many more are actually taking place. We very rarely hear, for example, about gang rapes being reported to the authorities in which the victim has a "bad" sexual reputation (as many of them do).

St. John's University Case Study

The rape trial involving members of the St. John's University lacrosse team was a highly celebrated case that involved alcohol, athletes, and a groupthink mentality. It will be presented here as a case study because it illustrates the very points we are making about campus sexual assault. The St. John's case includes many of the common elements present in the response to a campus sexual assault when the victim reports to the authorities.

> The three men on trial from St. John's University (Andrew Draghi, Walter Gabrinowitz, and Matthew Grandinetti) were accused of making a woman perform oral sex on them, using force at some moments and at other times taking advantage of her helplessness from liquor

that the victim says a fourth student (Michael Calandrillo) pressured her to drink. Not all of the men were tried together, because some of the defendants agreed to provide testimony against the other assailants.

The woman testified that she was told by Michael that he would drive her home from an evening college meeting, but that he needed to stop by at his nearby house for gas money. She agreed to that arrangement. According to the prosecutor, however, when they entered the house she was the victim of sexual advances by Michael and was forced to drink cups of vodka and orange soda, a mixture that caused her to fade in and out of consciousness. When she awoke periodically, she found Michael's housemates (and former teammates) shoving their penises, in turn, into her mouth. The woman asserted that she tried to ward off her attackers verbally but that she was too weak. A Queens, New York, jury in 1991 rejected her allegations, and the three defendants were acquitted.[25]

The facts in the St. John's case illustrate many of the issues that often contribute to not-guilty verdicts. The victim waited many months before she reported the incident, and there was another significant time period between the report and the trial. When she provided accounts of the alleged crime to her minister, detectives, and lawyers, there were subtle differences in her story, such as exactly how much liquor she drank (from one to three cups). As in most acquaintance rape cases, the major legal issue here was not whether the event in fact took place, but whether the woman consented. The victim said she did not consent; the jury did not believe her.

It is important to understand that a verdict of not guilty does not necessarily mean that the assailant is innocent. It simply means that there was not sufficient evidence to convince all the jurors, beyond a reasonable doubt, that he committed the crime of which he was accused. Although this is, of course, true for all crimes, the acquittal rate in rape trials is higher than for other serious felonies. Jurors often do not believe that the defendant committed the crime because he was a credible witness, or because the victim was a poor witness; because there was not enough corroborating evidence; or because they could not understand why such a nice, upstanding (often married) pillar of the community would have to resort to raping a woman of questionable character in order to have sex.

This last line of reasoning assumes that men rape for sex. Although sexual organs are used in rape, that does not make it sex. As Linda

Sanford, author of *Women and Self Esteem*, says, "If I hit you over the head with a rolling pin, you wouldn't call it cooking, would you?" In the same way, if a penis is used to commit violence, it does not make the act sex.

Stranger rapists often plan rape, whereas acquaintance or date rapists often plan sex. In acquaintance rape it is only when the assailant's plan for a perfect evening (ending with sex) goes wrong that he resorts to violence to get what he wants and may think he is owed. But even though the motivation may be different in stranger and acquaintance rape, the consequence is the same for the victim.

In many cases of acquaintance rape, the man may truly *not* believe that what he did was rape, or even that he did anything wrong. He may believe that a woman does not really mean no when she says it, and that all she needed was a little push, and she will be happy about the outcome. This scenario is played out in the media time after time, from *Gone with the Wind* to the soap opera "General Hospital," the television series "Moonlighting," and the movie "Baby Boom." Just because an alleged assailant believes he is innocent, however, does not mean that he is within the law. The law does not define the crime of rape in terms of what the defendant thought, but rather uses a more objective standard.

Newspaper accounts of the trial of the members of the St. John's lacrosse team suggested that this trial represented a miscarriage of justice, and that the legal system of the old South had returned because the victim was black, the defendants were white, and the defendants were found not guilty. Many feminists agreed that the verdict will have a chilling effect on the willingness of sexual assault victims to press charges.

Although the defendants were acquitted, St. John's University nevertheless expelled the three men. The university waited until after the trial, however, to pass judgment on the men through the campus judicial process. The university's president found that each of the students was guilty of "conduct adversely affecting his suitability as a member of the academic community of St. John's," noting that the court verdict acquitting the three of sodomy and criminal charges involved "different standards" from those related to the code of behavior that governs students' actions toward one another and toward teachers.

Many St. John's University students felt that this was a harsh verdict for a Catholic university and that better punishment would have been some type of forgiveness and rehabilitation, such as psychotherapy. Catholic colleges seem to respond more harshly, in general, than most other colleges in the judicial handling of sexual assault cases on their campuses. Sexual assault is considered immoral and is not usually tolerated there, even if other segments of society do tolerate or even condone those behaviors.

Although the St. John's case was typical in many ways, it differs from the norm because it actually went to trial. The victims of sexual assault rarely report either to the police or the campus judicial system. Approximately 90 percent of sexual assault cases involving people who know each other are never reported to the police. Some victims prefer to report the rape to the campus judicial authorities; however, the majority of victims of acquaintance sexual assault do not tell anyone about it.[26]

Why Victims Do Not Report

The St. John's case is similar to many other sexual assault cases in that it involved alcohol. Mary Koss found that at least 75 percent of sexual assaults reported to authorities involved the consumption of alcohol by the victim, the attacker, or both.[27] This estimate is probably low, because it does not include victims who passed out and can not remember what happened. It also does not include all those victims who believe that others will blame them for being drunk, and who therefore never report.

Other victims of sexual assault may observe or read about hearings such as the St. John's case and find numerous reasons not to report their sexual assault. Victims often feel as if it is their behavior that is on trial, and in fact, many victims blame themselves for doing something to cause the rape, such as drinking too much. Many victims are fearful that their names will be made public, or that their past sexual history may be discussed in court. During the St. John's case, the woman stated during cross-examination to the defense attorney, "Mr. Scaring, I'm not on trial."

What Happens When Victims Report to Campus or Criminal Authorities

Even when victims do report to the police, they are frequently disbelieved or blamed. This phenomenon was seen in the William

Kennedy Smith case, in which the victim did report being raped. Although this case was not a campus sexual assault case, the issues are similar; because it was so highly publicized, we will use it as an example for purposes of illustration. Patricia Bowman's character was called into question; she was criticized for being in a bar drinking, for going to his home voluntarily, and for using poor judgement. The same things happen when campus sexual assault victims report to the campus authorities. But in the campus system, because rules of evidence are more flexible than in the criminal courts, victims are also often asked inappropriate questions about their sexual behavior (for example, "Do you have oral sex with all the men you date? Do you like it?").

In most acquaintance sexual assault cases, the victim is usually blamed by her peers and her support system. Martha Burt found that a majority of Americans think that at least half of all rape reports are false and that they are invented by women to retaliate against men who have wronged them.[28] Many people believe that the charge of acquaintance rape or gang rape occurs because a woman feels guilty after a sexual encounter with a man and cries "rape" in order to ease her conscience. The fact is that only 2 percent of rape reports prove to be intentionally reported falsely to the police.[29]

> Mary, a graduate student, was raped by another student in her apartment and reported the assault to the police. (Because the rape was not on college property, it was not within the jurisdiction of that particular college.) The district attorney accepted the case and was preparing it for trial. In order to obtain information from the alleged assailant about another crime, however, the district attorney offered the assailant a plea bargain, and the latter received a light sentence. Mary was very angry and disappointed at having been denied the right to "have her day in court" or to see the man sentenced to what she considered an appropriate penalty. At least in her case, however, the assailant was sentenced for some offense and as a result will have a criminal record.

Many victims find it cathartic and healing to tell their stories in court and to play a role in their assailant's punishment. But a plea bargain is often negotiated for a lesser charge, and the victim feels cheated when the assailant pleads guilty to a much less serious crime than that which he committed against her.

The low reporting and conviction rates are generally characteristic of what are called *simple rapes* (those with no violence, a single attacker, and no other crime committed at the time).[30] Acquaintance rapes are usually simple rapes. The report and criminal conviction rates are much higher in the case of aggravated rapes, but those are far less likely than simple rapes to take place, especially on a college campus. Therefore, more assailants may be punished if acquaintance rape cases are heard by the college judicial board or officer, because the campus system can operate under different rules of evidence. Campus judicial processes are able to find more defendants guilty of sexual assault violations, all other things being equal, than the criminal courts, provided that the system is well designed and administered. The most serious penalty that may be administered in the campus system, however, is expulsion from the institution, which is not comparable to the loss of liberty that may follow a guilty verdict in the criminal justice system.

In many cases of sexual assault reported to the criminal justice system, the case is not accepted by the district attorney or indicted by the grand jury, which may make the victim feel powerless or very angry, especially if she wants to see her assailant behind bars. Victims who report their assaults to the campus criminal judicial system often also experience anger, frustration, and disappointment. For example, victims may be told that their case is not eligible for action by the campus judicial system because it occurred outside of the jurisdiction of the system. Other cases may fail because the victim is not taken seriously by law enforcement officials or campus officials, or because of long delays, among other reasons. These issues will be dealt with in greater depth in Chapter 6.

If the case is handled within a campus system, the result may be an acquittal. Although on some campuses the cases of campus sexual assault that are brought to the judicial body for hearing almost always result in a guilty verdict, this is not universally the case. The outcome depends, in large part, on the thoroughness of the investigation and the mind-set of the administrator(s) hearing the case. The way the campus code is written may also make a guilty verdict very difficult. Alternatively, there may not be enough evidence to convict the defendant, even when the rules of evidence are more flexible.

Even if the defendant is found guilty, he may receive an extremely light sentence (for example, thirty hours of community service). Additionally, the victim often has to face harassment by other students on campus who believe that she was not really raped, that it was her fault, that she is ruining the assailant's life, or that it was not "that big a deal." She may also be harassed by the assailant or his friends, especially if the former is a member of a fraternity that stands to be sanctioned if he is found guilty. Fear of this kind of harassment is more likely if the victim is on a small campus, where students tend to know almost everyone and everything that occurs on campus. All of these factors may contribute to reluctance on the part of women to report campus sexual assault.

General Problems with Trying Rape and Sexual Assault Cases

Rapes that take place on campus and are tried in the criminal courts experience the same difficulties that affect all rape trails. It is very difficult to prove to a jury that a rape really occurred, especially among acquaintances. In order to convince a jury, one needs to provide a clear, consistent account of what typically is a traumatic and disorienting encounter. This makes the criminal standard of proof difficult (if not impossible) to satisfy in sexual assault cases, where much hinges on the minutest of details being rendered with a detachment that defies the nature of the crime. When a victim attempts to recall her behavior after the fact, it does not always make a coherent, rational picture.

There are several factors that account for a victim's inconsistent recollections. If she is suffering from rape trauma syndrome (which is one type of post-traumatic stress disorder[31]), she is likely to have unconsciously repressed some of the events of the assault as a defense mechanism. Therefore, she may not be able to report the events exactly as they happened. In addition, she may have been intoxicated and therefore may have trouble recalling the events of the assault accurately, or at all.

Ann Burgess maintains that many people believe that rape must be a terrible thing, but that they also view it as sex rather than violence.[32] There may be a sexual component for the assailant, but the rape is not viewed as sexual at all by the victim. It is the violence that causes the traumatic response. This response may include denial that results in a time lapse between the actual event and the filing of a report. It also may mean that a victim may behave irrationally from the point of view of others, such as when she burns her clothes or takes a two-hour shower. Such acts work against the victim by eliminating concrete evidence of the crime; they also make the victim less credible in the eyes of the jury. Emotional strain also becomes a factor in the telling and retelling of the crime against an onslaught of fierce, dehumanizing questions posed by defense attorneys. Often the victim's story changes slightly because of the repeated retelling, which gives the defense an opening to argue that she is lying. All of these factors prevent the victim from presenting a clear and accurate account of the crime and weigh heavily in favor of the defense.

If the jury holds a rape victim to a standard of perfect consistency, most rape victims are going to fall short.[33] The defense attorneys in the St. John's case exploited the lack of consistency in the woman's story and made her look untrustworthy to the jury. Two lacrosse teammates of the alleged perpetrators corroborated her story, yet the jury found the inconsistencies too questionable to deliver a guilty verdict. Juries often equate inconsistencies with lies.

Some district attorney's offices have developed special units to handle sexual assault cases. As a result, victims are dealing with prosecutors who understand the issues and complexities involved with rape cases, and in those jurisdictions rape conviction rates are improving. For example, conviction rates for sex crimes now range from 50 percent to 75 percent in the Manhattan district attorney's office, which has such a unit.[34] But even though the statistics are getting better, one publicized acquittal (such as St. John's) dramatically diminishes the impact of these increased conviction rates. Many rape victims who know of the outcome of the St. John's case may be reluctant to report their sexual assaults.

Although the defense attorneys in the St. John's case believed that expulsion from college was an inappropriate punishment given the not-guilty verdict in the trial, we believe that it was a responsible one. The university has a responsibility to the women and men on its campus to condemn acts of sexual assault. With the prevalence of acquaintance rape on college campuses, messages that condone campus sexual assault should not be sent to students. It is important to show that there will be some form of retribution for acts of violence. The administration of St. John's provided such an example.

The Campus Judicial Response

Some cases, such as the St. John's case, result in action both at the college and in the courts. Of those that are brought to the attention of the campus judicial board, we are particularly interested in those cases in which one party, usually the alleged victim, is so dissatisfied that a civil suit ensues. Civil suits that follow reports of rapes on campus are usually against the institution for improper handling of a case. They may also be by a victim against an assailant for pain and suffering. An assailant may sue a victim, usually for defamation of character or slander. The assailant may also sue the institution for an inappropriate sentence or the improper handling of a case.

These cases illustrate the issues that are central to this book, and they address the fear many college administrators have of being sued after they have handled a sexual assault on their campus. We will discuss which factors and behaviors increase the likelihood of a civil suit against colleges, and what colleges can do to minimize that likelihood, in Chapters 8 and 10, respectively.

If victims are given only the option of reporting to the police, they may not be able to achieve any level of satisfaction. In many sexual assault cases, especially if the victim had been drinking or had engaged in sex with the alleged assailant before, the district attorney is unlikely to accept the case. In addition, the victim may feel assaulted again by having to go through the process of a medical exam and evidence collection by the police, especially if her case is then not accepted for trial.

In some cases, the victim is told by college administrators or campus police that she can press charges in the campus judicial process, but that because she was drinking while underage, she will also face a charge of violation of the college's alcohol policy. Because the vast majority of acquaintance sexual assaults on college campuses involve drinking alcohol, mostly by people who are under the legal drinking age, this approach could stop many victims from pressing charges.

Another approach used by an institution that does not want to deal with acquaintance sexual assault cases is to charge the victim with filing a false complaint if she drops the charges. She may decide to drop the charges if she is convinced by the authorities that she will never win her case because she was "asking for it" by drinking or by going to his room, for example. These are very effective victim-blaming statements that may cause the victim to doubt the wisdom of continuing with a legal case against the man.

The victim's friends and family may also blame her for the assault. Comments victims have heard from campus police, administrators, and medical personnel include, "Why did you go up to his room? Didn't you know what he wanted?" and, "Didn't you know that fraternity had that reputation?" Some fraternity brothers have reported that it is common knowledge that if a woman is in their house past 2:00 a.m., sex *will* occur. Therefore, if she does not leave earlier than that, she is viewed as being to blame.

College administrators must view acquaintance sexual assault as unacceptable and as a crime if they are to succeed in reducing this behavior on their campuses. Appropriate administrative responses must include evaluating and revising existing campus policies, judicial processes, personnel recommendations, services for victims, and public safety procedures and programs regarding acquaintance sexual assault. These policies need to be very specific and far-reaching to deal adequately with all the different types of sexual assault and rape that might occur on a college campus. A summary of the recommendations for handling campus sexual assault cases that appear throughout this book will be provided in Chapter 10.

Legislation protecting the rights of both victims and defendants and mandating education is necessary, because many colleges have handled these types of cases very poorly. Although legislation has been in place for several years in some states, it has not always been as successful as was hoped, because corresponding penalties have not been in place or applied to enforce the legislation. Current legislation will be dealt with in Chapter 9.

Public Attitudes About Acquaintance Rape

The role of public opinion in general and the influence of highly publicized cases of sexual assault in particular help to shape the way campus sexual assault is viewed. This book is about the problem of campus sexual assault in general, and those cases resulting in civil suits are but one small segment of the cases that occur. Case studies that did not occur on a college campus, involving the campus judicial process, or result in civil litigation are also included here if they are celebrated and have played a major role in developing societal attitudes about acquaintance rape. Examples of such cases include the William Kennedy Smith and Mike Tyson rape trials and the confirmation hearings for Clarence Thomas's appointment to the Supreme Court. Each of these events took place within a twelve-month period early in the 1990s and were instrumental in shaping public opinion about "real rape" and attitudes blaming the victim.

We have learned a great deal about how the American public views rape, sexual assault, and sexual harassment involving acquaintances from cases that have received wide publicity. The victim is held to a higher standard than is the assailant; her testimony must be perfectly consistent and impeccable. She is blamed for her behavior if she has been drinking, and for not being able to stop him. His drinking behavior, on the other hand, excuses his sexual needs ("He couldn't stop himself;" "He got carried away").

Most people in our culture are socialized to believe rape myths. Rape myths allow us to believe that a "real rape" is one in which a victim is raped by a stranger who jumps out of the bushes with a weapon, and in which she fought back, was beaten and bruised, reported the event to the police, and had medical evidence collected immediately. In a "real rape," the victim has never had sex with the assailant before, is preferably a virgin, was not intoxicated, was not wearing seductive clothing, and has a good reputation. If a rape occurred under those circumstances, most people would agree that the woman was indeed raped. Unfortunately, acquaintance sexual assaults contain few, if any, of those elements. In many acquaintance rape situations the victim had been drinking, did voluntarily go with the man to his apartment or room, was not threatened with a weapon, did not fight back, did not report the event to the police immediately, did not have medical evidence collected, and may have even had sex with the assailant voluntarily before.

In many of the highly publicized cases of 1990 and 1991, the verdict was simply based on the man's word against the woman's. It is a matter of whom we believe and why. Societal messages have suggested that men must always be ready and willing to have sex, that a woman who says no never means it, and that sex is a man's right if he spent money on the date.[35] Some men also feel that a woman is asking for sex if she gets drunk, goes to a man's apartment, or asks him over to hers. These ideas are in stark contrast to the legal definitions of rape and sexual assault in the United States. Most states have laws that define rape as a situation in which sexual intercourse is forced on one person by another against the victim's will and without the victim's consent, or if the victim submits out of fear for his or her safety or life. In theory, the victim does not have to say no more than once, and does not have to explain why he or she wants the offender to stop. Many people, however, do not believe that an event was rape if the woman is not bruised and hysterical, and if the offender was not a stranger.[36] Legally, these factors do not have to be present for a sexual assault to have occurred.

In some cases, members of society believe that the victim should have known better, such as in the Mike Tyson case. Even though Tyson was convicted of rape and sexual assault, the behavior of his victim, Desiree Washington, was still questioned, and victim-blaming statements were abundant. Many of the following comments were made by people who disbelieved the victim: Why did she go up to his hotel room unescorted? She must have known of his reputation. He was reported as having sexually harassed beauty pageant contestants earlier that day, and she surely must have seen that. In reality, most women have a hard time believing that men they know would hurt them if they have never hurt them before. If attacked, women often have a difficult time defending themselves against most men. In the case of the former heavyweight boxing champion of the world, she could never have fought her way out if he behaved inappropriately.

Tyson's reputation as a man who had previously been involved in sexual violence was very different than that of William Kennedy Smith, who was a physician and a member of a very influential family. Desiree Washington's background (as a pillar of the community, an upstanding member of her church, and a member of the National Honor Society), was very different from that of Smith's accuser, Patti Bowman. Bowman had obviously had sex before (because she was a mother) and was drinking in a bar where she met Smith. Undoubtedly, racial factors were also a likely contributor to Tyson's conviction, in contrast to the acquittal in the William Kennedy Smith trial.

The public often assumes that victims will make false accusations for some kind of personal gain. Anita Hill was accused of making up charges against Clarence Thomas because she was either a woman scorned, emotionally imbalanced, looking for a movie or book contract and a way to become famous, or a pathological liar. Patricia Bowman, the woman who accused William Kennedy Smith of rape was portrayed as a "wild girl" with a "taste for glitz" by the media. Sexual assault and rape victims are often charged by public opinion with trying to ruin a man's life; when a public figure is charged, the victim is viewed as being out for fame and fortune as well.

College students are aware of news events of this nature, and one can assume that they are influenced by them. Potential rapists may believe that they can rape with impunity as long as they choose the right kind of victim. Victims are likely to have learned the lesson that there are many factors, unrelated to the sexual assault, that will have bearing on whether their cases will be treated seriously. If victims do decide to report the assault, they must know that their chances of a conviction are not good, and that their chances of being further harassed and blamed are high. Current and highly publicized cases will undoubtedly have an important impact on the number of sexual assaults committed and the number of cases reported to authorities, both on and off the campus.

3

After the Assault

Colleges respond in a variety of ways to an allegation by a victim that she has been assaulted. As we have discussed elsewhere in detail, the way a college handles a case of sexual assault has a significant effect on issues that include the future rate of campus sexual assault, transfer rates, university-student relations, and whether the university will be sued by either victims or defendants. This chapter will focus on the effect of the school's different responses on the victim.

A significant proportion of those students who are victims of campus sexual assault do not remain at the institution where the assault took place. We do not know exactly how many of them transfer, but we have heard story after story of individuals transferring or dropping out of school altogether after an assault. It is also apparent from our research that a person is much more likely to transfer or to drop out if the college has failed to take her allegations seriously. This is especially true when the assailant remains on the campus. Our interviews with victims show that their major concern is avoiding confrontation with the assailant on campus; colleges that recognize this concern are much more likely to retain those students.

There are a number of ways in which the college can act to protect the victim. Before the case has been heard, the college can move either student (defendant or victim) from their living quarters, require that the defendant refrain from any contact with the victim, and try to ensure as far as possible that the two are not in the same classes. If the defendant is found guilty by the judicial hearing board and he is not expelled, his punishment should include leaving the victim alone. If he is not found guilty of sexual assault, it may nevertheless be possible to exert pressure on him to continue the type of arrangement made before the hearing, although this might be harder and will require careful negotiation. Our experience shows that it is the school's failure to implement any of these suggestions that makes victims more likely to transfer, drop out, or sue the school. If the threat is removed for the victim, however, she can get on with her life and her college career.

> Katie Koestner, who accused a fellow student at William and Mary of raping her, transferred to Cornell University because her assailant remained on campus after a hearing that Katie believed was biased in favor of protecting his interests (at the total expense of hers). During her first semester at Cornell, her assailant was suspended for one semester. On learning this, Katie decided to go back to William and Mary. Once the threat was removed, she decided that she would rather be at the school she knew with all her friends.

What Happens After the Assault

As mentioned above, colleges vary tremendously in their response to the victim's allegation that she has been assaulted. Many schools have a great number of different people to whom a victim can complain. Often, the first person who hears about the event is the resident advisor (RA) on the floor of the victim's residence hall. In some cases, she or he is not sure how to take the matter further. In one case, we were told that the RA printed out a big notice warning the other women on the floor to beware of the person about whom the woman complained. Though this is an imaginative response, it does not take into account the immediate needs of the victim. Nor does it recognize the risks involved in such publicity should the identity of the alleged assailant be mistaken; if someone is named incorrectly, or even if the charges have not yet been proven, he has a possible claim for defamation.

It is important that people on the front lines, as it were, be aware of the appropriate action they should take. They need to know to whom the case should be referred, both in terms of reporting and in terms of the victim's medical and psychological needs. In the case of obtaining medical evidence, speed is essential; in many cases, there are delays that make the collection of medical evidence worthless. If the delay is too great, no useful evidence can be obtained for the police should there be a criminal prosecution, nor is the evidence available to the judicial hearing board.

It seems sensible to have a number of possible places a woman can contact after the assault, given that women vary tremendously in where they feel comfortable reporting the assault. To limit the recipients of a complaint has the advantage, however, of standardizing the process and maximizing the chances that the case will be properly prepared for either a judicial hearing or a criminal trial. Some schools have moved in this direction by appointing a victim's advocate, who at the very least will support the victim, act to coordinate her various needs, and assist in the preparation of the case for hearing.

One of the sad facts of life that we have discovered in our research is how little students, faculty, and most staff know about what to do in such a situation. This is often so despite significant efforts made by the university to inform students about these issues. At orientation, they are overloaded with so much information that they cannot remember it all. They may therefore have actually been given the information but have thrust it aside as unnecessary because they cannot believe they are vulnerable. David Elkind postulates that adolescents consider themselves invincible because they have not had enough life experience to assess accurately the risks they face.[1] Students may also neglect information about reporting because although there are many sexual assault victims their age, they are ignorant of those assaults. As we know too well, most victims do not speak about their assault. Also, some young women have been victims of incest and child sexual abuse. They may feel safer at college because they have left behind those who have been abusing them. These women, however, have been shown to be most at risk for sexual assault at college.[2]

This problem is particularly acute because so many campus sexual assault victims are in their first year. They are the least likely members of the student body to know their way around the student service branch of the university and are the most naive about potential dangers. In addition, as noted, these students are at the age when they simply do not anticipate negative things happening to them. It is therefore especially important that all the people who come into contact with students are very much aware of the process for dealing with sexual assault cases, as the following example shows.

> At one university in the Northeast that has a very good record for dealing with campus sexual assault, someone broke into Penny's apartment and tried to rape her over the Thanksgiving vacation. When she appealed for help, she was apparently shunted from one person to another until it became clear to her that the people who were on duty over the holiday did not know the appropriate procedure in such cases. Getting what she saw as a runaround made her post-trauma adjustment harder and contributed to her belief that the school simply did not care about her welfare. If this is the result at a university with a highly developed system for handling such cases and a reputation for doing it well, imagine how easily such problems can arise at less well-prepared schools.

The Hearing

All colleges have some kind of procedure at which they decide whether a person is guilty of violating the school's code of conduct. As we shall see in Chapter 5, codes of conduct and the hearings held under them vary tremendously from college to college. Sometimes the hearing is conducted by the dean of students alone; sometimes the case is heard by a hearing board comprised of students, faculty, and staff. The formality of the hearing also varies greatly.

At this point, we want to focus on how the hearing looks from the point of view of the victim and what role the hearing plays in her post-trauma adjustment. Many of the victims we have interviewed have felt that the focus of the hearing was on the rights of the defendant, at the expense of their own needs. This is a common complaint of all sexual assault victims and stems in part from a misunderstanding of the legal process. In the U.S. criminal justice system, the victim's role is no more than that of the complaining witness; the charge itself is actually brought by the state against the defendant. So when a victim talks of the way in which "her" lawyer ignored her needs, her reaction is related to the fact that the lawyer is not *her* lawyer. Some district attorneys do a better job than others of explaining this to victims and of making them feel less alienated, and some states have recently passed legislation allowing the victim to have input into sentencing, but the victim nevertheless remains only a witness.

On the campus, the situation is usually similar. The college charges the defendant with behavior that is inappropriate for a student; thus, it is a violation against the school as well as against the victim that is being evaluated at the hearing. Because the college is not the criminal justice system, however, it has the freedom to give the victim a greater role, rather than treating her merely as a witness. As discussed in the chapter on judicial codes, some schools do recognize the victim's rights, as well as her needs.

We have, however, heard of many instances where this has not happened, sometimes at institutions that look very supportive for the victim on paper. One victim described a hearing at which both the defendant and one of the members of the hearing board, who were both Greek, spoke to each other in that language at one point during the hearing. Because she herself did not speak Greek, she was excluded from that portion of the hearing.

In other cases, victims were refused permission to have someone with them during the hearing, even though the defendant was accompanied. Or members of the hearing board made derogatory remarks about the victim in her hearing. Or the hearing, which was supposed to be private, was in fact overheard by outsiders. Or the defendant's fraternity brothers were permitted to be either in or just outside the hearing, and they harassed the victim for bringing the action against their brother.

All these situations, not surprisingly, had a profound negative effect on the women to whom they happened. It is this kind of behavior, either performed by the institution or sanctioned by it, that helped propel the victims in our sample into court. It is not, however, one experience alone that precipitates a lawsuit, but a pattern of behavior by a number of people within the institution. For the purposes of illustration, let us look at a case that was handled well and one that was handled badly by the college. The first example did not result in a lawsuit; the second case ended up in court.

The Well-Handled Case

Mindy was a student at a college in the Midwest visiting an East Coast university when she was gang raped at a fraternity party. She was collecting signatures on a T-shirt and was taken upstairs to get more. When she went into one of the rooms, the fraternity brothers were notified; they came into the room, and she was raped by five of them.

After it was over, Mindy was told to leave. She sat on the fraternity steps and cried, having been separated at the party from the companions with whom she had arrived. A young woman came to Mindy and asked her what had happened. When she told her, the woman called security, despite Mindy's reluctance to bring in the university authorities. She was taken to a local hospital where they examined her, in accordance with the rape protocols, in preparation for providing evidence for a future trial.

The university strongly encouraged Mindy to file a complaint with the local police. The people in the dean of students' office arranged for her to meet with the district attorney, who was anxious to press charges. Mindy met with the district attorney several times in the security offices on campus. Mindy was very reluctant to press charges, as she was intimidated by the prospect of cameras in the courtroom. This fear might have been heightened by the fact that this case received a great deal of local publicity; details about it were all over the papers and on local television stations.

Mindy ultimately chose not to pursue the case in the criminal justice system, but decided to press charges through the campus hearing mechanism. She felt that this avenue was a more protective process than the criminal justice system could offer her. The district attorney held a press conference to inform the public that the university was handling the case with the assistance of his office, because of her choice to press charges within the university system. Although both the district attorney and the university would have preferred Mindy to proceed with criminal charges, they were glad that they had at least been able to persuade her to go ahead with the campus hearing.

Mindy was flown back from her midwestern campus on two separate occasions and put up in a local hotel. Someone from campus security and someone from the dean of students' office stayed with her at the hotel to help her feel safe. The first time she provided information for the hearing board, Mindy was allowed to give her testimony on videotape, wearing a wig and sunglasses, rather than in person at the hearing. This agreement had been reached after one member of the staff had told her, "We need you so badly; how can we get you to testify?" Later, however, as a result of counseling provided by both the university where she was raped and her home institution, Mindy had gained enough confidence to be able to appear without a disguise. She answered the questions of the accused, which were required to be in writing or funneled through the hearing board members so that they would be less confrontational.

Mindy gave a waiver to the director of the student health service so that he could review her medical file and present the evidence obtained from the hospital examination after the rape. This was arranged so that the number of outsiders involved would be at a minimum. This university did not allow any lawyers to be present at judicial hearings, nor did they require that hearsay be eliminated. For example, Mindy's statement to the person she encountered after she left the fraternity house was admitted into evidence.

There was so much press publicity surrounding the case that the hearing had to be moved around the campus and held at several secret locations in order to protect the privacy of both Mindy and her assailants. The university also held a number of public meetings to describe its plans for dealing with the case. These meetings were for both the university and the community, because the publicity had spread off campus.

During the entire period from the rape to Mindy's second trip to testify, the person from campus security in charge of the victim assistance support program was in touch with her and with the security office at her own university. She helped Mindy arrange for a new phone number, as she was getting upsetting calls.

The hearing board found some of the men guilty of sexual harassment (which was the way this university defined sexual assault). Some of them were expelled as a result. In addition, the fraternity was banned from campus for a period of ten years. This decision did not go unchallenged by the national fraternity organization, which sued the university (although it later abandoned the suit, and the decision remained in force). The young men apparently felt that they had received due process, and they did not object to the methods or results of the hearing. They, too, had quite a lot of contact with the judicial officer before the hearing and were well aware of the details of the hearing process.

One of the interesting aspects of this case is the fact that Mindy was not a student at the university where she was raped. Because of this, one might have expected the university to be less concerned about protecting her interests and more concerned about protecting the interests of the defendants. In this case, however, the university was primarily concerned with punishing its students for their unacceptable behavior. To do so, it was particularly important that the school make it possible for Mindy to do something she initially shied away from because she was afraid the process would only exacerbate her trauma. Instead, the process strengthened her and helped her recovery after the rape. The university later incorpoated into their rules for conducting judicial hearings the option that a victim could, in appropriate cases, testify on videotape.

The Badly Handled Case

When Laura was sexually assaulted by Matthew in her freshman year at a midwestern university, she did not go directly to seek help. Rumors spread about a rape on the campus, and when Laura locked herself in her dorm room and would not come out, the resident advisor (RA) on her floor figured out that she was the victim. When the RA and some friends approached Laura and she admitted that indeed it was she, they suggested that she report it to the university.

The next day Laura went to see the woman who was in charge of residence life. This administrator told Laura what all her options were; these included telling the campus police, doing nothing, having the assailant's name placed in a file (that was buried unless he did it again), writing him a letter that campus security would deliver, or filing charges through the university arbitration board. In the last option, she was told that Matthew could be expelled, and that she would never have to see him again. She was not told that she could file charges with the local police. Laura said she was not really ready at that time to file campus charges, so she asked the dean to talk to her assailant to tell him to keep away from her because she was terrified of him. It was not until the following night that Laura went to the hospital because the dean of students told her she should "get tested," although she was told that they would not need a rape examination for evidentiary purposes.

Shortly thereafter, Laura decided to tell the campus police about the incident, but they did not contact the local police at this stage either. That night she received a message from Matthew to call him. When she did not call, he called everyone on her floor to get them to find her so that she would call him. At that point, driven by her fear of Matthew and his phone calls, Laura called the dean to say that she had decided to press charges through the university system. She was told that there would be no problem getting Matthew out of school. After the charges had been filed, Laura received a lot of crank calls that may have been from Matthew, though she never actually found out who made them.

During the preparation for the hearing, Laura was asked if she would take a lie detector test. She agreed, and she took and passed the test. Matthew refused to take such a test until several weeks later, at which time he failed it.

When Laura's parents finally found out that she had been raped (she had told only her sister previously), they asked if she wanted to press criminal charges. This was the first time she had been told of this possibility. After further consultation with the dean, Laura and her parents decided to continue with the hearing board procedure. They were told by the dean that it would be faster (ten days) and that if Matthew were criminally charged, he would never get into another college, nor would he ever find a job.

The hearing was held in the library during "Greek Week," when the library was full of fraternity members, all of whom knew what was happening. The university had promised Laura privacy, but the door of the hearing room was not locked, and one person came in by mistake. Laura felt very exposed by the number of people nearby when the hearing was being held. During the hearing, Laura gave her story and was questioned by Matthew and the members of the board. When Matthew gave his side of the story, he said that he could not remember because he had drunk about four beers. He had two witnesses, both of whom offered conflicting stories. The discrepancies came out when Laura was questioning them as she was required to do under the hearing rules. "It was really obvious that they'd lied," she said later. The hearing board members then questioned Laura and told her that she was not really sure what happened. "They made me stand up and give a demonstration of how he had held me down with him standing there," she recalled later, adding that she found it very distasteful.

The following day Laura was given the verdict that there was not enough evidence to find Matthew guilty of rape, sexual assault, or sexual harassment. He admitted to being "really pushy and aggressive." Laura was told that the board had decided to make an exception for her by allowing her to appeal to the provost of student affairs. They made it sound as if such an appeal was within the discretion of the board to grant, though the student code of conduct provided a right of appeal to the provost. Laura took the board's encouragement to appeal to mean that they had not been definite in their decision to acquit. "You'd think they'd be firm in their decision," she said.

The appeals process was supposed to take fourteen days; instead, it took two months. During this time, Laura was reassured that she would not be disappointed with the decision, although by then the dean with whom she had dealt before was reluctant to talk to her. The school kept collecting more information, questioning the two men who had testified at the hearing. It was at this point that they finally persuaded Matthew to take the lie detector test.

When the provost of student affairs finally announced his decision, in the presence of Laura's entire family, he emphasized how he realized that sexual assault was a growing problem on campus. With some reluctance, he then handed Laura an envelope containing the verdict. He had decided that he could not overturn the decision and could not take into account any new evidence (including the failed lie detector test that the university itself had ordered). Laura was amazed, especially as she felt that this result was entirely at odds with what she had been told by the authorities all along. "When it came down to the end, they said, 'Well, we lied, see you later,' " she noted. The provost had apparently consulted the university's lawyer, as he kept saying "Legally we can do this . . ." When Laura asked if she could appeal the decision further, the provost said no, though Laura later found out that she could have appealed to the president of the university.

Laura now feels, among other things, that the trust she put in the dean of students was violated. "I later found out that half the things she told me were either lies or not correct information." The dean is no longer speaking to her. One of the things the university told Laura was that they would pay for her medical bill. She has had a bill for more than five hundred dollars, but the school has not paid it. "Nothing that's been promised has happened," she complains.

Matthew is still on the campus, and so is Laura. "They are not happy with me at school," she says. She is seriously thinking of transferring, because she feels alienated and unsafe and is forced to see Matthew all the time. Nothing has been done to separate them, and she feels that Matthew goes out of the way to cross her path. For example, he got a job working in the box office of the theater where she rehearses and where many of her classes will be held next year.

Laura and her family are very angry about the treatment she has received from the university. They believe that the university discourages women from filing charges. In Laura's case, the university initially failed to tell her of this option and later told her that the police would not be interested in pursuing the case. The campus recently conducted a study that indicated that whereas approximately one out of four women had experienced an attempted rape or were raped on campus, no one had ever reported it. Many young women filed the names of their alleged assailants, but did not report it to campus security.

Laura and her family have consulted a lawyer, who has filed a complaint against Matthew in civil court. The lawyer is afraid the university might destroy the tape recording of the original hearing and has filed a motion to prevent it from doing so. He is also filing a separate action against the university, arguing that it is a "co-conspirator."

Laura's case is by no means the worst story we have heard. We have heard of cases in which the victim is not permitted to press charges at all, either through the criminal justice system or through the campus judicial hearing process. As mentioned earlier, we have heard of cases in which the women who complain are themselves charged with violation of the school's alcohol policies because they had been drinking at the time of the rape. We have heard of cases in which the victim was humiliated during the trial in a variety of ways, including having it revealed that she had slept with another person in the same fraternity or that she had previously had an abortion. We have heard of schools that never find defendants guilty of accusations of sexual assault, regardless of the strength of the evidence against them. We have heard of schools where the president or dean of students routinely overturns verdicts of guilty in cases of sexual assault, and schools that may find the defendants guilty but do very little to punish them. These defendants are never expelled, instead being asked to do community service of some minor kind that is usually not checked in any way.

What is important about Laura's case is that it is very typical of the bungling that occurs in sexual assault cases at many schools. The reluctance to offer her the option of going to the police is common, as is the failure to encourage her to get appropriate medical testing so that there will be evidence for a later trial. Misinformation of the type provided to her is all too frequent. Although the legal requirements of due process were apparently adhered to, Laura was given nothing that would have helped her feel that the hearing was a fair one. The use of a lie detector seems to be entirely inappropriate, especially as the defendant chose not to submit to one and benefited from his refusal, whereas the fact that Laura both was willing to take the test and passed it seemed to have been ignored as a measure of her credibility. If a school uses lie detector tests, it should use them properly. In this case, it made the claim that the campus hearing was not supposed to be a criminal hearing, yet at the same time it used the trappings of the criminal justice process with no benefit to the hearing process.

The campuswide effect of this type of handling is also clear from the illustration. Several women at Laura's university who had been raped waited for the outcome of the hearing before they decided whether to proceed or not. Naturally, in the circumstances, they decided not to proceed. The message to victims was that they could not expect any redress from this university, and that it was therefore pointless to press charges. The message to potential defendants was that this school did not take rape cases seriously, so they did not need to worry about whether their behavior might fall into the category of rape. We are not suggesting that this is the effect every time a hearing results in a defendant being found not guilty; inevitably, some cases will have that outcome. The problem arises when the victim is treated badly and everyone knows about it.

The other effect of this kind of handling is that the risk of the school being sued is increased. At this stage, the outcome of Laura's lawsuit against the university is unknown. What is known, however, is that the university is placed in a defensive position as a result of the case. It has received adverse publicity, and possibly faces the loss of funding and potential students. It also has to expend its resources on fighting a lawsuit, whatever the outcome. If Laura had been advised honestly and consistently, she would have been far less likely to sue. Instead, her whole family has been involved in a traumatic and drawn-out experience. Despite their continued determination to proceed with the lawsuits, they told us of the burden of having this legal battle hanging over their heads, dragging along in the way that is customary for lawsuits. Whether the university wins or loses this case, the damage to the victim and her family, as well as to the university as a whole, has already been done.

Conclusions and Recommendations

In this chapter we have shown the effects on the victim of the different ways a school responds to her charge of sexual assault. These effects may be both psychological and educational. A victim who is dealt with well will have a better recovery in general and will be able to resume her life and her education more easily. A school that responds well will be more likely to retain that student and less likely to be sued. Solutions to the whole problem of rape on campus are discussed in detail in the Chapter 10. What follows, however, is a checklist specifically focused on the victim's needs in the response to her charge of rape on campus.

Checklist for Assisting Sexual Assault Victims

1. Make sure that potential victims know as much as possible about what to do if they are raped.
2. Make sure the frontline people (RAs, counselors, nurses, faculty advisors, and those in the dean's office) know what to do immediately upon receiving information about a charge, or at least where to go to get such information.
3. Train people to respond fast and sympathetically.
4. Be consistent in what the victim is told. If you do not know information for sure, then find out; don't tell her something that later turns out to be untrue.
5. Make sure the victim receives all the medical and psychological treatment she needs as soon as possible. Have policies in place to deal with cases that arise on weekends and holidays as well as when everyone is in their office.
6. Keep the victim informed at all stages of preparation for the hearing, as well as afterward.
7. Be sure to deal openly and sympathetically with the victim's parents.
8. Make every effort to ensure that the victim and the defendant do not come in contact.
9. Hold the hearing as soon as possible after the event.
10. Make sure that the victim understands what will happen as the case proceeds, especially if she chooses to press charges in the criminal justice system.
11. Be sure the victim understands her role as witness, not plaintiff, in both the campus judicial system and the criminal justice system.

From Victim to Crusader

How Campus Sexual Assault Victims End Up in Court

In the last chapter the reader saw the different ways colleges handle campus sexual assault and the effect these have on the victim. This chapter will focus on why some victims decide to sue the college where the rape took place. What is it about the college and the young women that precipitates such a drastic decision? We believe that by understanding more about these victims and the process they go through, one can learn much about the problem of campus sexual assault. Colleges can learn how the process looks from the victim's point of view and how they can prevent a lawsuit, and campus sexual assault victims can learn about the costs and benefits of mounting a lawsuit against their school.

Who Sues?

Our interviews indicate that there are several variables that seem to affect whether a young woman will buck the system by suing. We call these victims *crusaders* because that is how they see themselves: pressing for change that goes beyond their own immediate concerns. The factors that influence whether a victim will sue have to do with parental involvement and support, institutional mishandling, psychological variables that affect the young women themselves, and the role of lawyers. Table 4–1 shows how these factors affect the likelihood that a campus sexual assault victim will sue. Before

TABLE 4-1

Factors Associated with the Decision to Sue

1. Parental involvement and support (increases chance of suit, especially when variables below occur)
   a. Parents are lawyers or know lawyers
   b. Parents become involved as activists in campus sexual assault prevention
2. Institutionalized mishandling (increases chance of suit)
   a. reduces rate of reporting by others
   b. general attitude that such behavior normal
   c. procedures which might make it very difficult for a finding of guilt
   d. intervention by high authorities to overturn findings of hearing board
   e. punitive attitudes toward those who report
3. Psychological variables that increase chance of suit
   a. If victim has been socialized into assertive role
   b. If pressing charges and suing help victim in postrape adjustment
4. Psychological variables that decrease chance of suit
   a. If victim needs to "put it all behind her" as part of her postrape adjustment
   b. If victim believes that her behavior was a contributing factor in assault (e.g., if she was drinking)
5. Role of lawyers (variables that increase chance of suit)
   a. The participation of a sympathetic lawyer
   b. A lawyer who will work on contingency basis
   c. A lawyer who thinks it is a "good" case

discussing differences between victims who sue and those who do not, however, it is important to look at the ways in which the crusaders are *not* different from the typical victims of campus sexual assault.

The details of the crusaders' sexual assaults are fairly typical of all campus sexual assaults. More often than not, the crusaders know the assailant. Usually the event took place at or after a party. These victims, too, often do not realize initially that what has happened to them is a sexual assault and therefore a crime; it may take a friend or a counselor to change their perceptions of what happened to them. As awareness of sexual assault on the campus grows, the recognition that the experience was rape may take place earlier and with less input from others. Most of our sample, however, were assaulted at least a year before we first talked to them in 1991—and in some cases several years earlier, before much of the recent publicity about campus sexual assault. This awareness increases the risk to the college of a lawsuit resulting from bad handling of a case.

In contrast to so many victims of campus sexual assault, the women in our sample who sue *do* report the assault to the campus authorities. Though they may leave the institution, it is all too clear why they have done so. Crusaders also "go public" at some point by revealing their names and what happened to them. They manage to find a lawyer who works with them on a further redefinition of the event as one in which the college bears some legally actionable blame. Finally, they make the decision to fight the system and take their grievances against the college to court.

Parental Involvement and Support

With people so young, it is important to examine the role played by the victim's parents in the journey to becoming a plaintiff. As we have mentioned elsewhere, victims are usually between the ages of eighteen and twenty-one; most of them, however, are raped during their first year of college. Contrary to what might be expected, the parents of these young women do not always play a significant part in their daughters' decision to sue. Although most parents are supportive of the decision, parents have often not been extensively involved. Some parents have been central to the whole process, whereas others were peripheral to it. For example, in one case with several plaintiffs, the motivation for seeking a lawyer and ultimately filing a suit came from being part of a support group of women who had been assaulted. In that group there were apparently also several women who decided not to sue; those who did sue spoke in varying ways about the advice and input their parents had (one discussed it extensively with her mother, another merely informed her parents of the decision to sue when it was made, and another's parents were initially "mildly opposed" to her suit).

Some victims initially avoid telling their parents what happened. Like many sexual assault victims, they are afraid that they will be blamed for the assault. In some cases, the young woman finally does tell her parents quite a while after the assault; in others, the parents find out in some other way. Many victims do not tell their parents because they are afraid of being pulled out of school.

> For Barbara's parents, the ultimate discovery that their daughter had been raped answered many questions. They knew very well that the girl who came home at Thanksgiving was not the girl they had sent off to college at the beginning of the semester, and they had no idea why. They had imagined all sorts of possible reasons, such as drugs or a serious psychological problem, and were glad finally to know why Barbara had changed.

> Susan told her sister initially, but not her parents. When her mother saw the sister in tears while watching a television program on date rape, she guessed that something was amiss and "dragged the information out of" Susan's sister. Clearly much depends on the nature of the relationship between parents and their children.

In some of our cases, though, it is clear that it is really the parents who are the motivating force behind the suit. When they learned what had happened, they were outraged not only by the assault itself, but also by the subsequent treatment their daughter received from the college. One victim said she could not decide which was worse: the rape, or the way the college handled it. A mother described her daughter's postassault experience as being "raped again" by the college. For Barbara's parents in the example above, the discovery of the nature of the problem gave them something to focus on, so that they could finally act in a way that would help her. They consulted a lawyer and are now engaged in lawsuits against both the perpetrators and the college.

As more sophisticated adults, usually paying tuition to the college that they felt had mistreated their daughter, parents decided that this was a situation in which a lawyer should be consulted more quickly than those victims who found their way to a lawyer alone. In more than one case, in fact, either the father or a close relative was a lawyer. In some cases, the parents were anxious to sue but were prevented by their daughter from doing so.

> Sara called her mother the day after the assault took place. Her mother immediately flew a thousand miles to her daughter's college, having paused only to call a doctor and a lawyer to obtain information as to how to proceed. Sara decided that because she had consumed a great

deal of alcohol and because the defendant was not found guilty at the campus judicial hearing, she would not sue civilly or press criminal charges. Although Sara's mother respected her decision, she clearly would have preferred to take further action against the assailant and/or the college.

The definition of the event as an actionable wrong is much quicker on the part of the parents than in the case of the women themselves. In some cases, it is the parents who are the first to point out to the victim that what happened was a crime. In fact, often it is the parents who become the crusaders, as well as or instead of their daughters. For example, one father has set up an organization called "Prosecute All Rapists," which works for more effective prosecution of alleged rapists. He gives lectures, attends conferences, appears on talk shows, and engages in networking with others who are having difficulty getting the authorities to prosecute rape cases.

Other parents work with established organizations or on their own to attempt to remedy what they see as a broader problem of which their daughter's case is an example. Sara's mother, in the case described above, has also become an activist in the field of campus sexual assault prevention as a way of dealing with the problem. She even donated thousands of dollars to the college where her daughter was raped to bring in an expert to help provide sexual assault education and prevention programs and to make recommendations to the campus authorities.

Institutional Mishandling

As discussed in Chapter 3, there seems to be a relationship between the way cases are handled on campus and the willingness of victims to report either to the campus authorities or to the police. As was noted in the case of Laura, there were several other victims awaiting the outcome of her campus judicial hearing to decide whether they would come forward. When the young man was found not guilty, they decided that there was no point in reporting the assaults. By contrast, when a young man at Cornell was indicted on rape charges, several other women came forward to allege that the same person had also assaulted them; both the criminal case and the campus hearing in this case are pending.

Many institutions treat cases of sexual assault on campus remarkably lightly. Often the administrators have a "boys will be boys" attitude that assumes that what a victim has described as sexual assault is nothing more than ordinary party behavior. At such colleges, students are discouraged from pressing charges either through the campus judicial process or in the criminal justice system. Those students who do press charges through the campus judicial process often find that the hearing board does not take their charges seriously, and that the defendant is not found guilty. If the defendant is found guilty, the decision may be overturned on appeal by an appeal board or a high-level administrator of the college. At one college, convictions for sexual assault were routinely overturned by the administrator who dealt with appeals, because he "didn't want to ruin the boy's career or shame him in front of his parents." When the hearing board does find the defendant guilty, the sentence is often trivial. In our research, we have heard of many cases (as mentioned earlier) where a man convicted of sexual assault is given a few hours of community service, often unsupervised. An article in the *Wooster Voice*, the campus newspaper for Wooster College, reported that "in some cases, the College Judicial Board has been more punitive with those found guilty of verbal harassment than those who allegedly committed sexual assault."[1]

For the crusaders in our sample, such attitudes and behavior seem to have a close connection with the decision to sue. It makes them angry, which is an emotion that drives them to action. It makes them begin to see their experience as part of a general problem, rather than one that has only affected them. For some victims, it is the college's effort to keep the case as quiet as possible that makes them feel that they are being badly treated. This effort to contain the case is usually part of a package in which the victim's interests are neglected.

Margie told us that one of the main reasons she decided to sue was the way the university handled the case. "My parents and I sat down and said, 'we've got to do something.' " The school's reaction was mainly to keep it within the school and not to let anyone know about it. For Margie, it was "a lot of little things that started to build up that made me sue. You don't realize it at first, but then . . ." The school never returned calls and kept postponing the hearing. On one of the supposed hearing dates, Margie was prepared to go, but she was told that they had "more important" cases to hear. One of the young men involved was a senior and they allowed him to graduate. The university asked Margie to leave school before the hearing, because it would be "in her best interests." When the hearing was finally held, the defendants were allowed to stay in the room and have lunch with the members of the hearing board, while Margie and her witnesses were told to leave.

It is not only when students are assaulted that the college can engage in such serious mishandling that they push the victims into suing. We do not have many cases in which other members of the college community are raped, but those we know about provide salutary lessons of their own. In the case of *Martin* v. *USC*, described in detail in Chapter 8, the university's behavior is a model of mishandling. This continued even after the victim decided to sue, when the university chose to fire her right in the middle of the court hearing. That victim is now suing USC for unjustifiably firing her.[2]

> After Professor Joyce Honeychurch was raped in her office at the University of Alaska, the university was very anxious to pay her off by offering her a settlement (albeit a modest one) if she would only leave the campus. Having just received tenure, she was appalled by what appeared to be their view that her presence was now somehow unacceptable. The university pushed for her departure even though there was no question of the validity of her charge. The rapist was convicted on another charge, which led to the police decision not to pursue charges in Professor Honeychurch's case.

Psychological Variables

The women whom we have interviewed come across as remarkably mature and strong young women. This is clearly a necessary quality in one who is willing to buck the system as a victim crusader does. Some of the women have a history of activism.

> Maggie told us about several political battles in which she had engaged in high school. "I was always active in causes," she said with some pride.

> Laura's mother described her daughter as "very idealistic and a fighter." According to her mother, she may have learned to fight at the Catholic school she attended, where "some of the nuns were very strong" and were apparently role models of activism.

Another important psychological factor that may distinguish those who sue from those who do not is the way in which pressing charges and going to court feature in the victim's perception of her postrape adjustment. Those who sued felt that taking such action was a central element in their adjustment, without which they would feel that nothing good had come of a traumatic experience. For others, it was not necessary to sue to gain this sense of benefit; in one case, a victim who had considered suing became actively involved in political antirape activities and felt that there would be no additional gain from a lawsuit. For those who contemplated suing but decided not to do so, it was frequently, as they told us, because they "wanted to put the experience behind" them. They felt that a lawsuit would impede, rather than facilitate, their postrape adjustment.

An additional set of factors has to do with the victim's perception of the "quality" of the case and her evaluation of her own behavior. Those who felt that they were to blame in some way (as, for example, in the case of those who had been drinking at the time of the rape) were both less likely to report the assault and less likely to sue. One of the victims who had pressed charges at the campus judicial level ultimately decided not to sue because she felt that more would be made of the fact that she had been drinking than she could tolerate.

The Role of Lawyers

The lawyer's perceptions of the merits of the case was also a significant factor in the decision to sue. An enthusiastic and supportive lawyer is a necessary but not sufficient condition for a lawsuit, as is shown by the fact that we are aware of several cases in which the lawyer was keen to proceed but the victim decided against it. Several victims saw more than one lawyer before they found the one who represented them in the lawsuit. Such persistence accords with the activist personality of crusaders mentioned above.

The best lawyer for a victim to find is one who is committed to pursuing the suit for moral and ethical reasons as well as for the financial gain. Some of the better lawyers we have encountered are concerned as individuals about the problem of campus sexual assault. Their attitudes toward women are egalitarian, and they believe that institutions have an obligation to treat women in such a way that rape does not occur on campus. In addition, good lawyers are realistic. They make it clear to the victim (and her parents, if they are involved) that taking on an institution that has already shown itself to be unsupportive is a major undertaking. They make it clear that the investment of time, money, and emotion is considerable. Thus, although good lawyers encourage the victim to sue, they do not bully her into doing so, especially if they believe that the facts of the particular case are not as strong as they might be.

In a number of the cases we are following, in addition to filing a civil suit, the lawyer has also worked with the victim and her family to see that the case is pursued in criminal court. Very often, the college has discouraged the victim from pressing charges in the criminal justice system. From the point of view of the lawyer, this has both moral and practical implications. If there has been a criminal conviction, any case against the assailant is easy to pursue in civil court. In a lawsuit against the college, it underscores the serious nature of the case that the college is trying to sweep under the rug. It also takes away from the college any defense that relies on the consensual nature of the event about which the victim is complaining. A good lawyer, if the facts look strong enough, will encourage the victim (and indeed fight on her behalf) to have the case dealt with criminally as well as civilly.

Why Buck the System?

The young women we have interviewed who have decided to fight back in the civil courts after their sexual assault and its aftermath are, not surprisingly, very unusual people. Many consider themselves to be activists, acting not only for their own benefit but even more for the benefit of other young women in a similar plight. When a young woman has been sexually assaulted on the college campus, her immediate concerns are usually related to her own recovery. As part of that recovery, most victims are interested in removing the source of the problem by trying to get the assailant off the campus. Later a victim becomes involved in a lawsuit for reasons that have much less to do with her own interests and more to do with a general social concern for the problem of campus sexual assault.

As crusaders, campus sexual assault victims make atypical plaintiffs. They share the characteristics of other plaintiffs described by Merry and Silbey, in that they too want vindication, protection of their rights, or for the "truth" to be revealed, but the women in our sample also want more.[3] Our plaintiffs see themselves as agents of social change. They assert that they are in it not to win damages, but "so that the school will stop treating women like they treated me." Whether this is true or not, it does affect the behavior of the victims. Often they have already been working with groups on campus to effect change in the methods used to handle complaints of sexual assault. They see a lawsuit as an effective addition to this work. By the time they have become involved with lawyers, they have taken on some of the language of the legal profession and can be heard to argue that, although they are not interested in the money for its own sake, making the school pay for its bad behavior is the best way of forcing it to change its approach.

When the women have reached the stage that they consult a lawyer and begin thinking in terms of legal action, they are far beyond being satisfied with anything other than a victory in court. For them, the journey has been even longer than for the average plaintiff. They are very young and they start out being rather naive; by the time they have been sufficiently badly treated to have come full circle in their perceptions of both the event and the institution to which they once gave their loyalty, they are after something that only the traditional legal system can give them. In fact, the redress they seek cannot be obtained through pressing charges in the criminal justice system, because that is not really a direct remedy for the grievance they have suffered. The learning process has been a long and difficult one for the victim we have interviewed. It has been a process of personal growth and change at a crucial age, and it has often involved extensive therapy as well as significant legal counseling.

For the victims who sue the college, the claim is not one for personal damages; rather, it is for a recognition of the validity of what they suffered and an attempt to obtain social justice from the college. For many, money comes to represent the route to achieving their goals; they think it is the ony thing that will hurt the college enough to make it change. It is for this reason that so many of them say that they are not interested in the money damages, except insofar as the latter will aid in the achievement of this goal. In several cases, it is the recognition of the inadequacy of the administration of the criminal law and of efforts for legislative reform that pushes these women in the direction of using the civil legal structure to force social change.

These goals make victims difficult adversaries, because their interests are diametrically opposed to those of the college. Once it is sued, the college is likely to be anxious to cut its losses by a quick and quiet settlement. The college would ideally like the victim to be silenced by a "gag order," without its having to admit any responsibility for what happened. The victim, on the other hand, wants all the publicity she can get, as well as an admission of responsibility and an undertaking by the college to change the method of handling cases such as hers.

For these women, as noted earlier, the civil lawsuit is part of a more general effort to bring about social change. Most of them are also actively involved in various organizations, both on and off campus, that are working to obtain better treatment for campus sexual assault victims. In addition, others have received extensive media publicity and have used this personal attention to publicize the issue. There have also been, as part of legislative efforts to recognize the rights of campus sexual assault victims, a number of national and state hearings at which the women have testified.

In this social change effort, the women have been supported in substantial ways by their lawyers, who are often quicker than the victims are to see the significance of having the right lawsuit at the right time. As one of the lawyers in the Carleton case said,

> I remember clearly them coming to me so that this would not happen to anyone else at Carleton . . . still full of hurt, not realizing how serious this case was and what its nationwide consequences were. . . . When we got this case, we knew what it was. We knew how the press would play it, and we developed the case as a historic case that, if done right, would have the kind of impact the women want it to have. You have an obligation to prepare clients (especially if they are coming to effect social change) to be spokespeople, to be banner carriers.[4]

Media attention is in itself one of the goals of those who sue. They are aware that such attention is an important source of pressure for change by the college. Ironically, it is exactly this fear of media attention that encourages colleges to minimize the seriousness of sexual assault cases. Those few recent cases that have placed the victims at center stage have had the effect of shifting public attention from the behavior of individual students (including the victims) to issues of morality and responsibility toward those students who have placed themselves in the hands of the institution, so to speak, by choosing to come to it for their college education.

How a Victim Turns into a Crusader

It is a long road for a victim of campus sexual assault between the actual assault and the filing of a lawsuit against her college. At each step of the way a victim faces difficult choices about how to conceptualize the event and how to choose a remedy. Figure 4–1 shows how events and the victim's reaction to them increase or decrease the chances that she will end up in civil court.

There are several different options that are available to a victim of campus sexual assault once she recognizes that she has suffered a wrong. The first choice is to do nothing, known as "lumping it."[5] As discussed above, this is clearly what happens in most cases. Like sexual assault victims everywhere, few victims come forward to make a claim. The reasons are likely to be the same as those for rape victims generally; Holmstrom and Burgess found that the most common of these include escape from the ordeal of court proceedings, fear of the assailant's revenge, distaste for sending someone to jail, and a feeling of uselessness that the person would "get away with it anyway."[6]

The second choice available to a victim of campus sexual assault is to proceed through the judicial hearing process on campus. This

**FIGURE 4–1: WHAT HAPPENS WHEN
A VICTIM REPORTS CAMPUS SEXUAL ASSAULT**

* Denotes outcome more likely to result in civil suits.

is a very attractive option for those victims who do not want to "lump it" and who believe they will receive fair treatment from the college. They avoid what they see as the harsh realities of the criminal justice system, and they avoid making a criminal out of the defendant—a sentiment that is surprisingly strong among victims. They can use the campus system to do what for most of them is the first priority: to get their assailant off the campus.

The third option is to proceed through the criminal courts, and the fourth is to file a civil suit against the assailant. The victim's final option is to sue a third party, such as the fraternity or the college where the assault took place. These options are not mutually exclusive. In all the cases in our sample where the victim has filed a lawsuit, she has been through the campus judicial system. In several cases the victim is suing both the assailant and the college, or both the assailant and the fraternity. All these options have different advantages from the point of view of the victim; these will be discussed below.

The Lawsuit as Empowerment

For any victim, filing a complaint and taking a case through the criminal justice system can be seen as a kind of empowerment, though it is much more effective in this sense if there is a conviction.[7] This method has severe limitations, however, as is well known. The victim often goes into the process with the mistaken impression that it is her prosecution; she finds out to her dismay that she is merely a central witness whose power is extremely limited. A victim may be told that the hospital charges associated with evidence collection will be paid for by a victim assistance program or the college. Sometimes this turns out to be untrue; she is billed for the charges and feels tricked. Many victims end up disillusioned with the whole legal process because of both their lack of power and control and its delays and often unsatisfactory (to them) results. As is also well known, many victims (usually women) feel that they are victimized once again by the traditional, male-oriented legal system.[8]

The civil process offers a victim a greater sense of power, because it *is* her suit and she thus has the power and control of a plaintiff. This sense of empowerment is evident in both the victims who sued their assailants and those who sued the college. It is clearly strongest for those who win, but even those who lost felt that at least they were in control to a much larger extent than those who proceeded through the criminal courts. Suing the college, however, has several advantages over suing the assailant. First, there is the obvious one that the institution (or its insurance company) has deep pockets, whereas the assailant is likely to have few assets.[9] But more important to the victim is that suing that institution gives her the opportunity to remedy a wrong done to her, both individually and on a more general level for the benefit of other potential victims. By the time she considers a lawsuit, her grievance is no longer with her assailant but with the system that, in her view, has treated her so badly.

In many ways, suing the college is an excellent way to move away from a sense of powerlessness, which is central to the post-traumatic stress suffered by a sexual assault victim, toward emotional strength. She can make the events public and may be able to precipitate social change. She can achieve these results without inciting the assailant's anger, the results of which she so much fears. This fear is of both his personal violence and the possibility, albeit remote, that he might use the court system against her. There have been several cases in which the assailant has sued the victim as a result of her charges agaist him, whether for defamation, intentional infliction of emotional distress, or abuse of the legal process.[10] To our knowledge, none of the cases have been successful in court, but they nevertheless remain a risk for victims.

Another advantage to the victim (whether she sues the assailant or a third party) is that she as plaintiff sets the framework for the case in terms of the harm to her. She tells her story instead of having the prosecution frame it for her (as is the case in a criminal trial), with all the reorientation and distortion that implies. When she sues the college, there are also implicit general issues about duty and moral obligation to the institution's students. A victim can thus focus the case on the violence and the intrusion rather than the sex, as happens in a criminal case.

Central to the victim's use of the civil courts is that her primary identification changes from victim to plaintiff or (even more empowering) social change agent, claimant, or crusader. As Bumiller found, some people who have suffered discrimination are unwilling to sue because it means taking on the unwanted label of victim.[11] For the women in our group, using the civil court, especially if the case is framed as one in which college policies are at issue, is the way the victim can shed that label. The sexual assault has made her define herself as a victim; the lawsuit liberates her and provides her with a replacement role. In that sense, an important purpose has been served regardless of the outcome of the case.

In those cases where the victim chooses the civil rather than the criminal system, and sues a third party rather than her assailant, she sidesteps definitions of power and sex that are central in the criminal arena. The issue is no longer her responsibility versus his, but the responsibility of the institution. In most of the cases, the claim is that the college did not fulfill its responsibility to its students, either by negligently maintaining an environment in which sexual assault could take place or by handling cases so badly that its likelihood is increased. As the reader will see in the chapter on civil suits, many of these cases are successful in terms of both changing college policy and winning the lawsuit or obtaining a satisfactory settlement.

> Dana is suing a university because she was raped by her instructor, a clear case in which the institution is responsible for the behavior of its employee. Whatever the details of the legal claims, Dana's lawsuit has shifted the focus from her behavior to that of the institution. The talk is now about what responsibility the university has in hiring and supervising its employees, and not whether she "asked for it," as is so often the case in criminal cases.

In this example, the focus has shifted from the narrow legal definition of rape to issues relating to the damage the victim has suffered as a result of the rape. In a criminal case, the harm suffered by the victim is only relevant to the extent that it helps prove that a rape took place. In all civil cases, it is central to the question of proof, as well as to the question of damages.

The Institution as Enemy

One of the things that changes on this journey for the victim is whom she sees as her enemy. When she first defines herself as a victim, the agent of her victimization is the assailant. *He* is the person who has caused her harm, and it is on him that she focuses her fear and, later, her anger. In the period following the assault, the victim is involved in the judicial hearing process. The members of the college with whom she interacts are initially seen as supportive helpers whose business it is to counsel her and to see that the judicial process is properly conducted so that her assailant can be punished for his behavior. In cases that end up as lawsuits, however, there is a gradual erosion of this view of the college and its agents. She begins to recognize that the staff may be protecting interests other than hers, and that the college is not as benign as she had originally perceived it to be.

This process may be a long one, because the victim needs to undergo an about-face in her view of the institution. As mentioned above, many of the victims of campus sexual assault are in their first year of college. The decision to choose this particular college is probably the first major decision they have made in their lives, and it is usually made after long deliberation and discussion. The victim thus has an investment in the "rightness" of that decision. Because she has invested so much in this choice, she is likely to feel that the college is definitely the best place for her to go.

> Dana told us that she had given up a full scholarship at another institution because she was so enthusiastic to attend the university she later sued, even though she was not offered a scholarship there.

Given her loyalty to and identification with the college, the victim may ignore or deny the first signs that the authorities are not acting in her best interests. Any ambiguity will initially be interpreted to show the institution in a benign light. In our interviews, victims often spoke of the dean of students as initially offering support and promising that he or she would take quick action to make sure that the defendant was removed from the campus. Because this is usually the major concern of the victim in the aftermath of the assault, it is very important for her to hear. Often it turns out that for one reason or another the assailant is not removed, and the victim feels that her trust was misplaced because the administrator has misrepresented the situation to her. This realization, however, generally does not come until quite a while later, when her trust is beginning to erode after encounters with other members of the campus community.

When the victim first realizes that the institution has interests other than her own, she moves from a positive view of its actions to one that is more complex, in which some of the people she encounters are seen as benign and others as malign. Gradually this process comes full circle, as she moves beyond individual judgments to a global view of the whole institution as malign. It is only when this happens that the victim is ready to take legal action.

The perception of the institution itself as the enemy, rather than a place composed of helpful and harmful individual members, may come from the outside. Often it is the victim's parents (who, as mentioned above, are quicker in general to see the event in legal terms) who plant the idea that the institution is treating her badly. The victim's parents have a very different relationship with the college; because the choice of a college was less central to their lives and because they pay the bills, they are likely to become disillusioned with it sooner than the victim does. They demand accountability for the thousands of dollars they have invested in their daughter's education. This is why it is so important for administrators to pay careful attention to the concerns of the victim's parents.

It is often the continued presence of the assailant on campus that is responsible for the change in the victim's perceptions. After all, she reasons, if the institution "allows" the assailant on campus, knowing that his presence is her greatest fear, then how can the institution be anything but her enemy?

In most cases, the victim has to remove herself physically from the college (by either transferring or dropping out) before she is able to distance herself enough emotionally to sue the institution. In only one case that we know of is a victim still a student at the university she is currently suing. Generally the victim finds it impossible to sue the college while she is still part of the community; this is true for practical reasons as well as because of her need to have distance to frame her grievance appropriately. These cases inevitably become the subject of extensive publicity on campus as well as elsewhere, and it is very difficult for the victim to remain on campus while she is the subject of gossip. She may also worry about how fairly she will be treated academically by an institution she is suing. (In fact, though, the opposite may be true. The college may bend over backwards to treat the victim well so as not to alienate her more and risk another suit.)

Conclusion

As we have seen, the victims who sue the college are a very small number of special young women. Their impact is disproportionate to their numbers. One extensively publicized case, like the Carleton case, can have a huge impact on the way colleges handle campus sexual assault. For those young women who are willing to take on the institution, the pain is significant, but the rewards can be major.

As discussed in Chapter 8, there is a body of law on the subject of the college's responsibility to its students. The legal bases for the lawsuits in the current cases are usually rather different, because they address a much broader question of responsibility that may be more moral than legal. In some cases, the legal basis for holding the institution liable is not well developed yet. Despite this, these cases are using the law to define a social and moral responsibility, especially to women. The victims thus become, perhaps unintentionally, the agents of legal change as well.

Checklist for Victims and Their Parents

1. If you feel that the college is not handling your case properly, first try to do something about it directly with them. If you decide to sue, it is important to show that you have tried all other options.
2. If that does not work and you are considering a lawyer, select one carefully. If you are not happy with your initial choice, change immediately. Look for the following things:
   a. Do not choose anyone who seems to have any association with the college (in some small towns, this is harder than you might think).
   b. Choose someone who seems to have a commitment to fighting on behalf of citizens who are wronged by big institutions.
   c. Choose someone who has egalitarian views about women and who seems genuinely supportive of your case.
   d. Choose someone who seems to have a realistic assessment about the merits of your case. If the lawyer says it will be a piece of cake to collect vast sums from the college, be suspicious. These cases are almost never sure bets.
   e. Choose someone who encourages you to pursue the charges in criminal court, if that is appropriate.

f. Choose someone you *like*. This is very important, as you will be likely to spend a great deal of time over a long period with this lawyer.

g. If you try one lawyer and are rejected, do not give up right away. Get a second opinion. You may not find the right lawyer on the first try.

3. Tell your lawyer *everything* pertaining to the case, even if you think it is insignificant or if you are embarrassed by some elements of the assault or your behavior. The lawyer cannot make a realistic assessment unless he or she has *all* the information.

4. Remember that you will need to be very committed to carry your case through. You need determination, patience, and strength. A lawsuit is easier for the college, which has far more resources than you do and less of an emotional investment. You need to turn your emotional investment into strength of purpose to continue over the several years it might take.

5. Use all the support that is available. Victims who sue tell us that the support of family, friends, and therapists was essential for them to go the distance.

5

The Disciplinary Hearing

Codes, Law, and Practice

It is customary for a college to have some written document in which it outlines what it considers to be acceptable academic and personal behavior. The details of this document are very important both legally and in terms of the message that the college sends to the campus community. From a legal point of view, recent cases have shown that a college that has a carefully drafted code to which it routinely adheres is almost always able to defend itself against attacks by students who feel that they have not been treated fairly. As we shall demonstrate, problems arise when the college either has no written procedure for dealing with behavior like sexual assault or does not follow its own procedure.

The first part of this chapter will look at different aspects of judicial codes of conduct that relate to campus sexual assault. The second section will examine a number of important cases that have dealt with issues arising from codes of conduct. The final section will consider the process of changing codes of conduct and the reasons for doing so; it will conclude with a number of recommendations for clauses that a college should consider including in its code of conduct.

The Nature of Campus Codes of Conduct

There are those who argue that it is a mistake for a college to have a code that looks too much like a criminal code.[1] The more legalistic the code, the more the college looks like the legal system. *Colleges cannot and should not hold themselves out as an equal alternative to the criminal justice system.* As is discussed in Chapter 6, the role of the college in disciplinary hearings is very different from that of the criminal justice system, even though the campus judicial system may be chosen as the better option by many victims. Georgetown University makes its role very clear when it states, "The student discipline system is designed to be an educational system and does not function as a court of law. Therefore, the rules of evidence and various other procedures are handled in a manner consistent with the educational focus."[2]

On the other hand, it is important that the codes be specific enough both so that students know what is expected of them and to satisfy legal requirements. For example, as we shall see later in this chapter, codes that do not list offenses at all are likely to be at risk of being declared unconstitutional by the courts.

Definitions of Campus Violations

Colleges differ in the nature and specificity of possible violations in their campus codes. Some codes are quite detailed and are modeled on a criminal code in which all offenses are outlined specifically; Bard College in New York actually cites the relevant section of the New York state penal codes.[3] These codes have an offense of sexual assault clearly described in them. Brown University has an offense it calls "sexual misconduct," which the code defines as "non-consensual physical conduct of a sexual nature."[4] Duke University uses even more legal language that divides sexual assault into two categories. The more serious offense covers actual rape and sodomy, whereas the lesser one includes "the touching of an unwilling person's intimate parts."[5]

The other model of a campus code does not list offenses at all, but has broad proscriptions of inappropriate behavior. In such a case, the code will say that no student shall behave in a way that is unfitting for a student of that college. Stanford University, for example, defines the "Fundamental Standard" as one in which students "are expected to show both within and without the University such respect for order, morality, personal honor and the rights of others as is demanded of good citizens."[6] The code does include a list of specific circumstances in which this standard has been applied, but it is implied that this list is not all-inclusive.[7]

Codes that do not specify charges but do outlaw such conduct as "inappropriate behavior" are becoming increasingly uncommon. There have been some cases in which the courts have held that a regulation that simply prohibits "misconduct" is unconstitutionally vague. This happened in the case of *Soglin* v. *Kaufman* in the late 1960s, in which the University of Wisconsin charged a student who engaged in protest activity with "misconduct" and argued that it had an inherent power to discipline that did not need to be exercised through specific rules.[8] The court agreed with the student that a greater degree of specificity was required by the law. Many codes, like that of the University of California at Los Angeles (UCLA), deal with the need for a general standard and the due process need for specificity by having a combination of both specific and general language. UCLA charges a student both with rape and with conduct that interferes with the health and safety of another.[9]

Some codes describe as prohibited behavior only that behavior that would be classified as sexual assault in the criminal code, while others have a broader definition. For example, the student handbook of St. Norbert College in Wisconsin defines sexual assault as follows:

> Sexual assault consists of actual or threatened sexual contact which is not mutually agreeable to both parties. Sexual contact is not limited to intercourse but includes any touch that may reasonably be construed as invasive and inappropriate. This includes any such action toward a person which damages his or her physical or psychological well-being. Such conduct (by other students or any other member of the college community or visitor to the campus) is expressly prohibited by the College and is considered a serious violation of human rights. Date and acquaintance rape are included in this definition of assault.[10]

This section is much more specific than the usual criminal code definition, especially with its emphasis on contact that is not "mutually agreeable," its concern with psychological damage, and its holding visitors accountable.

The emphasis on mutually agreeable sexual conduct is taken to the extreme in the proposed revisions to the "sexual offense policy" of Antioch College in Ohio. In these revisions, *consent* is defined as the "act of willingly and verbally agreeing to engage in specific sexual contact or conduct." The proposed revisions then describe in detail the responsibility of the person who initiates the contact or conduct to get the verbal consent, which is described as "an ongoing process in any sexual interaction," thereby requiring verbal consent with "each new level of physical and/or sexual contact/conduct in any given interaction."[11]

Although it is clear that Antioch College has good intentions in its attempts to get its students to communicate about sex to avoid the misunderstandings so common in date rape, these proposed revisions are a legal and practical disaster. It is unlikely that a hearing board would be able to deal satisfactorily with the cases that would come up under such vague and demanding definitions.

A number of the codes we have seen do not have a special section for sexual assault, but instead include it in a general prohibition against physical assault. Given the increase in concern about the problem of sexual assault on campus, we believe that it is much better to specify the type of sexual behavior that the college considers to be unacceptable.

We have found much confusion in some codes about the extent to which sexual assault and sexual harassment are to be treated as part of the same offense or whether they are defined and treated separately. Many schools include sexual assault as part of their prohibition of sexual harassment. The code of Luther College in Decorah, Iowa, in an article prohibiting violent, abusive, or obscene acts, defines sexual harassment as including "insults, threats, obscene gestures, coercion, or assault." As examples of prohibited behavior, it lists acts ranging from verbal sexual innuendo to coerced sexual intercourse.[12] Southern Methodist University in Dallas, Texas, also includes assault in the section in their code on harassment (of all kinds, not only sexual), although they do have a separate clause stating that "Southern Methodist University will not tolerate sexual assault in any form, including 'acquaintance rape.' "[13] St. Lawrence University in Canton, New York, asserts that sexual harassment can take many forms, from "unwelcome emphasis on sexual identity or sexual orientation to the actual coercion of sexual relations."[14] The emphasis on harassment about sexual identity or orientation is in fact different from what is legally defined as sexual harassment; it is really an example of general harassment, like that based on race or ethnicity. Thus, St. Lawrence is conflating three different issues: sexual assault, sexual harassment, and general harassment.

We believe that it only makes for confusion if sexual assault is treated as part of harassment. As discussed in Chapter 1, it is clear that there are similarities between the two areas, but there are enough differences to make it more efficacious to treat them separately. If they are treated together, there is a good chance that many people—especially students—will not see the issues separately and will not treat sexual assault with appropriate seriousness. In talking to members of campus communities where there is no separation, we find that the students (and some faculty and staff) do not understand the fact that sexual assault is different from and may be more serious than sexual harassment. In one case, it was not until students who had been sexually assaulted consulted a lawyer that they found, to their surprise, that they had been raped and not sexually harassed, as they had been led to believe by campus officials. Some institutions have taken steps to deal with this problem by specifically separating the two offenses. Brown University in Providence, Rhode Island, for example, states that "harassment without physical contact will not be deemed sexual misconduct."[15]

Our experience has shown that a college is more likely to have a specific statement and policy about sexual harassment than about sexual assault. Many of these policies are a recent response to publicity and lawsuits on the issue and make clear the college's position disapproving of the behavior. Colleges would do well to include a similar policy statement about the seriousness of sexual assault in their codes.

The Relationship Between the Campus Code and the Criminal Justice System

Some codes deal specifically with the relationship between the college hearing and the criminal justice authorities. One unusual provision, which we found in the code of the College of William and Mary in Williamsburg, Virginia, was a policy statement in which the accuser is encouraged also to "pursue appropriate remedies in the State judicial system."[16]

Colleges vary as to how they view the existence of a criminal justice proceeding against one of their students. On one side is the code of Carleton College in Northfield, Minnesota, which recognizes the obligation of all members of the college community to adhere to the laws but states that "it is not the role or obligation of the College to act as a law enforcement agency for these laws."[17] At the other end is the code of Duke University, which says that "acts in violation of North Carolina and United States law are necessarily in violation of the Undergraduate Judicial Code."[18]

Codes also vary as to what they do about the existence of a criminal justice proceeding. In the case of an off-campus violation, Carleton College states that such a charge or conviction is of "no disciplinary concern" and that it will act only if "it considers the alleged misconduct to be so grave as to demonstrate flagrant disregard for the rights of others."[19] The College of William and Mary states that violations of local, state, or federal law can be the subject of college disciplinary action only if it is determined that disciplinary action is necessary for the protection of other members of the college community. In the situation when the college also pursues its own remedy, the code states that it can do so without awaiting court action.[20]

The problems raised by the concurrent criminal trial and disciplinary hearing are not usually covered in the campus code. Rarely, a code will spell out how the college will deal with such a situation, as is the case in the code of St. Norbert's College (which covers in detail a number of issues not covered in most codes). In the case of concurrent jurisdiction, the code specifies that the college may go ahead with its hearing even if the criminal trial has yet to begin. The college retains the option to suspend the student until the decision of the criminal court. St. Norbert's is careful to maintain its distance from the criminal justice system, however, by stating that (1) the college will only participate in the trial when subpoenaed, (2) it cannot regard an arrest as a finding of guilt, and (3) even in the case of a guilty verdict, the college must reach its own conclusions through due process. Fifth Amendment issues are recognized in the clause that exhorts the college to be "scrupulous in respecting his/her rights as an accused person and avoid any effort to secure a 'confession' or evidence that may be used against him/her."[21]

Duke University, unlike most other schools, specifically addresses the issue of double jeopardy—the legal doctrine that prevents an accused from being tried twice for the same offense in the criminal courts. Its code clarifies this doctrine which legally only applies to more than one proceeding, both of which are criminal.[22] Given this definition, one wonders why Duke felt the necessity to put it in the code.

The Rights of the Accused

Included in some college codes is a section on rights that are recognized. Such a section has a salutary effect in that it emphasizes concern for the rights as well as the obligations of the accused. It makes clear that the school is concerned about fair treatment for all concerned. Some codes, like that of St. Lawrence University, have a special section in which the rights of the accused are listed, whereas others list the rights of all parties together.[23] St. Lawrence, for example, provides students with the right to remain silent, the right to be informed in writing of the charges, the right to have someone accompany them to the hearing, the right to call witnesses, and the right to appeal.[24] The State University of New York (SUNY) at Brockport is even more specific; it has a list of ten rights for those charged with violations of the code. In addition to those rights listed in the St. Lawrence University code, SUNY-Brockport provides such protections as the right to receive a list of the members of the hearing board, the names of witnesses, and access to the taped proceedings of the case.[25] These rights are basically the due process rights that are discussed later in this chapter, although any rights that are considered important can be listed, as we do in the recommendations at the end of the chapter.

The Rights of Victims

Contrary to the beliefs of many people, a sexual assault victim is accorded few rights in most college codes. This mirrors her status in the criminal justice system, although a number of states have recently passed "victims' bills of rights" that go some distance toward changing the situation. Just as in the criminal court, the victim is only a witness in the hearing procedure; thus, she has no right to legal representation in the hearing. (This is not to say that she would not benefit from having such a right, only that the law in no way demands it.) The Ramstad amendment, discussed in detail in Chapter 9, gives the victim the right only if the defendant is entitled to an attorney.

Even though the law does not provide the victim with rights, some campuses do include a list of victim rights in their codes. The campuses that seem to handle this issue best are those who recognize that it is appropriate to provide parallel rights to both the victim and the defendant. Thus, as the Ramstad amendment mandates, either both defendant and victim are entitled to an attorney, or neither. More common at present, however, is the situation in which each person is entitled to have someone (not necessarily a lawyer) present at the hearing. The purpose of this person's presence for the victim (most likely her mother or a best friend) is to provide her with the support necessary to get through the hearing and its inherent trauma. For example, in its list of victim's rights, Southern Methodist University includes the right "to have a person of his or her choice accompany him or her during the disciplinary proceedings. Such person is for moral support and has the same responsibilities as described for rights of the accused to have companions."[26]

In addition to the right to some kind of representation, there are several other rights that are very helpful. The victim should have the protection of the equivalent of the rape shield law, which bans discussion of a victim's irrelevant past sexual history.[27] These laws have become fairly common in criminal law, and they are equally applicable to the campus hearing. Many victims fear the disclosure of some past experience to such an extent that they are deterred from making a complaint at the campus level. Those states that have rape shield laws base them on the understanding that such information is generally irrelevant to the determination of guilt or innocence in the case at hand. This is no less true in the campus hearing.

A further right of great importance to the victim is the right to be able to make a "victim impact statement" to elucidate, if it is not already obvious, what the nature and extent of her suffering has been. In addition, she should be given the opportunity to state what she feels is the appropriate punishment for the defendant in the case of a finding of guilt. There is an increasing trend to involve the victim in the proceedings in criminal court to personalize the case for the jury and to give the victim the sense that she is not just a witness whose views are irrelevant. This is the result of the victims' rights movement, which has brought about statutes in many states. Once again, this right is no less important for the victim at the judicial hearing than it is in the criminal justice system. At Cornell, the victim can make an impact statement during testimony or after a finding of guilt (but before penalty determination).

The final issue relating to the hearing that is significant for the victim is her right to be informed of the outcome of the proceedings. It is remarkable how many institutions do not provide this information or do so only, as in the case of one university, on the condition that the victim tell no one. One exception to this silence is the College of William and Mary, which as part of the section in its code outlining "Modified Procedures for Cases of Sexual Misconduct" gives the victim the "right to receive written notification of the verdict of the hearing and any penalty imposed."[28] Cornell also provides this right.

There is a legal issue involved here that may account for the reluctance of colleges to inform victims of the outcome of the case. It relates to the confidentiality of a student's record under the Buckley amendment, which is dealt with in detail in Chapter 9. As we discuss there, we do not believe that the amendment prohibits providing information about the outcome to the victim of a sexual assault on campus.

Other rights mentioned in some codes have to do with the victim's needs apart from the hearing itself, such as the right to have the defendant leave her alone and the right to move out of her housing. In the section at the end of this chapter on recommended clauses for codes of conduct, we include a number of these rights that we have found to be very important for the victim.

The Law and Judicial Hearings

General Considerations of Due Process

We now turn to what the law requires of hearings held for infractions of a campus code of conduct. We have already mentioned that there is great variation in the specificity of the codes themselves. As the reader will see, there is also variation in the way in which hearings are conducted, who sits on the hearing boards, whether and to what extent lawyers are involved in the process, and what rights of appeal a student has and to whom.

The role of the court in overseeing the hearings stems from the constitutional right that a person has a right to due process of law under the Fourteenth Amendment of the U.S. Constitution. The relevant part of the amendment states, "nor shall any State deprive any person of life, liberty, or property without due process of law." For the Fourteenth Amendment to come into play, plaintiffs have to show that they have a property or liberty interest in their education, meaning that it provides a benefit to them that the state should protect. Although the Supreme Court has never specifically decided whether students at a private college have such an interest, it has stated that such an interest exists in the public elementary and secondary schools.[29] Also, in the lower federal courts, rulings have clearly indicated that university students do have a property and liberty interest in their education.[30] If the student can show this interest, then there must be some form of due process before he or she can be deprived of it. For example, a student could not be expelled (that is, deprived of his interest in his education) without some appropriate hearing. What the courts consider an "appropriate hearing" will be discussed in detail later in this chapter.

Because the Constitution requires state action before its interest is triggered, the right to due process only directly affects students at public institutions. In ordinary language, this means that you can not use the Constitution as a basis for your legal claim unless you can argue that some part of the government (federal, state, or local) has deprived you of your constitutional rights. Because private colleges are not part of the government in this sense, one cannot use the Constitution as the basis for a lawsuit when suing a private college. Recently, however, there has been a trend in the courts to apply similar rules in the case of private colleges under a standard of "fairness."[31] The most common basis for applying the doctrine of fairness to students at private institutions is one that relates to their contract with the students.[32] When a person enrolls at a private college, he or she enters into a contract with that college. In return for the fees the student pays, the college agrees to provide the student with an education. Having made this agreement, the courts argue, the college cannot fairly renege on its promise without some good reason. The school has to prove its justification in a similar way to the due process hearing that a public college must provide.

On the whole, the courts have left a great deal of leeway to universities as to what constitutes a satisfactory due process hearing under the Constitution. The problem is that there are no Supreme Court decisions that outline what is expected of universities. For this reason, one has to rely on lower court decisions, with results rather like a half-completed patchwork quilt. The courts also often do not distinguish between what due process they require and what they merely approve.[33] Further, the courts make a distinction between academic and disciplinary issues. They give greater freedom to colleges in the case of academic violations, such as cheating, as they believe that the institution is in the best position to decide such cases; thus, they are very reluctant to intervene.[34] Colleges need to provide more due process before finding a student guilty of a disciplinary violation than an academic one. Violations relating to sexual assault would all be classified as disciplinary and therefore subject to the higher standard of review.

In general, however, it is clear that the standards required by the courts are rather flexible, and most present-day codes of conduct have sufficient safeguards in them to provide due process to satisfy the constitutional requirements. The courts determine how much process is due in any situation depending on the nature of the interest at stake, that is, what someone can lose as a result of the hearing.[35] For example, if a student is at risk for expulsion, more due process is required than if she or he is placed on probation for a semester. Although the punishments that a college can mete out may seem very severe to a student, they are by no means as severe as other liberty interests protected by the Constitution. For a student to have a "conviction" for sexual assault on his college record could have serious negative ramifications for his future professional career, but it is by no means as bad as its criminal counterpart, where the liberty interest includes the possibility of going to jail (as well as the stigma of a criminal record).

What is important is that there be some standards of which the students are aware, and that these standards be adhered to in any given case. The classic case of due process in a college setting is that of *Dixon* v. *Alabama State Board of Education,* in which black students participated in peaceful demonstrations and attempted on several occasions to be served at a lunch grill during the early years of the civil rights movement.[36] Nine students were dismissed from the college without having been advised of any violations of the code of conduct or given any opportunity to be heard. It was clear in this case that there was no way in which the students could get a fair hearing, and no way in which they could defend themselves against the charges for which they were expelled. The court decided that they were entitled to some form of hearing to allow them to rebut the university's charges, although it made clear that it was not necessary to hold a "full judicial hearing."[37] Although the Supreme Court declined to hear this case, it gave its seal of approval later to the need for some kind of hearing in the case of *Goss* v. *Lopez*.[38] What this means for our purposes is that a college cannot punish a student for sexual assault without some sort of hearing, however bad the behavior or however "obvious" it is that the student did it.

A case decided in 1984 in which members of a fraternity at the University of Pennsylvania sued the university, arguing that their due process rights had been violated, raised the issue of hearings that did not have preannounced rules.[39] In that case, which is discussed in Chapter 8, the fraternity was disciplined as a result of a gang rape that took place in the fraternity house. The University of Pennsylvania is a private university which is not bound by the constitution but by a need for fairness. Even so, the judge in that case found that the hearing board's idea that it would make the rules up as it went along was entirely inappropriate.[40]

One of the difficulties with the lack of standards set down by the courts is that a college really does not know whether its procedures are in violation of due process until a court tells them, which is far too late. Our advice to a school is to err on the side of caution and to provide more rather than fewer rights. We also recommend, as will be discussed in greater detail later in this chapter, that the rights be enumerated clearly in the code of conduct. It is not enough, as Bradley University does, to have a rule giving appellate power to an arbitration board in cases "in which due process of law has been violated" without listing anywhere what due process entails.[41] Because these boards are composed of students and other members of the university, none of whom can be expected to be lawyers, one cannot imagine how they will decide that due process has in fact been violated.

The Role of Lawyers

On most campuses, there are no lawyers involved in the judicial hearings, and some codes of conduct specifically forbid them to be present.[42] The cases are conducted by a judicial administrator who is usually not a lawyer, before a hearing board composed of a mix of faculty, administrators, and students.

In relatively few institutions, by contrast, the judicial administrator is a trained lawyer. Cornell, for example, has a full-time legally trained judicial administrator who plays the role of prosecutor before the nonlawyer hearing board. In all hearings there is also a legally trained professor who plays the role of judge; the justification is that a legally trained person is better able to control the hearings and to advise the board of any legal issues that are relevant. It should be noted that Cornell allows a defendant to be represented by any advisor, including a law student, which risks making the proceedings unduly long and litigious.

Rutgers University currently allows lawyers to participate in the hearings at all stages, just as if it were a criminal trial. Administrators at the school are in the midst of a major revision of the entire judicial procedure and are considering minimizing the role of lawyers, because they find that this practice does not work very well.[43] It is too cumbersome, too lengthy, and too legalistic, in the view of those who have argued for a revision of the code of conduct.

One of the elements of due process is that of the right to counsel. In most cases, the courts have refused to require that a defendant in a campus judicial hearing have counsel, on the basis that this is not a criminal procedure and that a lawyer would serve no useful purpose.[44] There are two exceptions to the general rule. The first is that the student may be entitled if the college, as in the case of Cornell, has counsel. The second exception has to do with those cases in which the defendant faces criminal charges arising out of the same set of facts. In such a situation, a student may be given a lawyer if he or she is forced to choose between the risk of expulsion and the risk of self-incrimination. In that case, a greater issue of due process clearly is involved, as the behavior of the student at the campus hearing may affect the subsequent trial in criminal court. In the case of *Gabrilowitz* v. *Newman,* the court found that the university denied the defendant due process when it refused him permission to have an attorney on a rape charge. The basis for this ruling was the danger of self-incrimination and the student's "awareness of his inability to evaluate the effect" of his statements on the criminal charge.[45]

When legal representation is considered a part of due process, in the circumstances mentioned above, there is still disagreement as to the actual role of the lawyer.[46] Is the lawyer to be present in an advisory or an adversary capacity? Court rulings on this issue usually do not mandate actual defense at the judicial hearing, but rather only that the student have a lawyer available to advise him or her.

There are some other unanswered questions about the right to an attorney. For example, in the case where there is the risk of incrimination in a pending criminal prosecution, must the defendant be advised of his right to a legal advisor? The courts most likely would require that the defendant learn of this constitutional protection, though one case held that the university did not deny the student his right against self-incrimination when it offered him a choice between a polygraph test or a hearing.[47] The related question of whether the university has an obligation to provide a student with an attorney is less likely to be answered in the affirmative. Because the hearing is not itself a criminal proceeding, the right to be provided with a lawyer is less clear-cut than in criminal cases.

Dealing with Fifth Amendment Problems

The difficulty with this issue is that the defendant may be faced with the impossible dilemma of not testifying to exonerate himself at the campus hearing for fear that what he says will be used against him in the criminal hearing. This is a very real issue of due process that the university must recognize and deal with.

One possible solution is to postpone the campus hearing until after the criminal trial, although the courts have not generally required that universities do so.[48] The difficulty here is that often the criminal process moves at a snail's pace and there is an immediate need to resolve some issues before they are resolved by the legal system. The victim, for example, has an interest in having the matter concluded as soon as possible so that she can get on with her recovery. In many cases, the major interest of the victim is to get the defendant out of her life. If he is found guilty at the campus hearing, he may well be expelled, which effectively removes him from the campus and the victim's life. In addition, the college has an interest in dealing with a serious complaint as soon as possible in order to have a resolution of what may be a very volatile situation affecting the entire campus.

A further solution about which we have heard is for the college to work out an agreement with the criminal justice authorities that anything the defendant says in the campus hearing cannot be used against him at the subsequent criminal trial. It has been suggested that this should be extended to forbid the use in criminal court of anything that comes out at the campus hearing unless it is independently discovered.[49] This is usually an informal arrangement and may be feasible depending on the nature of the town-gown relationship at a college.

Evidentiary Issues

The courts have never required colleges to adhere to the same rules of evidence that are used in the criminal justice system. A number of colleges specifically state that they do not intend to do so, and will in their discretion admit any evidence that seems appropriate.[50] We believe that this is an important aspect of keeping the focus of campus judicial hearings educational rather than strictly legal. It also has the benefit of not requiring that the hearing board be trained in the finer points of the rules of evidence—a process that occupies an entire course at law school.

There has been one troubling twist to this freedom to use whatever evidence the college thinks is appropriate. In a case in 1992 at Old Dominion University in Norfolk, Virginia, several young men were found guilty of rape.[51] One of them, a student named Watts, was linked to the rape by the evidence of a young woman who heard him say that "he couldn't believe he did it with his boots on." The young woman had then asked, "What's going on up there?" and was told by a third party that "Watts did it, he definitely did it." This hearsay evidence was essential in the guilty verdict of the hearing board.

Watts asked the court for a permanent injunction prohibiting the university from suspending him as a result of the disciplinary proceeding. The judge granted the injunction based on a Virginia case ruling that where the court finds evidence that may be admissible in an administrative proceeding but not a court of law, it is not admissible when it is so prejudicial that it would decide the whole issue. Because the damning hearsay evidence was all that connected Watts with the rape, the judge decided that he was bound by the Virginia case. If the university had presented any other evidence, the hearsay would not have been as prejudicial. In fact, another of the young men involved, on seeing Watts's success in court, also tried to sue, but failed miserably because the university had other evidence on which to base its finding of guilt.

This Old Dominion decision is not as dramatic a departure from the general rule as it might seem. First, the judge applied a Virginia case, which would not be relevant outside that state. Second, the difficulty arose because the only evidence the university had to connect the defendant with the rape was the prejudicial hearsay. The victim was so drunk that she could remember very little apart from waking several times with different people in bed with her. Although such a situation unfortunately is fairly common, it is often possible to present evidence in addition to the kind available in this case.

Even though a college may not use the formal rules of evidence, the question remains as to who has to prove the claim (technically known as the *burden of proof*) and how decisively they have to prove it (technically known as the *standard of proof*). This is clearly one of the elements of due process. In all the codes that mention it (though few do), the burden is placed on the complainant or the representative of the college to prove guilt, and not on the defendant to prove his innocence. There is no law that addresses the nature of the burden of proof but a court would presumably follow the criminal rule, placing it on the college or the complainant and not on the defendant. One of the few colleges that mentions the burden of proof is SMU, which places the burden of "going forward with the evidence" on the dean of student life.[52]

We believe that the burden of proof should be on the college rather than on the complainant, as this latter method seems to make the case a private action between the victim and the defendant, rather than an offense against the college. We have been told by a number of victims who were supposed to present the case that they felt isolated and unduly burdened by this obligation.

As for the standard of proof, courts do not require the criminal standard of proof beyond a reasonable doubt in campus hearings. They consider that these hearings are not criminal in their process or their consequences, and therefore the criminal standard is neither required nor appropriate. If a college does use it, however, the law does not view it as unconstitutional. Stanford University is one of very few colleges that use this high standard; we were told that it works very badly, as it is virtually impossible to get a conviction.

Stanford administrators have been trying for some time to lower the standard to one that will work better, but have run into opposition from the student senate. The students see it as a bid for power by the administrators that will take away rights from them.

The second standard, which is the civil standard of a preponderance of the evidence, is the one used by most schools.[53] The third standard, of clear and convincing evidence, is used in other proceedings that are not criminal but involve greater liberty interests than civil lawsuits, such as civil commitment proceedings for the mentally ill.[54] It is more difficult to obtain a finding of guilt using this middle standard of proof than in the case of the preponderance of the evidence, but easier than when using the criminal standard. The courts do not require any particular standard to be used in judicial hearings; what they require is that the standard be articulated and that notice be provided to the defendant of the standard being used. The best way of doing this is, of course, to include it in the campus code of conduct.

Open or Closed Hearings

Whether the hearing should be public or private is a matter of serious concern to colleges. On the one hand, there is the importance of keeping information that may be damaging to either the victim or the defendant, or both, out of the gossip mills so common on college campuses. On the other hand, there is the model of the criminal justice system, which guarantees a defendant a public trial so that he can vindicate himself if the charges are unfounded. Because of these competing pressures, it is not surprising that a variety of different models are used.

Some institutions require that all hearings be closed.[55] Others, such as Carleton College, require that all hearings be public unless either party requests a private hearing.[56] Many campus codes do not deal specifically with the issue at all. As long as an institution's practice is consistent, it seems that it is not legally necessary to incorporate a statement in the code. When colleges reevaluate their codes in general, they should make a decision on this issue, bearing in mind the need to protect both the victim and the defendant, as well as other interests that seem significant.

We believe that the benefits of a closed hearing in the case of sexual assault outweigh any benefits of a public hearing. Many victims are only willing to press charges if they can do it in a closed hearing, rather than risk having all the defendant's friends there providing support at the time of the hearing and gossiping about it later. If the college takes care to protect the rights of the defendant, he does not suffer by having a closed hearing.

It is also important that the college exercise good judgment when selecting a room in which to hold the hearings, regardless of whether the hearing is open or closed. Administrators need to recognize that the victim will have difficulty being in the same room as the defendant; they should therefore choose a location where there can be some distance. We have been told of instances where the victim was seated right next to the defendant in a very small room, an experience the victims found terrifying.

For some victims, it is not enough that the hearing be private. For them, the very fact that they have to be in the same room as the defendant is too traumatic to bear. Because the victim is the main "prosecution" witness, her testimony is clearly necessary in all but the rarest cases. If the victim does not want to be in the same room as the defendant, her choices are extremely limited at most institutions: either she grits her teeth and testifies in the presence of her attacker, or the defendant goes unpunished.

A few institutions are working to make another option available in such cases. At the University of Rochester, the victim testifies in an adjacent room, and the testimony is taped and played to the hearing board and the defendant. The defendant has the opportunity to ask her questions on tape, which she answers in a similar way to her original testimony. This procedure, although cumbersome, has the benefit of keeping the victim and the defendant separate while providing the defendant with an opportunity to cross-examine his accuser, as is the case in the criminal justice system.

To our knowledge, this procedure has not been tested in court. It is presently used only by a few schools that also are very careful to protect the due process rights of defendants. There seems little doubt, however, that it would amply satisfy the due process standards required by the courts. Similar methods are used in some criminal courts without constitutional difficulty to obtain the testimony of children, so it is hard to imagine the courts objecting in a situation where the due process requirements are significantly lower. On a more practical note, however, one can see that such a procedure would hardly lend itself to the smooth and efficient running of a hearing. Some hearings take many hours even without the added burden of running back and forth between rooms each time a member of the board or the defendant wants to ask a question. An institution considering such a move might want to limit its availability to cases where the victim is particularly unwilling to be in the same room as the defendant. Good counseling may make it possible for many victims to face their assailants without major trauma.

The Appeals Process

Most institutions have some sort of appeals process for both the victim and the defendant. In some cases there is another hearing board, with different members, constituted to hear the appeals. In others, it is the college president or chancellor who reviews the evidence and decides whether the decision was correctly made by the original hearing board, as is the case at Carleton and SMU. In some large institutions that are comprised of several colleges, the appeals process may be from the individual college to the university. This is another situation where schools need to decide for themselves which approach best meets their needs.

The review by the president or chancellor is less cumbersome than the rehearing of a case by a separate board. The 1986 case of Tom Watson, a college football player at Syracuse University, shows how this can work. As part of a plea bargain, Watson pleaded guilty in criminal court to a charge of sexual misconduct. The hearing board at Syracuse heard the case and exonerated him, but the chancellor overturned the board's decision and forbade Watson to play the first five games of the season.

In several of the cases we know about that have resulted in civil suits, however, this same procedure contributed to the willingness to file a lawsuit. The victim-plaintiffs believed that the president or chancellor was far from disinterested in the outcome and therefore provided a biased review. College presidents have a great interest in the reputation of the college and in their ability to conduct fundraising operations. Such concerns may outweigh interest in the merits of a particular case. This is one example of the larger issue of conflict of interest in judicial hearings, which will be discussed shortly.

Notice and Record of the Hearing

Since the *Dixon* v. *Alabama* case, courts have decided that due process includes notice of the charges against the student. The courts do not say much about the nature of such notification, but do say that it must be "timely."[57] Most campus codes require that notice be given, but it often does not specify that details of the charges and the nature of the evidence against the accused be included. Picozzi described several cases in which universities have been very lax in the way they provide notice, including notice on the day of the hearing or without any information about the charge.[58] This kind of behavior on the part of an institution breeds an environment that is bad for the defendant, for the victim (whose rights are less likely to be protected), and for the entire institution. After all, part of the educational mission of a college is to teach students how to deal fairly and justly with one's fellow citizens.

The trend seems to be toward having a taped transcript of all hearings, though the court cases are not consistent as to whether this is required as part of due process. Some courts require that the college provide the student with a record of the proceedings, whereas others only require that there be such a record, and still others state that no record is required for due process.[59] The availability of the record is significant both for defendants and victims. In one recent case, the victim's attorney obtained a court order to prevent the university from destroying the record, an action he feared likely because the victim was suing the university for alleged bad handling of the case.[60] In another, the lawyer for three defendants found guilty by the campus judicial authorities claimed that due process was denied them because they did not receive a transcript of the hearing. This claim (and another) resulted in a rehearing of the charges.[61]

Conflict of Interest Issues

Our criminal justice system is set up so as to provide the checks that maximize the neutrality of the actors within the system. The investigation is conducted by the police, who are not responsible for taking the case to trial; the district attorney who does decide to take a case to trial is checked by the lawyer representing the defendant, the judge, and the public (through reelection); the judge shares the power of decision making with the jury in most criminal cases; and the judge is further checked by the appeals process in which his decisions are overseen. In addition, there are a number of rules that limit lawyers and judges from participating in a case in which they have some personal or financial interest.

A college simply is not geared to operate in a way that will avoid the problem of conflict of interest.[62] As a result, there are a variety of ways in which the personnel involved in the judicial hearing process may have such conflicts. On some campuses, a university administrator may fill the role of police (enforcing rules or identifying those who break them, as well as collecting information abut the alleged infraction), prosecutor (deciding who should be charged for breaking the rules and which charges should be pressed), judge (agreeing who should be charged and deciding on the fact-finding procedures), and jury (deciding if the individual is guilty as charged). In most cases, the situation is not this extreme, but nevertheless it is common for one person to play more than one role in the hearing process. Even in a large university like Cornell, the judicial administrator, who is legally trained, decides both who should be prosecuted and who will prosecute. She or he is also involved in the judicial role of advising the board (which has the role of jury here) about relevant legal issues. The courts have recognized the reality of such an overlap in judicial hearings and, conceding that a neutral fact finder is not necessary, require only that board members exercise "independent judgment."[63] Proving the absence of independent judgment is extremely difficult and would require strong evidence of bias.

When there are so many different roles being played by one person, or even more than one, there is an absence of the checking that is central to the functioning of the criminal justice system. In addition, there is the problem that one or more of the actors in the system may not be disinterested in the outcome of the hearing. A highly publicized sexual assault case may have a deleterious effect not only on future enrollments but also on fund-raising efforts. Administrators may have a great stake in the outcome of a case; if there is enough negative publicity, it is possible that heads will roll. We have often been told by victims and their families that they believed that the college administrators were by no means impartial, that they were anxious for the case to be handled so as to cause the least damage to the college (rather than to bring an offender to justice).

It is neither possible nor desirable for colleges, especially small ones, to set themselves up in a manner similar to the criminal justice sys-

tem and thereby avoid the problem of conflict of interest. It is, however, an issue that many administrators have not recognized. Many
of them feel that it is enough that they are acting in good faith and
are doing their jobs properly. The problem with such a view is that
things may look very different from the outside, and others may not
share their sanguine view that all is well as long as the administrator
acts in good faith. Sometimes the administrator has a view of what is
appropriate that is not shared by others within the system, whether
they are other administrators or members of the student body. Without sufficient checks on the decision-making power of that administrator, a college runs serious risks if a case is seen to be mishandled.
The issue of the overuse of power is an element in some of the cases
that have gone to court, as will be discussed in Chapter 8.

Changing Campus Codes

Many colleges have recently changed their codes of conduct, and
others are considering doing so. The first important issue to examine in such a process is to identify the purpose of the code. What is
the college's goal in drafting a code? Is it to prevent and punish specific acts of misbehavior, or is it to ensure that the students who are
part of the campus community adhere to appropriate general standards of moral and ethical behavior? The trend in the many colleges
that are revising their codes is to move in the direction of more specific language. We believe, though, that there are educational and legal advantages in including both general and specific language in the
code of conduct. The students are put on notice that certain specific
kinds of behavior are unacceptable. In addition, however, the college maintains its interest in the broader development of the student,
which demands an emphasis on treating one's fellow students with
consideration and maintaining a level of conduct above that expected by the criminal code of the wider society. As we have seen,
the law is flexible about exactly what should be in a code of conduct. In fact, courts do not always require that there be a written
code, although some courts have done so and are more likely to do
so nowadays.[64]

The advantages of a written code are obvious. It clarifies the college's expectations of student behavior as well as giving the institution a basis on which to charge students for violation of its mandates.

Both public and private institutions can, with a well-drafted code, avoid charges of unfair or arbitrary behavior.[65] The one important and possible negative aspect of having a written code is that "it provides a specific target to aim at in a lawsuit."[66] Because of this risk, especially in this age of frequent lawsuits, it is essential that a college adheres to the procedures outlined in its code. This may sound obvious, but we have seen several lawsuits in which the college has violated its own procedural rules in the conduct of the judicial hearing process. For example, as we shall discuss in Chapter 6, Carleton College was successfully sued in 1992 for expelling a student who committed sexual assault off campus, because the college had no jurisdiction to deal with off-campus behavior.[67]

There are several reasons why colleges need to change their codes. The first is the change in the age of legal majority. In the days before the reduction of the age of majority from twenty-one to eighteen, most of the students were legally minors. Now, on the other hand, most of the students are legally of age. This makes a tremendous difference in the amount of control a college can legitimately bring to bear on the student body. When students were mostly minors, the university operated under the legal doctrine of in loco parentis, in which the college was acting as a substitute parent. Thus, acts that would have been acceptable on the part of parents were also acceptable when undertaken by the college. This gave the college fairly broad latitude to regulate student behavior, as the law has always allowed parents considerable leeway in using their judgment to control the behavior of their children.

During the 1960s the courts began to move away from the doctrine of in loco parentis, as attitudes toward young people changed. The demise of the doctrine as applied to college students was completed as states lowered the age of majority for many purposes and the constitutional voting age was reduced by the Twenty-Sixth Amendment. Cases since then have repeatedly made clear that a college cannot act in loco parentis but must give the students the autonomy of the adults they are in law, despite any reservations it may have. As one judge put it in the 1991 case of *Tanja H. v. Regents of the University of California,* "College students are generally young adults who do not always have a mature understanding of their own limitations or the danger posed by alcohol and violence."[68] The courts, however, have not been willing to require college administrators to reinstate curfews, bed checks, dormitory searches, hall monitors, chaperons, and the other concomitant measures that would be necessary in order to suppress the use of intoxicants and to protect students from each other.

The change in the age of majority has been accompanied by other social changes in our attitudes toward young people of college age. We came to see them more as adults and allowed them the freedom to act as such. We no longer expect parents, let alone colleges, to control student behavior. This has been particularly true in matters of sexual behavior. Much has been written about the so-called sexual revolution and the rise in the number of people who are sexually active at increasingly younger ages, as well as the view that sexual activity is acceptable for women outside of marriage. This change in sexual behavior was reflected in the removal of curfews, the opening of mixed-sex dorms, and the greater freedom allowed to students to socialize in the absence of controls by the university. To the extent that these attitudes and the freedom that goes along with them are well entrenched in our society, it is hardly likely that a college will be able to turn the clock back in an effort to gain greater control over its student body.

Another change that has affected the ability of traditional campus codes of conduct to deal with the behavior of the current student population is the student body itself. Education is no longer the province of a privileged minority. It has become available to a wider and more diverse part of American society. There is no longer the clear agreement on social and moral values that comes with social and ethnic homogeneity.

A further reason that the college codes of the past are no longer suitable for today's world is that the world itself has changed markedly. Many colleges are discovering to their cost that codes developed to deal with panty raids and cheating are entirely inapplicable to the serious crime that now confronts them. The wider society is much more violent than it used to be, and campuses are not immune from that violence. The rate of campus sexual assault and its increase has already been dealt with in an earlier chapter; here it is sufficient to recognize that there is both an increased incidence and an increased recognition of sexual assault on the college campus. The movement toward the recognition of date rape as a felony similar to stranger rape is far from complete, either in the criminal justice system or on the campus, but nevertheless many institutions are now beginning to take it into account. This recognition of rape, whether by an acquaintance or a stranger, as a felony has serious implications for the structure of campus codes that attempt to deal with it.

Tempting though it may be for campuses finding it difficult to adapt to the changing world, one cannot turn back the clock. One hears the occasional story about a college that is considering reintroducing curfews or other such controls. No campus has yet done so to our knowledge; some schools, however, are moving to enforce existing policies that limit the free movements of students in and out of dormitories. In the fall of 1991, as a result of increased concern for the safety and privacy of its students, the University of Ohio began enforcing a policy that forbids students having guests of the opposite sex in their rooms overnight.[69] This rule had apparently been in the student handbook for years. Many religious schools, especially those with all-female enrollment, and some southern colleges have never given up rules banning opposite-sex guests in the dorms. Houghton College, for example, has rules about what it defines as "open house," a designated time during which students can have guests of the opposite sex in their rooms. The relevant condition is that the student's door "must remain open such that those in the room are easily visible to those outside the room."[70]

For most students in the 1990s used to the freedoms they have had at home and at college, however, such encroachments on their autonomy would not be received very enthusiastically. How could they tolerate being treated like the children they are convinced they no longer are? Another barrier to establishing greater control over the behavior of students is that the courts are unlikely to accept that a college has a right to do so. As with all these issues, the problem is much more pressing for a public institution, but private schools usually take their cue from the law developed for public institutions.

Conclusion and Recommendations

The climate on college campuses is in a state of great flux. To respond to this changed climate, it is important that colleges reevaluate their codes of conduct to see whether they still serve their purpose. Colleges that do not have a written code should think seriously about getting one. Those whose code has not been revised for a long time should see if it is still appropriate *before* a major case indicates that it is not.

Schools should also evaluate their codes to see if they are as clear and comprehensible as they should be. In the course of our research, we have read many codes; the worst problem we have found with them is that they are sometimes very confusing and difficult to follow. If we (a lawyer and a social scientist) cannot find our way around these documents, imagine how a student must feel. Often the codes are without any index or any way of finding the appropriate rules. The rules, when we find them, are scattered in amongst all sorts of other unrelated information. Sometimes parts of them simply cannot be found; for example, we have seen more than one code in which the punishments for violation are not listed at all. We have seen codes that are full of clauses and subclauses worthy of a piece of complex litigation, but sometimes these codes refer to clauses which do not exist. The best codes are those that are laid out in a separate section of the student handbook or in a brochure devoted to the judicial code. They provide a list of violations for which a student can be charged, along with definitions of those violations, procedures for hearings about offenses, and a list of punishments.

It is important that colleges recognize the differences between a code that is clear and concise and one that is overly legalistic. As mentioned above, we believe that it is a mistake to draft the code in legal language. Not only should the definitions and structure of the code be nonlegal, but colleges should also avoid mimicking other trappings of the legal system. In the St. Lawrence University code, the hearing board members are called "justices" (one of whom is designated "chief justice"), while the defendant has the right to bring "counsel" from the undergraduate student body.[71]

One of the ways of ensuring that the code of conduct is comprehensible to students is to include in it a section in which commonly asked questions are answered, as in the case at Stanford University.[72] For example, the Stanford handbook includes the answers to such questions as the following: What is the relationship between the several codes of conduct? Can the identity of a student witness to misconduct be protected during a judicial process? Is a misconduct conviction made public in any way? Each college can tailor such material to those questions that seem to be the most important to its particular students.

The process of changing a code of conduct is laborious and lengthy. It requires the cooperation of many people on the campus. Nevertheless, it is essential for the protection of both the students and the college in the current campus climate. The decisions a college makes about the contents of its code must serve its own special needs. For guidance in this decision-making process, we list below a number of recommendations of suitable clauses related to sexual assault.[73] Colleges may want to select some or all of these recommendations, or adapt them as appropriate. We are not providing a complete code of conduct, but rather covering those issues that we have found to be most important in protecting victims, defendants, and the college in the area of sexual assault. Some of the clauses are taken from different codes we have read, sometimes with modifications that make them clearer or more appropriate.

Recommendations for Clauses in a Code of Conduct

A. Definitions

OPTION I. (General, for handbooks in which sexual assault is part of a general prohibition against disruptive conduct)

This includes but is not limited to physical assault, rape or other sexual assault. Rape is forced sexual intercourse, whether or not a weapon is used.[74]

OPTION II. (Specific)

Sexual Misconduct. Nonconsensual physical contact of a sexual nature. Includes acts using force, threat, intimidation, or advantage gained by the offended student's mental or physical incapacity or impairment of which the offending student was aware or should have been aware. Harassment, without physical contact, will not be deemed sexual misconduct under these provisions.[75]

OPTION III. (Specific, where all aspects of prohibited sexual conduct are spelled out)

Sexual Assault I. By stranger or acquaintance, rape, forcible sodomy, forcible sexual penetration, however slight, of another person's anal or genital opening with any object. These acts must be committed by force, threat, or intimidation, or through use of the victim's mental or physical helplessness of which the accused was aware or should have been aware.

Sexual Assault II. By stranger or acquaintance, the touching of an unwilling person's intimate parts (defined as genitalia, groin, breast, buttocks, or clothing covering them) or forcing an unwilling person to touch another's intimate parts. These acts must be committed by force, threat, or intimidation, or through the use of the victim's mental or physical helplessness of which the accused was aware of should have been aware.[76]

B: Relationship Between Code and Criminal Justice System

OPTION I. (Jurisdiction limited to acts that take place on campus)

Acts in violation of state, federal, and local law are necessarily in violation of the judicial code. Such acts when committed on college premises are within the power of the judicial board.[77]

OPTION II. (Jurisdiction extended to acts on the college campus and some off-campus acts)

Acts in violation of federal, state, and local law are within the jurisdiction of the campus judicial board when committed on campus property. When committed off campus property, they may fall within the jurisdiction of the campus judicial board when they constitute a direct or indirect threat to the college community.

OPTION III. (Jurisdiction extended to acts of members of the college whether they take place on or off campus)

The university and its members are also subject to all [insert name of state], federal, and local laws. Alleged violations of local laws and statutes that occur on or off campus are subject to internal university investigation, review, and action in addition to any action by the proper civil authorities.[78]

C. Policy on Reporting Sexual Assault

As a matter of policy, the institution encourages the accuser in these cases also to pursue appropriate remedies in the state judicial system.[79]

D. *Policy in Cases Where a Student is Charged with Violating Both Criminal Law and the Campus Judicial Code*

1. Where warranted, the college may proceed with its case against the accused even though the civil process has yet to begin.
2. If a student is charged with a criminal offense, the college shall retain the option to suspend such a student until criminal courts have reached a decision. [alternative] An accused student shall have the right to be present on campus, participate in classes, and generally exercise all those rights and privileges associated with membership in the college community until found guilty of the charges, except when the accused's continued presence would constitute a threat to health or safety of the individual, other members of the community, or the educational process.[80]
3. The college cannot regard an arrest or indictment as a finding of guilt.
4. Because a student accused of violating both civil and college regulations may be subject to a trial, the college should be scrupulous in respecting his or her rights as an accused person and avoid any effort to secure a "confession" or evidence that may be used against him or her.[81]

   [alternative] As a result of an agreement between the college and the [name of country] County District Attorney, nothing that is said during the campus judicial hearing can be used against the accused in a criminal trial unless it has been independently discovered by the criminal justice authorities.

E. *Proof*

1. The defendant is assumed to be innocent until proven guilty.
2. The burden of proof in a charge of violating the code of conduct is on the dean of student life/judicial administrator.
3. Formal rules of evidence do not apply in judicial hearings.
4. The standard of proof shall be clear and convincing evidence [or, that the behavior complained of is more likely to have happened than not].

F. *Disciplinary Violation Transcript Record*

If the nature of the offense so warrants, the hearing board will record an individual's violation on his or her academic transcript. The notation will remain for the time he or she is enrolled in the university, and for three years following his or her graduation. If the student leaves the university before graduation, the notation is removed three years after the anticipated date of graduation from the university.[82]

G. *Rights of the Accused*

Anyone charged with a violation of the judicial code of conduct shall have the following rights:

1. The right to be informed of all of his or her rights before the hearing.
2. The right to be given written notice of the nature of the charges at least two days before the hearing.
3. The right to receive, upon request, a list of the witnesses who will appear at the hearing in support of the charges. The provision of such a list shall not preclude the testimony of witnesses who were unknown at the time of such request.
4. The right to receive, upon request, the names of the judicial board members. If the student feels that any member cannot objectively and fairly hear the case, the objection must be made to the judicial officer more than twenty-four hours before the hearing. The judicial officer shall determine the merits of the complaint and will decide whether or not to replace the board member in question.
5. The right to bring a personal advisor of his or her choice, but not legal counsel, to the hearing.
   [alternative] The right to have legal counsel present at the hearing. If the accused exercises his or her right to counsel, counsel may be present to advise the accused, but may not represent the accused nor directly examine or cross-examine the witnesses.
   [alternative] The right to have legal counsel present at the hearing.

6. The right to remain silent.
7. The right to examine the witnesses presenting the case against him or her.
8. The right to present witnesses and documentary evidence, and an explanation or argument on his or her own behalf.
9. The right to a written [or taped] transcript of the hearing [at his or her own expense].
10. The right to appeal the decision to an appeals board [or the dean of student affairs, president, or provost].[83]

H. Rights of Victims

Anyone who is a complainant in a case of sexual assault shall have the following rights:

1. The right to decide whether he or she wishes to press charges.
2. The right to have a person of his or her choice accompany him or her during the hearing.
3. The right to request to have his or her living arrangements (if in campus housing) modified pending the outcome if the accused lives close to the victim.
   [alternative] The right to request to move from his or her college dormitory. The dean of residence life [or student housing office] shall make every effort to accommodate the complaint's wishes.
4. The right to make up academic work he or she has missed because of time lost due to the assault and the hearing.
5. The right where possible to have the defendant's classes re-assigned so as not to share classes with the complainant.
6. The right to file for a no-contact order prohibiting the defendant or his or her friends from contacting the complainant.
7. The right to be present at the hearing.
8. The right not to have his or her sexual history discussed during the hearing.
9. The right to make a victim impact statement.
10. The right to be notified immediately of the outcome of the hearing.[84]

11. The right to request that the proceedings be conducted so that the defendant and the complainant are never in the same room together. On receipt of such a request, the judicial administrator shall make suitable arrangements to accomplish this purpose.[85]

6

Campus and Cops

The college campus is in an unusual position in our society in its control over those who live and learn on it. Each campus has a system for dealing with inappropriate or illegal behavior; much of this outlawed behavior is also illegal under criminal law. Many institutions have great difficulty in determining how best to deal with the police, and there is great variation in methods and results. Some of the reasons for this diversity have to do with the wide range of differences in the status of the police on various campuses, whereas others appear to be idiosyncratic. Campus police also have some tensions about the extent to which they should be a service unit or a policing unit. Are they "real" police officers who just happen to work on a college campus? Or are they more like security guards, or a kind of student assistance office, or part of the maintenance staff (as they were at Wells College until only a few years ago)? On many campuses, there seems to be a move in the direction of campus police being "real" police, but our research indicates that here too there is great variation from one campus to another.

Such divergent opinions also occur among various units of the campus about the role of the campus security office, with the officers seeing themselves more as "real" police, while other parts of the campus see them in a more service-oriented role.[1] This difference of opinion can lead to conflicts within the institution, both in general and in the handling of particular cases.[2]

The nature of the campus security force has important implications for the way sexual assault is handled on campus. Whatever type of campus security force a college has, however, it is very important that it be well trained and able to do a good job within the limits of its powers. We have heard of several lawsuits that have, in part, resulted from inappropriate handling of cases by campus security.

> In a recent case at the University of Southern California that is discussed in detail in Chapter 8, only one officer was actually in the field at the time the victim was raped. Four officers were apparently on meal breaks, two were running errands off campus, and two others were inside the security office for unknown reasons. Despite the facts that the victim was raped at a place that was known to be dangerous and that the assault took thirty to forty minutes, no security officer came to her aid.
>
> In the case at Clarkson University discussed in Chapter 2, a young woman was raped and murdered on campus. Two security officers passed the place one evening where the attack was taking place, but thought it was consensual sex and did not intervene.

The penalties for such incompetence can be high. The victim in the USC case was awarded 1.7 million dollars, including punitive damages.[3] In addition, the case received nationwide publicity at a time when the school, because of its proximity to a crime-ridden area, was having difficulty convincing potential students that it was a safe place to live and study.

The Status of Campus Security Officers

Our experience shows that the nature of the campus police system has a significant effect on the relationship between the campus police and their civil counterparts. College security forces range all the way from regular police officers who are legally members of the city force in which the campus is located to security forces made up entirely of students. Table 6–1 shows the different types of campus security arrangements that we have found most frequently, and the effects of the type of security force on campus sexual assault.

Many state university systems have sworn police officers in their campus security departments.[4] These schools do not generally have much difficulty with their relationship with police off campus. There is generally a sense of mutual respect and cooperation that is similar

TABLE 6-1

Types of Campus Security Arrangements and Their Effects

Type of Campus Police	Type of School	Type of Training	Characteristics	Examples
Regular state police	State school	Regular police training	(1) Well-trained officers (2) Broad powers (3) Good cooperative relationship	Penn State University Rutgers University
Regular city/local police	Local public institution	Regular police training		University of Idaho (services contracted through municipal police department)
Security officers (not deputized)	Private institutions	Many experienced police officers with regular training		Bates University Cornell University
Student or partly student force	Private, small	Informal on-campus training	(1) Personal contact (2) Cheaper	Moorehead State University

to the cooperation between any two police forces. Because the campus security force is made up of sworn and deputized officers, it does everything that a regular police force does, including its own investigations. These officers are likely to be better trained than those who are not part of the police force. Because of this greater professionalism, there is likely to be less of the bungling in investigations about which one hears sometimes in other cases. For example, sworn officers are likely to be more conscious of the need for a victim of sexual assault to be examined medically within the shortest possible time. They are less likely to miss important pieces of evidence, or to allow witnesses to disappear before they have given a statement. In our research we have heard cases in which all of those inappropriate things have happened, but none at schools with a "real" police force.

There are a variety of campus security systems apart from this police model. At many institutions, the campus security office is not part of the police force, but nevertheless most of the officers are former police. The college can benefit from the training these officers have had before joining the campus force. In some cases the college can also benefit from rapport they have built up if their employment was with the local police force.

> The assistant director of public safety at the University of Hartford spent a number of years on the local police force. During those years, he naturally got to know the other officers and developed good rapport, to the benefit of the University.[5]

On the other hand, previous training does not always work to the advantage of the public safety office. It may be easier to train a rookie than to "untrain" an experienced police officer.[6]

Some colleges have a security force that is made up of both officers and students. In Minnesota, many of the schools use this combined system.

> At Moorhead State University, which is part of the University of Minnesota system, *all* members of the security force are students.[7] They seem to have a good relationship with the local police force, perhaps because they are in no way in competition with the police. Whenever there is a violation of the law, the students who are running the dispatch office call the police to handle it. The system seems to work satisfactorily, even though it may seem amazing to those used to "real"

police and plenty of "real" crime. It is clearly significant that there is evidently very little crime on the campus in northern Minnesota, especially during the winter. Nevertheless, occasionally one of the students does get injured in the line of work, though it has apparently never been serious enough to warrant alteration of the system.

This willingness to have the police deal with the lion's share of the criminal violations, even those that take place on campus, seems to have a positive effect on the relationship between the campus security force and the police. At Johnson City Community College, for example, after a crime occurs on campus, the public safety office sends a report of it to the local police, and "they take over."[8] This is apparently not the result of any formal college policy, but a method that the security office has devised to serve its needs best.

In some institutions the cooperative relationship may work differntly. For example, at Cornell University, where the police are sworn police officers but not part of the local force, there is a very strong sense that felonies are appropriately handled only by the criminal justice system after investigation and arrest by the campus police. Thus, when a case of sexual assault takes place on the campus, it is referred to the criminal justice authorities as soon as possible to be adjudicated there, although the campus police assist in collecting evidence even after the case has been taken over by the civil police. The Cornell public safety department has a very good reputation with the local police force as a department that investigates sex crimes to the fullest extent before sending them to be adjudicated in criminal court. Its officers may also have an advantage over the local police in that they have training in sensitivity and crisis intervention as well as the usual police investigative training.[9]

Other institutions have worked out a different kind of cooperation. At Rutgers, each campus has an agreement with the local police under which the campus police handle all cases involving students that take place on campus or in adjacent areas where many students live. In effect, the campus officers take over the role of the police in collecting the appropriate information, which they then hand over to the authorities for prosecution just as the police would. The local police—overworked, as are most police forces—are very happy to have some of their work done for them.[10]

At Pennsylvania State University, the police for the campus and the town of State College are one and the same thing. The police can therefore act both as protectors of the interests of the university and as representatives of the state. This is not uncommon at state universities when the police are actually part of the regular police force.

Some of these relationships are informal, whereas in other instances the campus security office has worked out a formal memorandum of understanding in which the respective roles are spelled out in some detail. For example, Santa Clara University has had a memorandum of understanding with the Santa Clara Police Department since 1990 that has served them well.[11] The purpose of the memorandum is "to establish policy and guidelines on matters of mutual concern regarding law enforcement, including the uniform reporting of criminal activity, on the Santa Clara University Campus." It is made clear that members of the Santa Clara University Department of Public Safety are not peace officers as defined by the California penal code, so that they are not considered the appropriate agents to investigate criminal activity by students on or off campus. Accordingly, the memorandum of understanding deals with issues of notification, as well as making it clear that crimes will be investigated by the local police department rather than by the university. With respect to sex crimes, it is agreed that the police will be notified and requested to investigate all sex crimes reported to the university public safety department, regardless of the victim's desire to prosecute.

In our experience this is very unusual, and it seems to be a good approach. Though it does not force the victim to prosecute, it does send a message that a sex crime is something that is the responsibility of the police department and thus is something to be taken seriously. The one potential disadvantage is that a victim might refuse to cooperate because she does not want the police involved at all. Alternatively, knowing of the relationship between the two police forces, she might decide not to report to the campus police in the first place. This is always a risk in such cases, and colleges should do what they can to encourage students to report cases to both the campus and the civil police. As discussed elsewhere in this book, the goals of charging assailants in a campus and criminal setting are different from reporting it as a record-keeping mechanism. Even if a later decision is made to pursue the charge only in the criminal setting, at the very least the campus police need to know about any criminal activity that takes place on the campus.

The relationship between the campus and the local police is much less satisfactory at other colleges. Many of them have come to an uneasy truce, whereas others have a bad relationship. This seems to be as much a matter of personality and idiosyncratic factors as the type of force that exists on the campus; it may be part of a bad town-gown relationship. We have heard police maintain that college kids are not treated seriously enough, and that they are protected from the criminal justice system by the college.

> In the case in which a campus sexual assault victim sued Stetson University, we were told by the victim's father that the local police and the district attorney hated the university because of what they saw as a double standard of justice in which the "rich white kids" from the college were protected from the law.

This antagonism is more likely to be expressed in the case of private schools, and also in those schools whose forces are not part of the civil system. In other cases, the opposite is true. At Stockton State College, as well as at Cornell University, the judicial hearing system is harsher on defendants than the criminal justice system. We are told that Stockton State students live in terror not of the criminal justice system, but of the campus judicial system.[12]

In some cases, the source of the problem is not so much the local police as the district attorney, who may simply not prosecute cases of acquaintance rape, especially if it happens on the college campus. We are told, for example, that sometimes at Stephen F. Austin University in Texas, after the campus police (a "real" police force) investigate the case and turn it over to the district attorney, they are told that "boys will be boys," and the case is taken no further.

Whether the unwillingness to press charges comes from the poilice or the district attorney's office, it can be extremely frustrating. It is especially true in situations where the department of public safety is working to have such cases taken seriously by all members of the college community. They can hardly encourage victims to report sexual assault when they know that the police will never press charges, or that the district attorney will never prosecute.

Conflicts Among Units of the Campus

On some campuses, the conflicts that exist are not between the campus public safety office and the local police, but between the public safety office and other units of the college. In many cases there are both general issues and problems that have to do with the handling of individual cases.

The general issue is usually one of goals and role perceptions. The officers in the campus public safety department are more inclined to see themselves as professional police with a law enforcement role similar to their counterparts in the criminal justice system. They recognize that there are definite differences in the way they do their job, but in general their self-perceptions are those of police officers. In many cases, they consider that the administration of the college is lagging behind in recognizing the realities of current campus security issues. The administration, on the other hand, sees the campus public safety office more in terms of the traditional security-guard role with a service orientation.[13]

Because of these differences in role perceptions, there can be disagreement on the campus as to how the security department should be doing its job. To what extent should the campus police work in conjunction with the local police? To what extent should they be involved in education or traffic control, as compared to enforcement of the law? If these and other related questions are not discussed openly and philosophical agreement reached, the campus security office will have trouble satisfying the needs of the administration. There will inevitably be some tension among the different parts of the campus administration, because the campus police lack the autonomy (both financial and administrative) of their criminal justice counterparts.

In some cases, this difference in philosophy is obvious. We have heard of several colleges where the campus police want to handle cases of reported sexual assault very seriously, whereas the administration wants to sweep the problem under the rug. Those officers we have talked to at such colleges express extreme frustration that they are not being permitted to do their work properly. Often they feel that if they do handle a case in the way they feel is appropriate given their law enforcement orientation, they risk losing their jobs.

In one case, a woman security officer vehemently disagreed with the dean of students about the appropriate way to handle a case of campus sexual assault. She described a situation in which the dean of students did not notify campus security about events that involved the sexual assault of several young women. Rather than refer the case ther to the campus security office or to the local police, the dean's fice attempted to keep them within its control. It was not until the cases received considerable local media coverage that both the campus and the local police were brought in.

The campus security officer also felt her hands were tied as she was not officially permitted to become involved in the preparation of the cases and the collection of evidence. At this college, the victims are responsible for collecting their own evidence for the campus judicial hearing. The security officer felt that everything she was doing for the victims—such as accompanying them to the local police station, providing them with information about their options, and collecting evidence—placed her at risk to lose her job, because it was so clear that the administration had a very different idea about how such cases should be handled.

The role conflict and job frustration of this security officer seemed to us to indicate a serious (but, unfortunately, typical) problem in that particular college. The dean seemed unwilling to allow the campus security department to do its job properly for fear of the bad publicity that might be generated. We believe that, on the contrary, a well-trained security force taking such cases seriously and handling them well would do less to damage the reputation of the college than an attempt to keep the events covered up.

When the campus security force is made up of former police officers, conflicts are more likely to revolve around the security force's relationship with the students and with other parts of the campus. We have been told of situations in which the officers lack an understanding of and sympathy for the special needs of students. Student *perceptions* of the understanding and sympathy of campus security officers are also important. If the latter are seen as unsympathetic, students' willingness to report sexual assault will be diminished. This again is a matter of training that many colleges have undertaken. It is part of the service model of law enforcement and involves a recognition that the campus community is the "customer" for the police services on campus.

We have also heard of a reluctance on the part of the security force to cooperate with or share any information with people in the office of the dean of students, although this problem could also occur at those schools with forces that are part of the civil system. Recent legislative changes are likely to improve this situation as security forces come to recognize their legal responsibility to provide mandated information.[14]

Jurisdiction

Different colleges have different definitions of the scope of their jurisdiction. Some campus codes, like that of Stanford University, cover the behavior of students both on and off the campus, whereas others cover off-campus behavior when that behavior is considered to have implications for the educational process or the running of the college.[15] Most codes, however, have more limited jurisdiction. As mentioned above, the code at Rutgers covers activity on the campus as well as in places where students live in large numbers. Others have more limited jurisdiction, like that of Cornell, which in general covers only behavior that actually takes place on the university's property. For some colleges, the limit of the jurisdiction extends to behavior on campus or during campus functions.

Stockton State College in Pomona, New Jersey, provides an example of the most extensive type of jurisdiction. This college has jurisdiction to act in any case that it learns about, wherever it occurs. This is made abundantly clear to the students when they enroll at the school. Using this tough approach, the college has had great success in reducing the criminal behavior of its students both on and off campus. The vice president of student services told us of reading in the newspaper of the conviction of a Stockton State student elsewhere in the state. He immediately took steps to deal with the case through the campus judicial hearing process.[16] He considered the crime to be within his jurisdiction even though it had taken place far from campus and in the summer recess. Stockton State College argues, as do other campuses, that because the student has not yet graduated, he or she is still a student during the summer and therefore is subject to student discipline.

The extent of a college's jurisdiction has significant effect on the issue of campus sexual assault. For example, if the college is one with limited jurisdiction, and a victim is raped in her off-campus apartment by another student, she must either make her complaint to the criminal justice authorities or let the situation go unreported. The college also has its hands tied if it wants to punish its students. If the rape takes place in an off-campus fraternity house (a relatively frequent occurrence), the victim is similarly limited in her options, though the college may have the power to punish the student through the fraternity. Colleges usually have the power to revoke the fraternity's charter or put it on social probation; they may also be able to require the fraternity members to attend some kind of educational program. Fraternities are coming under increasing pressure from their national organizations, out of concern for the reputation of the organization as well as insurance factors. Such pressures act to support the college in its efforts to punish inappropriate off-campus behavior. Many schools solve this problem by extending their jurisdiction to off-campus fraternity houses and college-sponsored functions.

It has been our experience that many students and staff feel that an assault in an area that is not technically college property is nevertheless campus business. They often have trouble understanding why the college, because of a "legal technicality," does not respond in a way they think is appropriate. Both students and staff are frustrated and angry when they find out that a university cannot use its code of conduct to handle the case. At Cornell, there has been pressure from the group responsible for coordinating rape education and prevention to change this part of the campus code, though their efforts have so far met with little success.

A broader jurisdiction has the advantage that it protects victims more fully. Colleges also then have control over behavior they consider unfitting, regardless of whether it took place on campus or in an adjacent area. Many colleges are, however, unwilling to take on the extra responsibility and expense that such an extension entails. The risks are evident in the case of *Estate of Linda Yalem* v. *State of New York*. In that case, a woman was jogging on a bike path adjacent to the State University of New York (SUNY) at Buffalo when she was raped and killed.[17] One of the central issues in this case, which is still ongoing, is whether the university can be held responsible for its failure to warn students that there had been previous rapes on the bike path where the victim was killed. SUNY-Buffalo argues that because the bike path was not university property, and its jurisdiction extends only to university property, it had no obligation to warn students of the risks. Regardless of whether this argument succeeds, it is just this sort of responsibility that makes colleges reluctant to broaden their jurisdiction. These fears may be the reason we do not know of any college where the jurisdiction has been broadened recently, although we have heard administrators involved with handling student behavior express the wish that it could be done.

Some colleges are afraid of expanding their jurisdiction out of fear that they have no legal ability to do so. The courts, however, have ruled otherwise.[18] Arguments that a college did not have the right to discipline students for off-campus behavior have invariably been struck down. Usually, the courts base the decision on the interest the college has in the character of its students and its right to regard off-campus behavior as a reflection of the student's character and fitness to be a member of the college community.[19] The courts also recognize the need of the college to protect the health and safety of other members of the community, which may be endangered by some off-campus behavior.[20]

Colleges should satisfy two requirements if they have expanded jurisdiction. First, it is important that the extent of the jurisdiction is made clear to the students when they enroll. Inclusion of the information in the code of conduct would appear to be sufficient; Stockton State College goes further by making the students sign a form indicating that they understand the extent of the college's jurisdiction. This is an excellent precaution against a student later arguing that his or her due process rights have been violated because he or she did not know how far the school would reach in discipline matters.

The second important requirement is that the school must make clear the connection between the behavior and the interest of the college. The school has to be able to argue that the offense relates to the character of the student and that the latter is an important part of the education process. This is not very difficult to do in the case of serious crimes like sexual assault. In general, however, the courts have been very liberal on what is required.

The need for a college to abide by its jurisdictional limits is illustrated in three recent cases that have been the subject of lawsuits.

At one college in the Midwest, a rape took place one block from the college. The administrators told the victim that they were proceeding with campus charges after her complaint against the assailant, despite a clear rule in the code of conduct that the college only has jurisdiction over events that take place on campus or are college sponsored. The victim's case fell into neither category. After many months, the college acknowledged that it was unable to proceed with the case because of the jurisdictional limitations. The victim is currently suing the college, in part because the college administrators wasted several months on the investigation without telling her that they could not proceed or encouraging her to take the case to the police.

In a recent case at Carleton College, a student was raped off campus by another student during an intercession. Carleton charged the assailant with a violation of the campus code of conduct despite wording in its code that "behavior of students off-campus is of no disciplinary concern to the College." He was expelled from the college as a result of a disciplinary hearing. The assailant then obtained a court injunction barring the college from expelling him, with the judge agreeing that Carleton had indeed exceeded its power.[21]

In the case of *Watts* v. *Old Dominion University*, the plaintiff was suspended for his part in a gang rape that took place after a fraternity/sorority social in a house in which several fraternity members lived.[22] He argued that because the activity had not taken place on university property, the school had no jurisdiction over his behavior. Old Dominion countered by arguing that the college clearly intended to regulate student conduct, whether on or off campus. The plaintiff's suspension was reversed on other grounds, but the case makes it clear how risky it is not to specify with the utmost clarity the extent of the college's jurisdiction.

However tempting it may be for a college to act in a case it considers important, it cannot do so in violation of its self-imposed jurisdiction. If a college wants to broaden its jurisdiction, it has to change its code.

The Legal and Practical Relationship Between the Campus and the Criminal Justice System

Campus security and the civil police have different roles in the case of a sexual assault that is reported on campus. For the college, there is the question of whether the accused student has violated the campus code of conduct. There is also the issue of determining the ap-

punishment and the best way of protecting the victim. The
so has a general interest in protecting the safety and sanc-
ts environment. Thus, one of its major goals is to remove
ne from the campus if he or she is standing in the way of the
fulfillment of this goal.

The police role, on the other hand, is to represent the state in its
goal of upholding the law. Campus police officers stand somewhere
in the middle: they are both law enforcement officials who in some
cases have taken the same oath as their civil police counterparts and
also college officials. It is these two roles that can cause conflict in
the relationship between the campus and the local police.

Sexual assault is a serious crime, and the state has a strong interest in preventing and punishing such behavior. Because their interests and goals are different, though overlapping, it is appropriate that
both the police and the campus have a role to play in such cases. Neither should automatically give its part of the process over to the other
institution.

Some schools feel a strong ethical and moral obligation to report
felonies to the criminal justice system. The college is a part of the
community and therefore shares the obligation of every citizen to assist the police in the latter's efforts to uphold the law. It is also concerned about protecting its student body. In some states, there are
also legal obligations that could place a college at risk of criminal or
civil liability for refusing to report cases. For a criminal prosecution
to succeed, for example, it would have to be shown that the college
was involved in obstructing government administration or in criminal facilitation or solicitation.[23] If a college willfully refuses to report cases to the criminal justice system, it runs the risk of a civil
rights claim under 42 U.S.C., Section 1983 based on a potential argument that the college denied the civil rights of a victim by refusing to involve the criminal justice authorities.[24]

There are some institutions that seem to see themselves as islands,
separate from the rest of the community, with the right and the obligation to handle matters of student misbehavior, regardless of whether
it is cheating or rape. Although this obligation is certainly true for
matters that affect only the student's relationship with the institution (such as cheating), it is certainly not the case with behavior that
is also criminal. It is these institutions that are likely to have the chill-

iest relationships with their local authorities and also to run the legal risks we have mentioned.

In some cases the college is under pressure to take on more of the policing role than may be appropriate. This pressure may come from the victim. There are many victims who refuse to bring charges, however seriously they are encouraged to do so. Many fear the trauma of a court trial, or they do not believe that the criminal justice system is the appropriate place to adjudicate cases of campus sexual assault. We have been told of many students who refuse to go to the police even when campus security makes every effort to persuade them to do so.

> In one case, a victim was being taken to the rape crisis center by campus security. On the way there, she was told that the rape crisis center had to report the case to the police. "Stop the car," said the young woman, who then demanded to be taken back to the campus.

In cases where the victim does not want to proceed, the university has an obligation to honor her wishes as well as to protect her from the pressures of the police. In these cases, however, campus security officers are placed in the difficult position of wanting both to see the defendant prosecuted and to do as the victim requests. We have been asked how to handle such cases by many officers who are very troubled by this conflict, and we have been unable to offer them any satisfactory resolution to the problem.

> In one case in North Carolina, the victim made a statement to the police but later changed her mind and refused to provide them with further information. She was then told by the police that she would be required to testify to the grand jury about the rape or, alternatively, to tell the grand jury why she was unwilling to testify. Campus security tried in vain to prevent this outcome, as they believed that it was unfair and counterproductive, even though the police were legally entitled to act as they did.[25]

If the victim reports the case to the campus security office but does not want to press charges, the college can technically proceed without her in the same way as a criminal court. The problem in both cases is that the prosecutor lacks sufficient evidence without the complaining witness's story. In some cases, the victim might report what happened to her but refuse to give the police or anyone else on campus any information about her assailant. In other cases the victim does not report to the campus security office at all, which means not only that they cannot press charges in the campus system but that they have no idea of the extent of sexual assault on their campus. It is with this latter concern in mind that MIT and other institutions have developed a third-party reporting form to obtain as much non-identifying information as possible about assaults.

Sometimes the pressure to replace the criminal justice system comes from other sources. Many institutions feel the need to control everything that happens on their property. To let an outsider take over, as they see it, is an indication of failure. Though this approach may have been true in the days when colleges did have more power over their students, for reasons dealt with earlier in this book, it is no longer possible.

The need of the college to control what happens on its campus may stem from another source: the need to control the dissemination of information about assaults. Negative publicity is particularly to be avoided in these days of higher costs and fewer potential students. The parent of one rape victim has assured us that this problem is particularly acute in the spring, when fund-raising drives usually take place and admission letters are sent out to prospective students. As long as cases of sexual assault and other criminal activity are handled entirely on campus, they are less likely to become public knowledge and to put off prospective students and their parents. Indeed, it is in an attempt to deal with this problem of concealing campus crime that Congress has recently passed the Student Right to Know and Campus Security Act,[26] which will be discussed in detail in Chapter 9.

Sometimes the campus police, like their civil counterparts, predict what will happen to a complaint once it is filed by a victim. The victim will be told, for example, that because she had been drinking, the district attorney will not take the case to trial. It is possible that the district attorney in question operates that way, even though the victim's state of sobriety is not a defense and indeed may be proof of rape as it is defined in some criminal codes. Nevertheless, this type of second-guessing is not the role a college should undertake. Quite apart from questions about who should be making decisions about which cases to prosecute, this behavior has a very self-serving ring to it. It gives the impression that the college, through its public safety department, is holding onto cases for reasons of self-protection rather than to protect the victim.

Another difficulty with a college that has extended its role into the territory of the criminal justice system is that the personnel have neither the standing nor the expertise to handle criminal cases, as we have discussed in the previous chapter. It is sufficient here to say that punishment and prevention of crime is the job of the public law enforcement agency, whereas the running of an institution of higher learning is the job of the college or university.

Political Problems and Solutions

The political implications for town-gown relations are a significant element in dealing with the issues discussed in this chapter. Often the college is limited in the amount of control it has; the school must take its local police force and district attorney's office as it finds them. There is a delicate balance to be maintained in not invading someone else's turf while cooperating in sharing information. Much depends on the professionalism of the campus security force. In some cases, there are many deficiencies in the way the campus security officers carry out their job. They may not be very well trained in either detective work or the relevant psychological issues involved. If this is so, the local police may not have any respect for them and therefore may be unwilling to cooperate. If campus security bungles investigations on a regular basis, then the local force cannot rely on them for help. We have heard many examples of less than optimum police work by the campus security office, some of which have already been mentioned.

> In one case, after a campus sexual assault, the victim sought help from a couple driving by in a car. They took her to the campus security office. The campus police officer neglected to take a statement from the couple and did not even get their address, thereby losing a source of possible information.

There are, of course, also many examples of incompetent or inappropriate behavior on the part of local police. In some cases, the police will not investigate complaints where the victim has been drinking, regardless of the seriousness of the sexual assault. Cases of ınce to prosecute are legion and are not limited to students. In se of students, however, the college has more power to remedy the situation than when the victim is an isolated individual. As an institution, the college can attempt to change the practice of the police by applying pressure at appropriate places in the system; the actual method depends very much on the community. Colleges can also attempt to develop the kind of cooperative relationship that exists in some areas, as exemplified in the memorandum of understanding of Santa Clara University discussed earlier.

Conclusion

This chapter has described the different campus security forces we have encountered in our research and has offered some suggestions for the appropriate role of campus security. Beyond some basic principles about how to manage the relationship among units on the campus and between the college and the civil police, each college has to work out the best kind of force to meet its needs. It is clear that a large urban university is in a very different position from a small rural college, and that what will work for the former could be a disaster for the latter. For many campuses, however, their needs may have changed since the current system was put in place. The most important thing colleges can do, therefore, is to evaluate their campus security systems to see whether they continue to meet their needs in the current campus climate.

7

Institutional Responses

All colleges deal with campus sexual assault—whether they think they do or not, and whether they do it well or badly. College responses to sexual assault range from being proactive and attempting to create a fair and safe environment for their students to ignoring the problem and blaming the victims for being raped. Based on our research, we have divided colleges into eight categories in terms of their management of campus sexual assault. They are being identified here from the most severe to the most lenient and are discussed in detail below.

1. *Victims' rights advocates* (primary prevention is the focus, with mandated extreme penalties for offenders found guilty by the campus judicial system)
2. *Ethical* (colleges that will not tolerate sexual assault)
3. *Concerned* (colleges that are primarily concerned about the quality of life of their students)
4. *There but for the grace of God* (schools that respond after observing a messy legal case from another campus)
5. *Barn-door closers* (colleges that attempt to decrease the problems associated with sexual assault after handling a case poorly themselves)
6. *Don't rock the boat* (colleges that make their decisions regarding sexual assaults on a case-by-case basis, rather than based on policy)
7. *Ostriches* (schools that do not believe that sexual assault is a problem on their campus, because no cases have been reported there)

8. *Victim blamers* (colleges that blame the victims for the sexual assaults perpetrated against them)

For the most part, the colleges in the first three categories base their behavior on ethical concerns for their students. The There-but-for-the-grace-of-God schools and the barn-door closers change their policies and codes of conduct reactively, after a rape has occurred on their campus or elsewhere. Colleges in the last three categories seem to base their behavior on the motivation to avoid negative publicity and to decrease potential revenue loss. As we will show, most colleges are struggling with these cases and are often handling them inadequately.

Victims' Rights Advocates

Antioch College has passed a policy that goes well beyond the intent or the letter of the criminal law in establishing expectations for its students. The standard that defines sexual assault according to the criminal statutes, and the one adopted by most schools, is sex against the victim's will and without the victim's consent. Antioch, by contrast, has decided to establish a standard of *explicit consent*, meaning that one person in the relationship must *ask* if the other wants to engage in sexual intercourse and must receive noncoerced verbal consent. Furthermore, verbal consent is required not only for sexual intercourse but for every other act of sexual interaction prior to intercourse. Violation of the requirement to obtain verbal consent carries with it a mandatory sentence of suspension or expulsion.

The problem with this approach is that students are expected to discuss sexuality openly, which is inconsistent with the messages most of them have received prior to coming to college. This approach also requires college students to behave in a way that is uncharacteristic for people at their age, with their life experiences, and with their level of maturity. Women are expected to say yes to sex when they want it, even though many women have been socialized to fear that they will earn a bad reputation by doing so. Although it is desirable for students to be assertive and honest about their sexual desires, it is probably unrealistic to expect them to be able to carry out these expectations without extremely comprehensive training that contradicts most of their earlier socialization.

Antioch is considering mandating participation in education programs on sexual assault prevention for all students each year they are at college. If the college adheres to its rules, Antioch is likely to have many cases brought before the judicial board for infractions of these policies, and numerous suspension and expulsions. Given the likelihood that many students will violate this policy, the administration may decide to be lenient with the penalties. One consequence of lenient behavior is that students will not be more assertive and honest about their sexual needs. Perhaps more importantly, some students may feel that the administration has deceived them, and a civil suit against the institution for failure to enforce its own policy could result. This type of policy will be very difficult to carry out effectively.

Ethical Schools

These colleges approach sexual assault cases from an extremely moral and ethical point of view, with the result being elimination of most assailants from their campus. Although private religious colleges are most likely to fit into this category, some public colleges have also dealt swiftly and harshly with people who clearly violate their sexual assault policies.

A quick expulsion may raise questions regarding the rights of the accused. Private institutions often have greater flexibility in their handling of these cases quickly and authoritatively, because they are not restricted by regulations tied to state funding. In addition, public institutions are often part of a larger organization, with guidelines and regulations handed down from the chancellor of the state university system or some other state body (such as the board of regents or the state education department). These regulations are often cumbersome and slow down the process of handling a sexual assault case. Public institutions tend to have much more trouble responding swiftly in these cases and expelling assailants because they are often part of a structure that prevents them from being able to change policy or make policy or regulations without a great deal of "red tape." It is nevertheless possible, however, for both public and private schools to handle these cases quickly and with due respect for the rights of the defendant, as the following case illustrates.

An Ethical School

Stockton State College in Pomona, New Jersey, is a public college that has responded very aggressively to sexual assault cases. It is a relatively new institution (less than twenty-five years old) and therefore the college has not had to change inappropriate policies written long before acquaintance rape was a problem. Many older college policies at other schools were written when judicial boards were traditionally called upon to handle such violations as cheating on tests and drunken brawls at parties.

One of the unique elements of the Stockton State College policy is that if one of its students is the assailant in a violation that would be classified as a felony in the criminal courts, the hearing board is composed of administrators only. In the event of a less serious violation, the hearing panel also includes students. The two-tier system results in more convictions in serious cases, with stiffer penalties from the nonstudent board. Students are often reluctant to convict and to penalize other students harshly.

One outcome of the two-tier system is that students know that serious offenses will be handled seriously and that they are likely to be expelled in such cases, so there are very few serious infractions on campus. Not only does the reputation of the judicial board have a deterrent effect, but also there are few recidivists on campus to commit further violations. By contrast, we have heard of many cases on other campuses in which the perpetrators commit more than one sexual assault over a period of months or years before any action is taken.

Stockton State College always handles sexual assault and other serious cases expeditiously, often dropping everything else to hear the case within one week of the event. The defendant is removed from the institution, and the investigation takes place immediately. In this way, the victim does not have to worry about being harassed by or even seeing the defendant before the hearing. If he is found guilty, he is expelled or suspended immediately. It is easier to handle cases quickly when the board is comprised only of administrators who see this as a high priority. This speed is an essential element of the strength of the program, because the evidence is fresh and neither the victim's nor the defendant's life is disturbed unnecessarily by a delayed hearing.

Case Study from Stockton State College (Text of Complaint)

I had known William for approximately one month. My roommate had introduced him to me. Since he lived in the same dormitory building as I, I spoke to him when I saw him, usually concerning classes and other school related matters. I genuinely thought we had a typical college friendship.

I began to see him as a questionable person when he began asking me personal questions whenever he and I would "bump into one another." On the night of April 10th, somewhere between 11:00 P.M. and 11:30 P.M., he came to my dormitory suite. My roommate let him into the suite, then she left.

He came into my bedroom which was located in the suite, where I was alone, dressed for bed, watching television. He neither announced himself nor had I heard him knock on the door. He asked to use the telephone because, he explained, his had been disconnected. I allowed him to call his friend. He spoke on the phone for about five minutes.

After he hung up, I wanted him to leave but he requested that I talk to him for a little while. I said that would be alright although I did tell him I had early class the next morning. During our conversation, we talked about what courses we were going to register for next term, and which professors we wanted to take. We also talked about our musical interests. He sat down on my roommate's bed across from my bed where I was sitting.

All of a sudden, without any provocation, he asked if I had ever seen a man "play with himself." I looked at him as if he were insane to ask such a question. I then asked him why he would say such a thing. He stood up, right in front of me, and began "playing with himself" asking if I enjoyed watching him do this.

Being caught off guard, I actually thought for a moment that the whole thing might be a dream. I was unsure what action I should take but what I did was I told him that if he didn't stop, I was going to call the resident assistant. He said he didn't believe that I would do that, and he continued to masturbate.

I left the room to tell the resident assistant what was going on. I could not bring myself to say what William was actually doing. All I told the resident assistant was that William was acting very strange. The resident assistant told me that I should tell William to leave my room if he was acting strange.

I went back to my room and asked him why he was acting this way, and told him to leave immediately. He kept "playing with himself" all the while, and then suddenly he pulled down his pants, exposing his penis to me. I again told him it was time he left. He kept insisting that I watch him. Finally he stopped and said that I shouldn't be afraid, that he had only been joking with me. I told him that I was going to tell my roommate what had happened, and he sort of laughed and said he would deny the whole thing. I then demanded that he leave, and he did.

Shortly after he left, my roommate returned and I told her the whole story. She suggested that I tell the resident assistant what had happened. After discussing the situation with the resident assistant, she suggested that I file a complaint.[1]

William was suspended for two semesters based on Donna's complaint. Prior to his reapplying, he was required to participate in mandatory counseling and to demonstrate that he successfully understands the appropriate male-female interactions. Donna has graduated from the college; William has never returned. In this case, the offender was removed from campus for exhibitionism, not rape or any sexual assault involving unwanted touching. This penalty is much more harsh than most other institutions. Many schools may find a person guilty of rape or sexual assault that involves unwanted touching, but not even suspend him. He may be put on social probation, required to do community service, or participate in mandatory counseling, or suspended for a semester. Ethical schools such as Stockton State College send a message to their students that sexual misconduct in any form will not be tolerated on their campuses.

Many of the cases we have researched that have been handled well have been at Catholic colleges. Jesuit colleges in particular handle campus sexual assault cases very quickly, often by an administrator without a hearing board. St. Norbert College of DePere, Wisconsin, for example, is one of many Catholic Norbertine Colleges that do not tolerate immoral behavior among their students. At St. Norbert College, a hearing board is not always convened in cases of this nature; the decision regarding who should hear the case is left up to the victim. If a student is found guilty of a violation of the campus code by the vice president for student life, or the college community board, he or she is usually expelled. One of the consequences of this policy is an unusual closeness among members of the student body, perhaps because they are less fearful that people who will rape or sexually assault are among them. The positive sense of community at St. Norbert College is amazing; our visit to the institution showed that the students, faculty, and staff seem to respect each other and interact as if they were members of the same family. Sexual assaults are less likely to occur between people who respect each other. Recently, another Catholic college, St. Ambrose in Davenport, Iowa, handled a case well. After the case had occurred, it publicized in the news media the stringent actions it had taken. Such publicity is likely to serve as a deterrent to future sexual assault on their campus.

Other religious institutions also tend to deal with assailants with a heavy hand. For example, the Hawaiian branch of Brigham Young University (a Mormon school) does not allow any alcohol consumption on campus. In addition, BYU has a policy that allows for harsh and swift action against assailants, although the university has never had to use it.

Concerned Schools

Concerned schools are those that have not themselves had a reported rape, but believe acquaintance sexual assault is a problem for students everywhere. Because of this belief, they take action before they are made aware that a sexual assault has occurred on their campus. This does not mean that sexual assaults never occur, but that the administration sets policy to address the problem rather than acting in response to a specific case. Furthermore, these institutions do not feel that sexual exploitation against men or women should be condoned or tolerated on their campus. Therefore, they take action to revise their campus codes of conduct and policies to reflect the complexities of this issue prophylactically. As a way of minimizing the risks to women on their campus, colleges in this group are also likely to revoke the charters of fraternities, for example, for condoning irresponsible sexual behaviors that may lead to sexual harassment or assault.

Cornell University is an example of a college in this category. In the early 1980s, before campus sexual assaults between acquaintances were widely recognized, interested professional staff and faculty began to implement programs, revise policy, and monitor reporting because of a concern about this issue. This was an example of grass-roots organizing that evolved into a very comprehensive universitywide program. An ad hoc sexual assault task force was created by members of the campus community with an interest in preventing sexual assault on campus. This task force included faculty, student services personnel, and representatives from the Cornell outreach theater ensemble, public safety, psychological services, students, the dean of student's office, Greek affairs, and the office of equal opportunity. This group worked tirelessly to educate the campus community about acquaintance rape prevention, and sexual assault incidence, as well as to change policy. After several attempts over several years to obtain official recognition, the president of the university was persuaded that this issue and the task force's approach were important. He made the group an official advisory committee to the vice president for human relations and funded a position for a university sexual assault prevention education coordinator.

There But for the Grace of God

These are colleges that have not yet had a poorly handled sexual assault case come back to haunt them. They have seen other colleges with similar circumstances sued civilly or receive negative publicity for mishandling cases, however, and have watched these schools revise their policies and procedures to avoid negative publicity or civil suits that may cost them significant sums of money. Many colleges undoubtedly began revising their policies after observing the outcome of the civil suit against Carleton College. In that case the school was sued and settled out of court for an undisclosed sum based on its handling of cases reported by four separate women who claimed to have been raped by acquaintances at Carleton. The motivation for change at schools in this category is usually more financial or legal (responding to legislative mandate) than ethical or moral. Behaviorally, however, they look much like the concerned schools.

Barn-Door Closers

These schools respond to rape reactively. Only after they had handled an event very poorly do they revise policies and codes of conduct. In much the same way that it is useless to close the barn door after a horse has escaped, it will not prevent a sexual assault or help the victim if policies are changed after a rape has occurred. Future rapes may be prevented, but this will be a case of too little, too late for those who have already been victimized.

Barn door closers sometimes respond to difficult cases of sexual assault allegations on their campus by hiring consultants to come to campus and present sexual assault prevention programs. One of the authors is often called in to conduct such large and small group presentations for college campuses. If the members of the institution are serious about preventing future problems, they are likely to create a college task force to continue to work on this issue; however, some colleges act as if bringing in one speaker to present a few programs will alleviate the problem. The latter type of response indicates very little understanding of the complex causes of campus sexual assault. Campus sexual assault is such a complicated issue that one large community presentation is not likely to make much difference in changing attitudes and behaviors of students, faculty, or administrators.

Frantic phone calls from colleges to the authors of this book often follow messy cases that resulted in very bad public relations. In these instances the college representative usually requests a program as soon as possible, without any discussion of follow-up programs, education of the members of the judicial board, or of groups most likely to commit sexual assault. This often means that the institution is interested only in minimizing liability by stating that it has done something to educate its community about sexual assault prevention. If the college were really serious, it would also be interested in developing long-term, ongoing programs, policies, and procedures that could honestly make a difference in the way sexual assault is viewed on the campus.

The policy in place at the time a violation is committed is the one that must be used to process the violation. Therefore, if a school has had a case that has resulted in negative publicity, if it has been sued, or if the victim or complainant has been treated unfairly by the system, the institution often will change its policies and procedures so as not to repeat the same mistakes. Although these changes are likely to help in subsequent cases, they will not undo the damage resulting from the problem case.

> Rutgers University has been involved in several well-publicized cases in the last few years. There have been almost a dozen disciplinary hearings over the last five years, although there have been no criminal prosecutions, apparently because Rutgers wants to handle the cases internally. It has been sued by at least one victim, although not successfully. Its methods of handling complaints of campus sexual assaults have been found to be both unduly cumbersome and unhelpful for victims. As a result, the school has placed more emphasis on publicity and education about the problem of campus sexual assault. It is also involved in a major reassessment of the judicial hearing process in an attempt to make it less protracted and arduous for all concerned. It is considering adding a specific charge of sexual assault, which does not presently exist, to its code of conduct. The university is also attempting to minimize the role of lawyers, who are extensively involved at all stages of the process, partly accounting for its complexity and duration.

Some campuses have developed institutional committees devoted to examining campus safety, including sexual assault. For example, Clarkson, as part of their response to the incident referenced, formed a Campus Safety Committee that was composed of students, faculty, staff, and parents. The charge of the committee was presidentially based and consisted of a thorough examination of all components of campus safety and security. The results have been very effective. Many changes have occurred, and a much greater awareness of safety issues is prevalent. As the committee has identified weaknesses in its system, the University has been very responsive to take corrective measures. When legislative edicts came down, they were already doing most of what the law(s) specified.[2]

Don't Rock the Boat

Administrators of colleges in this category decide how to respond on a case-by-case basis, regardless of what policies and procedures mandate. For example, if a victim is likely to "go public" and make the details of the incident known, then the administration will act to remove the assailant in order to silence the victim, especially if the institution has any culpability in the case. Institutional culpability includes not having enforced its alcohol policy or its nonhazing policy, having conducted the judicial hearing improperly, and so forth. If the assailant is threatening to sue the institution or if he is suspended or expelled, the administrator is likely to find a way to keep him on campus. The philosophy behind the decision-making process is to find a solution that makes the fewest waves (and therefore does not rock the boat).

As will be seen, this method is most likely to result in civil suits against the institution. A college that does not have constructive policies or does not enforce them consistently leaves itself wide open to charges or violations of due process by defendants, as well as suits for negligent handling by victims. This issue is dealt with in depth in Chapters 5 and 8; examples of colleges that employ this approach are also addressed in other chapters.

Ostriches

These are colleges who believe they do not have a problem with sexual assault on their campuses. The administrators at these schools do not believe, by and large, that acquaintance rape is a real phenomenon, or they may believe that it just happens elsewhere, perhaps only at colleges where the men lack the proper upbringing or where the women are "loose" sexually. They may also believe that many victims file false claims. Administrators of colleges in this category express similar views to those of Neil Gilbert, professor of social welfare at the University of California at Berkeley, whose views have received wide publicity and represent one widely held view of the issue of sexual assault. He believes that most cases of acquaintance rape are a result of misunderstanding between men and women, and that if a woman has sex with a man after he has allegedly raped her, it could not have been rape.[3]

Many schools in this category have not had reported cases, so they believe that sexual assault on campus is not a problem. They have also not conducted any research on their campuses to determine how many of their students have unreported sexual victimization experiences. It is clear, however, that having no cases reported does not mean that the problem does not exist. As soon as colleges start taking acquaintance rape and sexual assault seriously, their reporting rate is likely to increase. At Cornell University, for example, the first year a concerted effort was made to deal with this issue on a number of levels—through training of staff, programs for students, revising the policy and publicizing it, revoking the charter of offending fraternities, and handing down convictions in the judicial process—the reporting rate increased 450 percent.[4] This included reports to the dean of students, the judicial administrator, campus psychological services, campus safety, university chaplain, the office of equal opportunity, the sex counselor, the rape crisis center, and residence life.

Colleges in the ostrich category have probably not done much in the way of training or education, and their administrators are probably uninformed about acquaintance rape and sexual assault and unsympathetic to the needs of victims. They tend to believe (because they want to believe it) that if they do not hear about acquaintance rape on their campus, it must not be happening.

Victim Blamers

Schools in this category are likely to say that "we don't have a problem with sexual assault here, because we have not had one case that has stuck." The colleges in this category often do one or two things that are devastating for victims and that discourage any past, present, or future victims from reporting acquaintance rape and sexual assault cases. First, they may say to the victim, "If you insist upon filing these charges against this man, we will investigate them, but we will also bring *you* up on charges for violating the alcohol policy on campus." Most victims under those circumstances will drop the charges, because many victims consume alcohol shortly before the assault and are also under the legal drinking age. This will have the consequence of discouraging all future victims who were drunk and underage from reporting their assaults, and perhaps others as well.

The second victim-blaming practice employed by these institutions is to interrogate the victim during the investigation in the following way:

Q: Were you drinking?

A: Yes.

Q: How many beers did you have?

A: I can't remember exactly, six or seven.

Q: Did you get yourself drunk?

A: I guess so.

Q: Were you wearing suggestive clothes?

A: Yeah, but so was everyone else; it was a beach party. Everyone was wearing bathing suits.

Q: You didn't voluntarily go to his room, did you?

A: Yes, but I didn't think he was going to rape me.

Q: Then you voluntarily performed oral sex on him?

A: Yes, but I only did that so he wouldn't need to have sex.

Q: You expect us to call sexual intercourse after that a rape? You have got to be kidding. What did you expect any red-blooded American man to do? Look, do yourself a favor, don't get drunk and go back to a man's room anymore if you don't want to have sex with him. You're lucky that is all he did to you. Filing a complaint like this is just wasting our time and the district attorney's time. You are going to get crucified if you try to take this to court.

A: Okay, just forget it. Let's just say it didn't really happen. Can I go home?

The above dialogue is based on composite information from several cases in which this type of interaction took place. Sometimes victims have also been asked about previous sexual partners, numbers of partners, previous sexual experiences, and if they have ever had an abortion. This information is, of course, irrelevant to the sexual assault charge, but may be used like the above interrogation to blame victims and to get them to drop the charges.

After the victim drops the charges, she may nevertheless be brought up on charges herself for filing a false complaint. If women know that victims are treated like this by the person investigating (such as the dean of students, campus police, judicial administrator, chair of the hearing board, or local police) very few victims will ever report their rapes. This kind of behavior can only take place if it is condoned by the chief of campus security and other high-ranking campus administrators. Colleges that respond in this way primarily do so to protect the reputation of the institution. The accused thus remains unaccountable for his actions so that the institution can protect itself.

> Several years ago the campus police chief at a small college in Pennsylvania told us that he did not believe that acquaintance rape or sexual assault ever happened on his campus. He had only heard of one complaint in all his years as police chief, he explained, and in that case the women admitted that she had made up the charge. He believed that she had engaged sex consensually and then regretted it the next day, so she claimed it was rape. During his interrogation, when he grilled her for hours, she had finally recanted and told him that it did not happen. He then charged her with filing a false complaint. Once this information became public, there were no other sexual assaults reported to the campus police department.

Elements Necessary to Become an Ethical or Concerned School

A campus must have both a good written (explicit) policy and at least one ethical administrator to create an environment in which their students feel protected from both being victimized *and* being unfairly accused and expelled. The best approach is for colleges to have both a solid, comprehensive policy and an administrator (or judicial board) who is fair and consistent in handling the cases. The administrator in charge of carrying out the response to these cases must take the issue of student safety more seriously than the concern for the reputation of the college or dwindling applications that may result from a highly publicized sexual assault on the campus. It is our view that when an administrator dismisses assailants for clear violations of the sexual assault policy, the result is increased campus safety and positive student morale. To make the best decisions for the campus, the administrator must view sexual assault as morally and fundamentally wrong. As discussed in Chapter 8, civil suits have resulted in cases where the policies and codes of conduct have been inadequate, where cases were handled inappropriately, when institutions have failed to protect students, or when students feel that they have been treated unfairly.

Table 7–1 depicts the interrelationship between policies and administrators in the handling of sexual assault cases. For example, schools that have unrealistic policies but good administrators (victims' rights advocate schools) will probably provide severe penalties for the assailants. Schools with poor administrative philosophy will probably handle cases negatively, however, even though their policy may be acceptable (such as don't-rock-the-boat schools). The outcome column in the table provides the likelihood of positive or negative outcome. For example, victim-blaming schools will probably handle these cases least well (with the resultant worst outcome), whereas ethical schools will probably handle the cases most appropriately (with the best outcomes for the majority of people involved).

The outcome column indicates the appropriateness of the finding of the judicial process. A positive outcome is one that is morally correct considering the circumstances of the case and will probably not result in a civil suit against the institution. A negative outcome indicates an inappropriate finding of either guilt or innocence, which is more likely to result in a civil suit against the institution.

How Policy Changes in Institutional Response Come About

It is important to understand how policy changes come about and how they take place. This is especially valuable if one wishes to make changes at an institution regarding the issue of sexual assault. Policy changes are usually effected by people in traditional positions of power, such as administrators. Students and faculty may also be effective at creating change, however, if the proper approach is employed. Parents or others who are not part of the formal campus community may also be effective in creating change. Howard and Connie Clery, parent's whose daughter was raped and murdered at

TABLE 7-1

Systemic Approaches for Dealing with
Sexual Assault On Campus

Systemic Approaches	Policies	Administrators	Outcome
Victim's rights advocates	U	G	+
Ethical	G	G	+++
Concerned	G	G	++
There but for the grace of God	G/T	E	+
Barn-door closers	G/T	E	–
Don't rock the boat	E	P	–
Ostriches	E	P	– –
Victim blamers	E	P	– – –

U = unrealistic; G = good; P = poor; E = either good or poor possible; T = too late

Lehigh University, have been very effective in this endeavor. Lehigh has carefully reexamined its policy as a result of the case of Jeannie Clery and her parents' subsequent efforts. Policy change can come about as a result of top-down (administrator-initiated), or bottom-up (grass-roots-initiated) strategies. The internal decision-making structure of a college is usually composed of administrators.

There are three basic structural models that account for creating policies in colleges. The first is the hierarchical or closed (Figure 7–1) decision-making process, which occurs in colleges where there is a centralized focus of authority (that is, the administration has the power to make the final decisions). Other groups in the institution provide information, which may or may not be heard, to the administration. In this case, administrators are often unavailable to talk directly to members of special interest groups. Decisions thus will be made without much regard for their effect on the other members of the community; this is a top-down approach. In this situation, where the administrator is not particularly interested in the welfare of the members of the community, it is best to approach him or her with language he or she can understand. For example, administrators are more likely to agree with the position that policies must be changed and sexual assault prevention education should be implemented if they are convinced that they may be in danger of being sued civilly or losing federal dollars. If the administration is well educated and

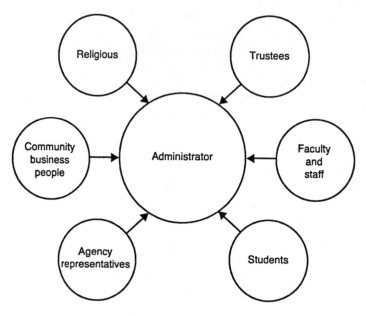

FIGURE 7-1: CLOSED SYSTEM

Administrators in the closed system are resistant to input
from external group when making decisions
Source: Parrot (1981).

informed on these issues, this approach may yield positive results toward making the campus a safer place regarding sexual assault.

The second approach is an open system (Figure 7–2), in which there is a high degree of communication among the administration, special interest groups, and related agencies. The open system is the best system for creating changes regarding sexual assault education and policies *if* members of special interest groups and the campus community are informed about and interested in this issue. The grass-roots approach, with the impetus for change from the bottom, would be effective in this type of system.

The third approach is the decentralized structure (Figure 7–3), in which special interest groups and agencies may alter the decisions made by the administration. There is a high degree of overlap between the administrator and the specific interest groups; decision making may be shared by the administrator with his advisers in the special interest groups. Any of these three systems may allow for effective policy development and educational approaches. The key is for the change agent to know which type of system operates in his

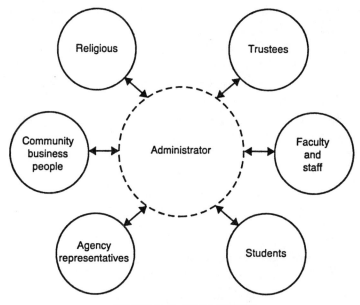

FIGURE 7-2: OPEN SYSTEM

In the open system the administrator is open to input and
suggestions from external sources for policy recommendations.
Source: Parrot (1981).

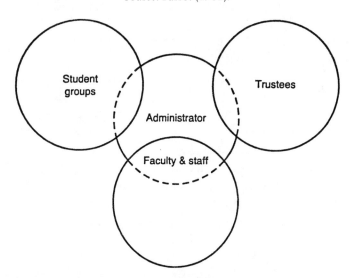

FIGURE 7-3: DECENTRALIZED STRUCTURE

In the decentralized structure, the administrator seeks
input and recommendations from other in making decisions.
Source: Parrot (1981).

or her college or community, and then to work to make changes in the most efficient way possible.

If the administrator is supportive, effective policy changes may come from a closed system through the top-down approach. The top-down approach will not work, however, if the system is closed and the administrator is unsupportive. In that case, one can work to remove the resistant administrator, create federal or state legislation or other outside pressures that will force the administrator to act appropriately, or hope that his or her colleagues at other institutions may be able to make him or her "see the light."

Conclusion

It is clear that the types of institutional responses to handling sexual assault on campus vary tremendously. The responses range from expecting students to behave in an uncharacteristically mature and moral manner to ignoring the plight of victims and attempting to sweep them under the rug. Many of the responses colleges have traditionally exhibited to sexual assault have been irresponsible and/or immoral. An increasing number of colleges, however, are handling these cases in a way that will protect all of their students and will also minimize the risk of civil litigation.

Unfortunately, there are far too few colleges with an ethical or concerned approach. These approaches are probably the best for student mental health and create a campus where students can do what they are at college to do: study, learn, and develop into responsible, ethical adults. Colleges can foster or thwart these elements of student life and growth by the way they deal with the ethical and moral dilemmas their students face. Parents of high school seniors and other prospective college students should know to which category the school they are considering belongs. The necessary information can be obtained through the student right-to-know legislation and by asking students and members of the college's women's center what they know about the way sexual assault is handled on that campus. For students already at college, if their institution's approach to sexual assault is not desirable, they can work toward changing the policies and procedures on a grass-roots level. But if change seems impossible, transferring to a more ethical institution may be the best option.

8

Civil Suits

There is in academe today, as in many other places, a great fear of lawsuits. In our research, we have heard many administrators say that they did or did not do something because they thought it would protect them from a lawsuit. Some of the actions (or inactions) were important and appropriate; some were not. In fact, in a number of cases, their behavior risked becoming self-fulfilling: the very behavior that they thought would protect them was the kind that precipitated some plaintiffs to file civil lawsuits. The purpose of this chapter, therefore, is to outline what we see as the risks of a lawsuit, as well as details of ways in which the university can protect both its students from sexual assault and itself from lawsuits. There are, of course, no guarantees that a university that follows all our suggestions and behaves in an exemplary way will not be sued anyway. It is, however, possible to minimize that risk dramatically.

Two cases in which the University of Southern California was sued by rape victims can serve to illustrate the kind of problems a college can face and how it responds. In the first case, *Martin* v. *USC* (which is currently on appeal), a nurse was stabbed and raped in some bushes one block from the campus security office. The jury awarded the victim $1.8 million in compensatory and punitive damages (reduced by the judge to $1.3 million, though the punitive damages were not reduced) for the rape, for several reasons. First, there had been a confidential report six months earlier from a crime prevention officer about the area where the rape took place, in which the officer said that there was insufficient lighting and the bushes should be cut back. The report was filed away without any action at all being taken. Second, there had been a series of rapes prior to the rape in question, and the security office put its members on "rape alert"—for which they got extra compensation, but did nothing extra. Most people did not know about the rape alert. Third, of the nine officers who were assigned to be on patrol at the time of the rape, eight of them were not doing their job.

The focus of USC's defense was that the victim had made up the rape complaint because she did not tell the police about it initially, though she did tell the physician who examined her. The jury clearly did not accept this, and it may have been a factor in the award. USC also fired the victim during the closing arguments, saying that the position had been eliminated. The victim is currently suing USC on that issue.

In the second case, *Weber* v. *USC*, the victim was awarded $2.7 million by the jury for a rape that took place near the off-campus student housing in which she was living. The victim, a music student, chose to come to USC because of a brochure she received showing that it had music rooms in which to practice and that the library was very near the dorm. When she got to the campus, it turned out that the music rooms were under construction and the library had burned down. She tried to get out of her housing contract, but was not permitted to do so. She decided to move anyway; she was assaulted as she was moving. The security guard was watching TV and heard screams, but thought it was a couple of students playing around. The rapist had committed another rape two nights earlier and was tried and convicted for both rapes. The university knew about the earlier rape, but did not report it in its internal documents until after the *Weber* case.

As a result of this rape, the student cannot play solos on her violin and is uncomfortable with other violinists. Her potential career as a concert performer is now in serious doubt. The jury found that the university was guilty of fraud in that it concealed the nature of the neighborhood from prospective students, as well as in not living up to its responsibility to students who were living away from home for the first time. In this case, USC argued that there was comparative negligence involved, as the victim had the opportunity to ask for an escort but did not do so. The jury accepted this rather unusual argument, in which the victim was held partly responsible for a rape at knife point, and reduced the award by 40 percent. The case was ultimately settled for a reported $1.6 million.

After these two lawsuits, USC had an external review committee write a report of recommendations for ways of handling sexual assault at the university.[1] This report is extensive and covers many issues relating to both prevention and handling of rape cases, although the committee was given very little opportunity to obtain data about what had been happening during the judicial hearing process on campus. It remains to be seen whether USC will implement these recommendations. If it does, (and it seems to be taking steps to do so), it will have a model program.[2]

Before we discuss ways in which the college can protect its interests and those of its students, it is necessary to describe the different types of lawsuits for which schools are at risk in the area of campus sexual assault. We will also describe other lawsuits that relate to campus sexual assault, where the victim may sue either the perpetrator or a third party. Although the college is not directly affected by these latter suits, they do result in negative publicity and further illustrate the scope of the problem.

As we discussed earlier, the changes in the doctrine of in loco parentis have made the university less responsible for its students; it no longer has any general obligation to protect them from harm. As one court has said of the new student-college relationship,

> A university is an institution for the advancement of knowledge and learning. It is neither a nursery school, a boarding school nor a prison. No one is required to attend. Persons who meet the required qualifications and who abide by the university's rules and regulations are permitted to attend and must be presumed to have sufficient maturity to conduct their own personal affairs.[3]

There remain, however, some specific bases or liability claims in both tort and contract law that may be brought against a university. These claims are either developments of established doctrine or, in some cases, attempts to develop new doctrines for cases of campus sexual assault.

Types of Lawsuits in Campus Sexual Assaults

There are a number of different legal bases on which lawsuits about campus sexual assault can be based. Which legal basis is used will depend on the facts of a particular case, as well as who is plaintiff and defendant in the case. So that the reader can better understand the legal grounds for suits in this area, Table 8–1 lists the various possibilities which will be discussed in the next section.

Victim Suing the College

A victim who sues the college at which the sexual assault took place can use several areas of the law as the basis for her suit.

TABLE 8-1
Possible Lawsuits Resulting from Campus Sexual Assault

Plaintiff	Defendant	Grounds

Victim	College	Tort law
		(i) Premises liability claims
		    (a) landowner-invitee
		    (b) landlord-tenant
		    (c) special relationship of college and student
		(ii) Other tort claims
		    (a) violation of alcohol policies
		    (b) responsibility to provide safe educational environment
		    (c) intentional infliction of emotional distress
		Contract law (breach of contract to provide safe educational environment)
		Civil rights claims

Victim	Assailant	Intentional tort
Victim	Other third parties (e.g., fraternities)	Tort claims (similar to those above against college, depending on circumstances)
Defendant	College	Violation of due process in dealing with campus sexual assault
Defendant	Victim	Defamation, abuse of legal process, intentional infliction of emotional stress
Fraternity	College	Violation of due process in dealing with fraternity

TORT LAW. GENERAL PRINCIPLES. Most of the lawsuits against colleges in this area have been based in tort law. A tort is a private wrong doing by one person or entity to another, for which the doer is legally responsible. There are two kinds of tort that are relevant in this chapter: negligent and intentional torts. When a victim sues the college, it is almost invariably based on a claim of negligence. When she sues the assailant, it is usually on the basis of an intentional tort. Under tort law, a number of factors must be present before the institution can be found to be liable for negligence. The plaintiff must show that (1) some duty or obligation exists, recognized by the law, requiring that the person conform to a certain standard of conduct for the protection of others against unreasonable risks; (2) there was a breach of this duty; (3) there is a reasonable causal link between the damage suffered by the plaintiff; and (4) the plaintiff has suffered real damage as a result.[4] A description of the various types of lawsuits that can be brought against the university and other parties follows.

PREMISES LIABILITY CLAIMS. In these claims, the plaintiff alleges that the defendant institution was negligent in not protecting its student from harm resulting from some quality about the premises. Suits can be based on either of two theories—that of landowner-invitee, and that of landlord-tenant. They usually deal with rather specific claims of obligations that the college arguably has neglected. For example, a number of cases have been based on the absence of adequate lighting and locks, which the victim argues fits into the four factors mentioned above. These cases are the most traditional, where the law is fairly clear.

Landowner-Invitee. Under the theory of landowner-invitee, the university is characterized as a landowner holding its property open for the public, who may come onto it for business purposes. Students are, of course, part of this public. In this situation, the landowner has a responsibility to exercise reasonable care toward the public. The nature of this responsibility is to use reasonable care in inspecting the premises to discover possible dangerous conditions and to warn and protect invitees from foreseeable dangers.

There have been a number of attempts by students who have been injured as a result of campus crime to use this theory to recover damages from the university. For example, when two students were abducted from a Florida campus and murdered, their families sued the state on the basis of the landowner-invitee theory of tort law.[5] Such claims have met with mixed success, at least for those about which we know from the law reports. It may well be that cases where the issue of liability was clearer were settled out of court.

In the reported cases, the courts do not allow recovery where there was insufficient evidence that the risk was foreseeable. This was what happened in the Florida case where the students were murdered. For the parents to have recovered damages, they would have had to prove that the landowner knew or should have known of prior similar criminal acts committed against invitees; because they could not prove this, they lost the case. In the case of *Brown v. North Carolina Wesleyan College*,[6] a college cheerleader was abducted from a basketball game, raped, and murdered. In the suit by her estate, the court said that "a college can be liable for a criminal assault upon one of its students under certain circumstances. Foreseeability of a criminal assault, however, determines a college's duty to safeguard its students from criminal acts of third persons."[7] In this case, the college had not had many incidents of violence and had only experienced one attempted rape two years earlier. Thus, the court stated that there was insufficient basis on which to impose on the college a duty to warn or protect its students.

Landlord-Tenant. A second theory under which a victim can sue is by arguing that the university, as a landlord of the property in which the student lives, has the same responsibility as any landlord to keep the premises safe. Students who live in campus housing owned by the college would be covered under this doctrine. It has been fairly limited in the past, but as the rate of crime on residential property increases, both in general and on the college campus, it is becoming a more common basis on which to sue.

Under common law, the landlord has the duty to warn tenants of any dangerous conditions on the premises. There is no requirement that a landlord protect a tenant from the criminal behavior of third parties merely by virtue of the landlord-tenant relationship; however, if the plaintiff can prove special circumstances, the university may be liable. Examples of special circumstances would be such things as previous attacks on tenants because of faulty security, or even faulty security that the landlord knew about but took no action to remedy. As one court said, "A landlord who recognizes and assumes the duty to protect his tenants from foreseeable criminal conduct may be liable if he fails to take reasonable precautions to prevent injury to his tenants from this conduct."[8] The issue of foreseeability is all-important. In the case from which this quote is taken, Carol Cutler was raped in her dormitory room at Florida Agriculture and Mechanical University. She argued successfully that the university knew or should have known that other rapes had occurred on the campus.

A similar rule was enunciated in the New York case of *Miller v. New York*.[9] In that case, a student was abducted from her dormitory at the State University of New York at Stony Brook and raped twice at knife point. The courts said that the university would be liable if the plaintiff could prove that "there was a reasonable foreseeable likelihood of criminal intrusion into the building, that the State negligently failed to keep the outer doors locked, and that the failure was a proximate cause of the injury."[10] In this case, there was evidence that strangers were often seen in the hallway, the lounges, and the women's bathroom. There had also been reports of criminal activity of various kinds in and around the dormitories. Given these facts, the court held the university liable, arguing that the crime suffered by the plaintiff was reasonably foreseeable.

Special Relationship. In the above situations, the university is treated like any other landowner in its duty to students. A few courts have held colleges to a higher standard, arguing that, despite the inapplicability of the doctrine of in loco parentis, colleges have a special duty to protect their students. In the case of *Mullins v. Pine Manor College*,[11] the court made a distinction between the role of a college in policing the morals of its resident students and its role in ensuring their physical safety. Though the former role was no longer necessary, this did not mean that the university could abandon the latter: "Parents, students, and the general community still have a reasonable expectation, fostered in part by the colleges themselves, that reasonable care will be exercised to protect resident students from foreseeable harm."[12] In this case, a student was abducted from her dorm, taken to an unlocked dining hall, and raped. The college had taken some precautions to protect its students, thereby raising the expectations of students and their parents. Because these precautions were inadequately implemented, the court found the college liable both under tort law and on its special student-college relationship. This illustrates the dangers of bad prevention. If a college does nothing, it risks being found negligent; if it does something but does it inadequately, it also risks a lawsuit.

The issue of foreseeability, however, is still central. One wonders whether any of these cases would find the college liable on the special relationship theory if there were not also issues of responsibility under one of the other two theories. In a case where there have been no previous crimes of a similar nature, it is hard to imagine a court requiring the college to prevent such activity.

The situation nevertheless has changed rapidly in the last few years. In the first place, because there has been an increased incidence of crime on campuses generally, it will presumably become easier to argue that a university should have taken some steps to protect its students. Thus, liability will be more likely in a suit based on the special relationship between the college and the student, as well as on the other two theories previously discussed. In addition, awareness has been heightened by the publicity about acquaintance rape both on and off campus. It therefore is much more difficult for a school to argue that there was no foreseeable risk, even if it has not had a reported case. This is especially true in light of the material we have documented elsewhere, which makes clear that this is not just a problem of stranger rapes on urban campuses, but one that can affect all schools. Too many colleges are far more willing to assume that the problem involves only outsiders and can be prevented by a lights-and-locks prevention program.

The cases in our sample of victims who are currently suing, or whose suits have recently been resolved, are more often based on a broader responsibility than the premises liability cases discussed above. In the case of *Leonardi v. Sanders and Bradley University*, which is currently in the pretrial stage, the plaintiff alleges that Bradley University had a special relationship of business inviter–invitee with her and that therefore the university had a duty to exercise a high degree of care toward her.[13] The plaintiff, Angenette Leonardi, was raped at a fraternity party on campus soon after her arrival at college. Her foreseeability argument is framed in terms of the general problem of campus sexual assault. The complaint lists studies showing both the widespread nature of the problem and the rate of the campus sexual assault on the Bradley campus. Thus, Leonardi argues, the university knew of the danger and failed to warn the students of it; it failed to provide appropriate education programs and failed also to develop an appropriate course of investigation and punishment of prior sexual assaults committed by Bradley students. Because this case has not yet been tried in court, we cannot say how the court will respond to these arguments. Like so many of these cases, Bradley may see it as being in its interests to settle out of court and require as a condition of settlement a gag order on the parties to prevent them from discussing the case.

In *Coverdale* v. *Rutgers University*, the court decided that the university was not negligent in failing to prevent the sexual assault of one of its students, nor was there evidence to support the claim that it had covered up the charges. This case involved a student who did not report the assault until several months after the assault. The university said that Ms. Coverdale had failed to attend mandatory rape prevention instruction in her first year. She alleged that Rutgers had been negligent in training residents to supervise dormitories and in failing to take action to protect her; The court, however, denied her claims.[14] When these cases do get to court, the strength of the fact situation is crucial. In this case, there was enough evidence that Rutgers University did make efforts to deal with the problem of campus sexual assault to answer the claim of negligence. Ms. Coverdale also sued the students involved and recently settled her claim against one of them from his family's homeowners insurance.[15]

Another case illustrates that the obligation of the university may extend beyond educating and warning its students. In the case of *Zick*, v. *University of Minnesota*, Louis Sabin, who sexually assaulted Ms. Zick, was employed by the university as part of the ROTC program.[16] The plaintiff was a student in a rifle marksmanship class taught by Mr. Sabin. The suit was based on two counts, *respondeat superior* and negligence. The first doctrine is one in which an employer is responsible for the actions of its employees when they engage in wrongful conduct in the course of their employment. In the second count, Ms. Zick's complaint argued that the university was negligent in failing to screen and train personnel adequately, as well as to investigate and punish the behavior promptly when it was first reported to them. This case has not yet been resolved, but it serves to illustrate the need to include all members of the university community in prevention and education programs. This has been done in a few institutions, and will be discussed further in Chapter 10.

In another example of the doctrine of *respondeat superior*, Luther College is being sued for the professional malpractice of its psychologist and social worker. The plaintiff argues that these members of the college community failed in their duty toward her by not treating her case appropriately. She also argues that the college was negligent in inadequately training residence advisors and in hiring people it knew to be incompetent. This case is still in a pretrial stage, so it is as yet unclear how far the liability of the university for the behavior of its employees will extend.[17]

Many campuses are aware of the need to take a wide variety of precautions in the area of campus sexual assault. The risk of being sued should a crime occur is clearly only one of many reasons colleges are actively involved in crime prevention. Increased pressures as a result of federal and state legislation also have had an effect on the behavior of colleges. The nature of this legislation and the obligations it places on colleges will be discussed in detail in Chapter 9. At this point it is sufficient to mention that the obligation to provide secure premises for students is now clarified and somewhat expanded under this legislation.

OTHER TORT CLAIMS. There are several other claims in tort that a victim can use in appropriate circumstances. The more recent cases we have followed seem to be relying more on these legal bases as a way of expanding the reach of the law in campus sexual assault cases to cover the facts of current cases which are not adequately addressed under the more traditional legal doctrines.

Violation of Alcohol Policies. There have been some recent attempts to tie the alleged negligence of the university to violations of its alcohol policies and the provision of alcohol to minors. Because the legal drinking age has gone up to twenty-one, colleges are faced with the problem of their responsibility to enforce this law on campus. Several suits have argued that a university that knowingly allows alcohol to be served to minors and allows extensive drinking to take place is responsible for the criminal activities that result. So far, such claims have not generally been successful in the courts. For example, in the case of *Baldwin* v. *Zoradi*,[18] a student was severely injured in an automobile accident that was caused by other students in an auto race. The students were underage and had become inebriated as a result of drinking alcohol on the campus. Although decrying the egregious nature of the actions of the students, the court refused to hold the university responsible for the illegal drinking; such behavior was not sufficiently heinous nor unusual as to require special efforts to stamp it out. In that case, the court refused to acknowledge the existence of a special relationship between the university and the student.

A similar result was reached in the case of *Tanja H.* v. *Regents of the University of California*.[19] In that case, the plaintiff was raped by four members of the football team at the University of California at Berkeley. The rapes took place after a party in a dormitory. Again, the court acknowledged the "outrageous and reprehensible conduct of the perpetrators," but refused to find the university responsible for their behavior. The court stated that the university could not be held liable as an insurer for the crimes of its students. Again, there was no acknowledgment of the special relationship between the university and the student. It is possible that in a case such as this, another court might place responsibility on the university in an appropriate factual situation. For example, the school would have to be well aware of both the illegal alcohol consumption and the possibility of sexual assault, as proven perhaps by previous incidents. It would have to be shown that the university, despite its awareness of these facts, did not make sufficient effort to control the behavior of its students. These facts would be sufficient to show that it was reasonably foreseeable that doing nothing or very little to curb underage drinking could result in sexual assault. At this point, there are no reported cases like this; however, there are some that are currently in the pretrial stage. If these cases go to trial, more will be known about the development of the law in this area.

One of the allegations in the case of *Buxton* v. *Colgate University et al.* is that the university was negligent in failing to control or halt the fraternity party at which the plaintiff was assaulted.[20] The fraternity in question had repeatedly violated college alcohol and party regulations to such a degree that it had been placed on probation for these violations. The party had been permitted only if certain conditions were met, such as only allowing invited guests and not serving alcohol to minors. These conditions were extensively violated by the fraternity. The plaintiff was raped in a bedroom at the party by several men who were at the party, some of whom were underage and all of whom were intoxicated. Thus, Colgate is charged with knowing what had been going on at the fraternity but nevertheless failing to supervise its rules about alcohol use at the party, thereby maintaining a dangerous environment. This is another case that has not yet been resolved.

Responsibility to Provide a Safe Environment. Other new cases have attempted to argue a more general claim of negligence, under which the university has a responsibility to protect students from danger by virtue of its obligation to provide them with a safe educational environment. This is very similar to the claims made regarding premises liability, but it relies more on the need to provide a safe educational environment than on the safe premises required of a landowner for invitees or a landlord for tenants. This can be combined with a similar claim that is based in contract (rather than tort) law, which will be discussed below.

INTENTIONAL INFLICTION OF EMOTIONAL DISTRESS. One case filed at the end of 1992 is the first we know of to argue that the way the university handled the victim's rape complaint was sufficiently insensitive as to intentionally cause her emotional distress. She argues that the university conducted a "brutal, insensitive, and humiliating, interrogation," and refused to allow the presence of a counselor during questioning.[21] In addition, the school attempted to coerce the victim to withdraw from the university, implied that she "asked for it," bungled the collection of evidence, and behaved as if it were an acquaintance rape even though she had never before seen her attackers. As this case is still in the pretrial stage, it is not known how successful this claim will be. If it is successful, it will open a wide area for victims to use as a basis for their suit based on the handling of the case, rather than the conditions which caused the assault.

CONTRACT LAW. The second major basis for claims against universities can be found in contract law. Under this theory, the plaintiff claims that the university has breached a contractual relationship, and that as a result she has suffered harm. Often these claims are made alongside the tort claims discussed above, and recovery may be on either or both grounds. For example, in the case of *Peterson v. San Francisco Community College District*,[22] the plaintiff was attacked in the campus parking facility. She sued the university for breach of its duty to warn her of or protect her from reasonably foreseeable danger. Peterson's suit, which alleged that her attacker attempted to rape her, was also based on the breach of a contractual relationship. She argued that the college had an implied contractual obligation to provide its students with safe premises in which to obtain an education. The fact that the assailant was able to hide behind a high bush and attack her in a place that was insufficiently lit was evidence that the college had been in breach of its contractual obligation. The opinion was for the most part based on Peterson's tort claim, but the court did say that

> in the closed environment of a campus where students pay tuition and other fees in exchange for using the facilities, where they spend a significant portion of their time and may in fact live, they can reasonably expect that the premises will be free from physical defects and that school authorities will also exercise reasonable care to keep the campus free from conditions which increase the risk of crime.[23]

In the case of *Bradach et al v. Carleton College*, the plaintiffs also argued that the college had a contractual relationship to provide an environment reasonably free from physical danger, sexual harassment, and criminal sexual assault.[24] This was seen as a central element of the college's obligation to provide its students with an education, particularly as the college required that its students live on campus for their first two years. Since this case was settled out of court, it cannot be determined whether the legal argument would have been successful.

A specific aspect of a claim of breach of contract is illustrated in the case of *Weber* v. *USC* (discussed earlier). The claim of fraud made successfully by the plaintiff was related to the contractual relationship between the University and the student. As the plaintiff's lawyer stated, "They enticed students to live at that facility by not revealing the dangerous area."[25] This case sends a message to campuses located in dangerous areas that they had better not gloss over the dangers.

The contractual obligation used in these cases is buttressed by the recent legislation at both state and federal levels, which is discussed in Chapter 9. It is possible that in the future there will be more lawsuits based on the breach of a contractual relationship in accord with the requirements of the legislation.

CIVIL RIGHTS CLAIMS. In the case of *Coverdale* v. *Rutgers University*, the plaintiff claimed that the university had violated her civil rights under 42 U.S.C., Section 1983. This argument is used in many other contexts, but this is the first time we know of it having been used in a case of campus sexual assault. The claim rested on the argument that Rutgers had a policy or practice that deprived the plaintiff of her constitutional rights, in this case her right to be free from invasion of personal security through sexual abuse. Coverdale argued that by maintaining a "policy, practice, or custom" that prevented her from bringing a suit against her assailants in criminal court, Rutgers deprived her of her civil rights.[26] Coverdale lost her case on other grounds, but this argument represents an interesting new approach that is already being followed in other cases.[27]

Victim Suing Her Assailant

There has been a lot of publicity recently about rape victims who sue their assailant in civil court. For many victims there are advantages to a civil suit either in addition to or instead of pursuing the case through the criminal courts. The main advantages to a civil rather than a criminal proceeding is that, in the former, the victim is in control and may receive some money as a reward for her pains.

A further advantage to a civil suit is that the standard of proof is lower. The state must prove a criminal case beyond a reasonable doubt—a standard that is hard to meet in cases of rape, where very often there is little by way of evidence other than the testimony of the victim. In a civil suit, on the other hand, the standard is only that of the preponderance of probabilities. This means that the plaintiff has to show that the events on which she bases her claim are more likely than not to have taken place as alleged.

There are, however, some disadvantages to the civil suit by a victim against the perpetrator. The major one is that the latter probably has no assets to make the case financially worthwhile. Although for many victims, winning a civil suit is not primarily a matter of money, it is nevertheless somewhat pointless to sue someone against whom one has no hope of recovering anything. In one case, Jean Murray, a student at the University of Florida, sued her assailant and won a judgment for $1.7 million dollars. The assailant, who did not defend the case at all, was also convicted in criminal court. He is now serving a substantial prison sentence, so the chances that Ms. Murray will receive any of the award are distant at best, as she very well knows. Nevertheless, the victim and her family decided that it was very important that they proceed in order to "send another message, to people in general, to him and to his family."[28]

A further problem in suing the assailant is that the legal fees involved may be considerable, which may prevent many victims from suing in civil court. In cases of campus sexual assault where the perpetrator is a student, it is possible that he does have some money and also that he has good prospects of money in the future, perhaps making a suit worthwhile. In the case of *Davis* v. *Bard College*, the victim is suing the perpetrator (as well as the college) because he apparently comes from a wealthy family.[29] There is also the possibility of using the perpetrator's family's homeowners insurance as discussed earlier in the *Coverdale* case.

Another disadvantage of a civil suit from the point of view of the victim is that the recent laws designed to keep out evidence of the victim's prior sexual behavior do not apply in civil cases.[30] Thus a victim runs the risk of very nasty cross-examination by the defense on the subject of her sexual behavior.

Victim Suing Other Third Parties

The most likely targets of a lawsuit in a case of campus sexual assault have been the fraternities where the assault took place. The benefit of suing fraternities is that they often have money (or insurance) with which the victim may be compensated, especially if the victim is able to add the national organization to the list of defendants. In addition, it is often the case that the fraternity is seen by the victim as the villain in the assault because it encourages the kind of activities that end up as cases of campus sexual assault.[31] Related to this fact is the concern on the part of the victim to use the civil suit as a means of initiating social change. If this is a large part of the victim's motivation, the fraternity that may encourage inappropriate behavior is a much better target than the individual himself.

In the *Buxton* case discussed above, Kristen Buxton is suing not only the university but the national and local organizations of the fraternity she alleges is responsible. The basis of the fraternity's responsibility is that it sponsored a summer party at the fraternity house to which the plaintiff was invited. Because the fraternity was on probation for violation of college rules about drinking, it needed permission for the party, which it obtained. The conditions under which it was given permission to hold the party were extensively violated by the fraternity. In providing alcohol to underage drinkers, the fraternity (and the other defendants) also were in violation of several New York statutes.

Defendant Suing the College

There have been some suits by defendants that have also had an impact on the issue of campus sexual assault. Because these cases may affect the college in very different ways than the suits by victims, some administrators may feel themselves caught in a no-win situation where they risk either being sued by the victim or by the defendant. Though there is indeed such a danger, we believe that it is possible to minimize risks from both sides simultaneously; appropriate strategies for this will be discussed after we describe the nature of the lawsuits by defendants and their organizations. In addition to the cases that follow, many cases dealing with defendants' suits against universities for violation of due process rights generally are discussed in Chapter 5.

These suits are generally based on the actions taken by the judicial hearing board. In most cases, the defendant has argued that his due process rights have been violated. At the University of New Hampshire, a basketball player named Antonio Steadman was expelled for assaulting a female student. He took his claim to court, arguing that he had been unfairly treated by being expelled after a hearing that did not protect his rights.[32] The judge ordered him reinstated; the university appealed to the Supreme Court of New Hampshire but dropped the appeal when it became clear that Mr. Steadman would contest the case, despite the fact that he had already transferred to another college in Florida. In his opinion, the judge agreed with the student that a number of aspects of the hearing violated his due process rights. This case is unusual in that the plaintiff was able to prove his claim, unlike many of the cases dealt with in Chapter 5.

Defendant Suing the Victim

There have been several recent cases in which the defendant has sued the victim in a campus sexual assault case for libel and slander (based on the allegation of sexual assault by the victim). In the case of *Rosenboom* v. *Vanek*, a visiting professor was accused of rape by a student.[33] In addition to the alleged victim, he also sued the workers at the University of Michigan's rape counseling center who were counseling the victim. The case was dismissed by the lower court; the professor appealed without success as far as the Michigan Supreme Court. In addition to this case, there was another case involving students at the University of Michigan that was based on allegations of defamation, intentional affliction of emotional distress, and abuse of the legal process. The case was eventually settled out of court.[34] These cases resulted in the state of Michigan passing legislation, discussed in Chapter 9, that prevents such actions until the criminal case has been resolved. The Steadman case at the University of New Hampshire (discussed in the previous section) also gave rise to a suit against the victim for slander. That case was dropped as part of the agreement between Mr. Steadman and the university in which the latter dropped its appeal of his due process suit.[35]

Many of those who work with rape victims are very concerned that these cases represent a trend that will have a chilling effect on the already small proportion of victims who report their assault to the authorities. One commentator recommends that other states pass legislation, similar to that passed in Michigan, that would delay any such action until after the criminal case has been tried.[36]

Fraternities Suing the College

There have been some cases in which a fraternity has sued the college for actions taken against it after a campus sexual assault case. The assault usually takes place at an event in the fraternity house and is perpetrated by fraternity members. This was the case at the

University of Pennsylvania, were the university took action against a fraternity after a gang rape. The case went to court before Judge Lois Forer, who, in a strongly worded opinion, set up due process rules for appropriate methods of hearing the charges rather than the ad hoc methods used before the case went to court.[37] The rules were based on the cases discussed in Chapter 5 and included notice of the charges, presentation of evidence in the presence of fraternity representatives, an opportunity for the fraternity to present witnesses and documentary evidence on its own behalf, and the right of the fraternity to consult with counsel during the process.

When Can a College Be Sued?

Sovereign-Governmental Immunity

The liability of a college will depend in part on whether it is a public or a private institution. It is much easier to sue a private institution than a public one, because there is a doctrine called *sovereign immunity* that we inherited from English common law. Under that legal doctrine, the king was immune from suit. We have, of course, come a long way in the law since the time of English common law, and the doctrine has changed with the times. Indeed, it is very difficult to say with any precision exactly when a public college or university is protected and when it is not. The availability and extent of the doctrine varies from state to state. In our experience, it is the kind of information that the university attorney will have about his or her own state, but not about any other, so anyone who is concerned about whether a college is protected from suit would do well to consult that university's attorney.

It is possible to say a few things about the doctrine. In general, it is much less extensive than it used to be, though an institution of higher education is still likely to be immune from suit in at least some circumstances. The doctrine has been narrowed both by legislation and by judicial decisions that vary from state to state and are in a state of flux.[38] For example, Pennsylvania has created legislation that narrowly defines those instances in which tort action may be brought against the state.

There are several exceptions to the doctrine that are fairly widely accepted. The major one is the distinction between ministerial and discretionary immunity; in plain English, this means that a public institution is liable for torts committed if they were part of the ministerial activity of the institution, which is the specific function for which the institution was set up. In the case of a college, the ministerial function is education. If the action complained of is one that involves discretionary activity, the institution is protected on the grounds that imposing liability would jeopardize the quality and efficiency of the school. For example, in a case where the parents of a football player sued the team physician and trainer after the player collapsed and later died on the football field, the court held them both immune because they were performing discretionary medical treatments on the student. Unfortunately, however, the distinction is extremely confused in the courts and in legislation, so that it is impossible to describe the situation clearly.

It is unclear whether the area of campus crime falls within the ministerial or discretionary area. In one case in Florida, the court found the university immune from a suit brought by parents of three students who were killed after being abducted from a university parking lot.[39] Some courts, however, look to whether the harm was foreseeable, in which case "the duty to warn of a known dangerous condition . . . has been recognized . . . to be an operational-level function of government not subject to sovereign immunity."[40]

In the case of *Coverdale* v. *Rutgers University*, the university defended itself against Coverdale's claim that it was negligent (in its hearing procedures and in allowing violations of its alcohol policies) by claiming tort immunity under New Jersey law.[41] The plaintiff responded that the activity complained of was not governmental but rather in the interests of the university; therefore, under New Jersey law, absolute immunity did not apply. The plaintiff also argued that the individual employees were acting outside the proper realm of their discretion when they tried to keep the case within the university, and accordingly, they were also not protected under the doctrine of discretionary immunity. Although Coverdale lost her suit on other grounds, it seems clear that Rutgers was not immune, especially from the claim that it violated her civil rights (discussed earlier in the chapter).

In some states, it is still possible to sue a public institution in circumstances such as campus crime, but there are restrictions as to the court in which the action must be brought, the time limits for bringing the suit, and the amount of damages that can be obtained. In Illinois, for example, one can sue a public institution in the Court of claims, for up to $100,000 in damages. In New York, the trial must be before a judge alone rather than before a judge and jury, and the limit is $50,000.[42] In Colorado, the plaintiff must file a written notice within 180 days after the discovery of the injury. All these limits are designed to circumscribe the extent of the state's liability without making it immune altogether.

Some courts and legislatures have held that the purchase of liability insurance constitutes a waiver of immunity. Presumably, this undercuts one of the justifications for the immunity in the first place: that the state could not afford to pay for the damages in a lawsuit.

Charitable Immunity

In some states, a private college might be immune from suit or liable only to a limited extent by the doctrine of charitable immunity. Again the law is in a state of flux; this is also, therefore, a question that should be put to the attorney for the college. The law here also is moving in the direction of limiting the immunity so that, in many cases, a private college is liable to the same extent as an individual or private corporation. At the very least, the doctrine only applies to the charitable activities of the school. In some states, the doctrine has the effect of limiting the liability of the college, as is the case in Massachusetts, in which it is limited to $20,000 for personal injury.[43]

The Law and Reality

As shown above, there are a number of legal bases on which a plaintiff can sue the institution for harm arising out of a sexual assault case on the college campus. From a practical point of view, administrators must also be aware of the risks of being sued and defending a lawsuit, successfully or otherwise. The difficulty here, as in all lawsuits, is that the mere filing of a suit may have serious negative effects on the college in terms of bad publicity and potential loss of financial support, regardless of the merits of the legal claim. The damage can be greater than for other institutions, as so much of the college's enrollment and reputation depends on public opinion.

Without exception, as discussed in Chapter 4, the cases we have collected in which colleges have been sued by victims show that the lawsuit was the final remedy sought after all other efforts to get redress had failed. Invariably the victims go through the judicial hearing process, which often has an unsatisfactory result. They often appeal and fail to find satisfaction through that mechanism either. The institution takes a defensive stance and refuses to recognize any problem, and the victim feels belittled and cheated. Her family usually has become involved, and they share her outrage at the treatment she has received; the officials often respond badly to the parents as well. Typically, the parents decide that they will not tolerate more of the treatment they and their daughter have received, and they take the matter to a lawyer. At this point, the legal merits of the suit are less significant to them than the feeling that they must right a wrong that has been done to them.

In most conflicts involving the college and students, the interests of the student are pitted against the interests of the college. In the case of interstudent campus crime, there are three parties with conflicting interests, and problems often arise in such cases when the institution misjudges how to balance the conflicting interests. As seen in earlier chapters, many of the cases in our sample ended up in court largely because the victim felt that her interests were ignored in favor of those of the defendant. Some of this feeling may stem from a misunderstanding of the roles played in the judicial hearing process, in which the victim is merely a witness (just as she is in a criminal trial). The college can, however, do much to make the victim feel that her interests are not being ignored and that the institution is not unduly protecting her assailant.

The message here is obvious: when a school takes a case seriously and makes every effort to collect evidence and to have a fair hearing, whatever the outcome, lawsuits usually do not follow. Research in other fields, especially in the area of medical malpractice, shows clearly that people are less likely to sue those with whom they have a positive relationship. In such situations, they usually decide that even though the outcome was bad, it makes sense to view it as an unfortunate occurrence for which no one should be held responsible. So they shrug their shoulders and decide to put the matter behind them. In the case of campus sexual assault, victims may see it the same way. It was a terrible experience, but the college did its best to avoid it by providing appropriate education and security. After it happened despite the school's best efforts, it provided sympathetic help for the victim, kept her informed of the situation, and held a fair hearing. In such a situation, the victim and her parents are more likely to say that the college should not be held responsible for the bad behavior of the assailant; if anyone is to be sued, it should be the assailant himself.

Similar reasoning can be applied to the case of potential lawsuits by the defendant. If an alleged assailant feels that he has been fairly treated, he is not likely to sue. It is when he feels that his rights have not been considered that he will take action; the ways in which a defendant's due process rights can best be protected are dealt with in Chapter 5. From a study of the cases in which defendants in campus sexual assault cases do sue, it is clear that the institutions being sued had dealt very shabbily with the rights of the defendants. Many defendants in this litigious society may *threaten* to sue, a threat that frightens many schools. In fact, many of those threats are simply a way of venting spleen after an outcome with which the defendants are not happy. In most cases, this threat means nothing and is not followed up by legal action. In those cases in which the defendant does consult a lawyer, there is often very little action, and the case eventually peters out. We have been collecting cases for some time now and have been able to accumulate relatively few cases that have gone as far as the defendant filing a complaint, let alone resulting in a court decision or a settlement.

Some institutions do seem to be able to balance the interests of both the victim and the defendant. At the University of Rochester, for example, the emphasis is placed on equality of treatment to protect the rights of both sides. The accused is permitted to have anyone he chooses to testify on his behalf. The judicial officer spends time with him before the hearing so that "he becomes a real person" to the officer.[44] At the same time, the people in the office of the dean of students are concerned with the victim, especially with providing her with emotional support. In addition, the University of Rochester has developed a system whereby it is possible for the victim, if she so chooses, to testify in a room adjacent to the hearing room so that she will not have to be in the same room as her alleged assailant.

Neither the victim nor the defendant is permitted to have a lawyer present at the hearing.

Areas of Special Concern in Avoiding Lawsuits

Personal Safety of the Victim

Many of the victims we have interviewed named personal safety as their primary concern after a sexual assault. They are terrified that the defendant will return and assault them again. A rapid response to her desire for safety is perhaps the best example of how a college can protect the victim and make her feel that her concerns are being taken seriously. As discussed elsewhere, some schools have the equivalent of a temporary restraining order that they can use to order the defendant to keep away from the victim pending the hearing on the merits of the case. If the judicial hearing officer thinks there is enough evidence to make what in the criminal justice system is a prima facie case (in other words, there is enough evidence to take the case to trial), then he or she can order the defendant to stay away from the victim. A good procedure of this kind needs a real punishment for failure to obey this order. At Cornell, the judicial officer can suspend or even expel someone who disregards such an order.

Similar approaches that exhibit concern for the fears of the victim have to do with efforts to move either the victim or the defendant from student housing if they are living in inappropriate proximity. This approach, which has been discussed elsewhere, is also emphasized in the Ramstad amendment (see Chapter 9).

Initial Response to the Victim's Complaint

It is important that the victim's claim is not denigrated by the university when she first makes her complaint. Too many institutions have a way of playing down the seriousness of her charge either by making her feel that the assault was not very important or, worse still, by blaming her. A victim who is made to feel that it was her fault has a difficult time adjusting to the assault. Her psychological well-being can be seriously harmed for a long period of time; many such victims drop out of school, transfer, or have serious psychological difficulties. This, of course, has a number of implications for the nature of the problem of sexual assault. For our purposes here, however, there is the risk that when the victim understands the nature of the process whereby she was blamed for the assault, she is more likely to sue the institution that, as she sees it, put her through so much psychological distress by its response to her complaint.

Alcohol Policies

Often the way in which the college makes the victim feel responsible for the assault has to do with her alcohol consumption. Many victims we have interviewed told us that the college told them that because they were intoxicated at the time of the assault, no crime was committed. This is a misstatement of the law, which is actually the reverse: rape takes place when a victim is unable to consent by virtue of her state of intoxication.

The relationship between sexual assault and excessive drinking is an important one, and it is discussed in Chapters 2 and 10. The significance of this relationship here has to do with the potential legal liability of a college that does not adequately monitor alcohol policies on the campus. As shown above, there is a risk of a lawsuit resulting from such neglect. We believe that the issue will only become more important as the connection between violence and alcohol on the campus becomes better known, thereby raising the risk of lawsuits.

Physically Safe Environment

The obligation of the university to provide a physically safe environment is a central one to minimize the risk of suit. It is penny-wise and pound-foolish to attempt to save money on such issues as lighting and security, in terms of both dollars and the mental health of students. Actually, aside from the financial issues, we have found that these security issues are the easiest to resolve, because they do not require any attitudinal change on the part of college administrators. Everyone recognizes the importance of having the campus free from crime in general and such solutions as proper lighting, maintenance, and policing are simple to implement. It is those areas that require a reorientation of college administrators' attitudes that present many colleges with difficulty. This is especially true for acquaintance rape cases that occur within a party setting or in dorms where students regularly socialize, which many administrators find difficult to take seriously. Not taking such complaints seriously can be very costly for a university, both financially and in terms of lost reputation, should a lawsuit result.

Conclusion

Colleges that take complaints of sexual assault seriously and do not attempt to sweep cases under the rug for fear of bad publicity are less likely to be sued as a result. We have seen the efforts to keep such cases quiet backfire on more than one occasion. Somehow the facts have a way of getting out, which may lead to more bad publicity than would have resulted if the case had been dealt with publicly in the first place. In addition, the resentment that such behavior generates in the victim is exactly what sends her into the office of a lawyer.

By taking cases of sexual assault seriously, colleges will gain a reputation that will be extremely beneficial to them, especially in today's climate of fear of crime. A college cannot guarantee to parents that their children will never be involved in a crime; what it can promise is that it will do what is possible to avoid such a situation, and if it happens, it will be treated seriously and not hidden from view.

Checklist for Colleges to Avoid Lawsuits

1. Check your campus carefully for safety problems. If possible, hire a safety expert to walk around showing you vulnerable spots. If you find problems, *fix them.*
2. Make students aware of safety policies. Punish students who sabotage the system (for example, by propping open doors).
3. Make sure your code of conduct clearly spells out what behavior constitutes sexual assault. Be sure students know of the expectations for appropriate behavior.
4. Be sure your code of conduct provides due process to students who are charged with violations of the code of conduct. It should list rights available to the accused.
5. Include a list of rights for victims of sexual assault in your code of conduct.

6. Be sure that you adhere to the policies outlined in the code, especially those in items 4 and 5 above.
7. Treat victims and defendants with respect.
8. If someone does threaten to sue, *do not panic*. Most threats will be only that. If you say, "Go ahead," most people will not bother.
9. If you hear from a lawyer representing a defendant or a victim, *do not panic*. Even those cases in which someone has consulted a lawyer often fizzle out one way or another. Tell the lawyer you are waiting to receive any papers he or she is ready to serve on you. Do not let lawyers intimidate you.
10. If you do receive either a call from a lawyer or legal papers, consult your college attorney immediately, and then channel all communications through him or her. Do not let anyone try to get you to make statements or admissions; simply say, "Please address all your questions to the college attorney."
11. If the lawsuit does not fizzle out, remember that you have done your best by following the above suggestions. If anything you did turns out to be relevant, remember that it is better to have taken the high road. At least you will be able to sleep at night knowing that you did what you thought was right, regardless of the legal outcome.

9

Legislation

The problem of sexual assault on campus has been getting a great deal of publicity. Much of the media attention and pressure on legislators has been initiated by Howard and Connie Clery, whose daughter Jeannie was raped and murdered in her residence hall room at Lehigh University in 1986. They have been instrumental in getting the following three Federal laws developed and passed: Student Right to Know and Campus Security Act—PL 101-542[1]; Ramstad Amendment to the Higher Education Act—PL 102-325[2] (introduced as the Campus Sexual Assault Victim's Bill of Rights Act of 1991); and Clarification of the Buckley Amendment. They also created an organization called Security on Campus, which monitors college campus security issues and keeps the public informed of problems that arise. The Clerys, Frank Carrington, Margaret and Tom Baer (whose son was stabbed to death at the University of Tennessee), Genelle and Jack Reilley (whose daughter Robbin Brandley was stabbed to death at Saddleback Community College in California), and so many others, have been attending and speaking at legislative hearings about campus sexual assault. The function of these hearings, both the national and state levels, is to determine the extent and the scope of the problem of sexual assault on campus and to create legislation that will reduce it.

Legislators on both the state and national levels are addressing this issue by introducing legislation that requires colleges to keep accurate records of the number of sexual assaults occurring on campus. These statistics must be made available to students and prospective students. The legislation also mandates education on sexual assault prevention, as well as revisions to policies, procedures, and protocols relating to how sexual assault cases are handled on the campus.

Federal Legislation

The earliest relevant legislation, which deals with students' privacy rights, dates back to 1974 (the so-called Buckley amendment). The first legislation related specifically to sexual assault and violence issues dates back to 1987, when the Student Right to Know and Campus Security Act was introduced. The Campus Sexual Assault Victims' Bill of Rights Action of 1991 (HR 2363), sponsored by Congressman James Ramstad of Minnesota, was revised and signed into law in 1992 as an amendment to the Higher Education Act.

The Ramstad Amendment to the Higher Education Act

Drafted by Frank Carrington and Howard Clery, this legislation was given to Congressman Ramstad for sponsorship in the House and Senator Joseph Biden for sponsorship in the Senate. This amendment derived from H.R. 2363, the Campus Sexual Assault Victims' Bill of Rights Act of 1991. It eventually gathered 192 cosponsors from both parties, and was supported by many victims rights and law enforcement groups. Representatives Ramstad and Susan Molinari attached a revised version of the bill the "Higher Education Amendments of 1992," which was signed into law as Public Law 102-325 by President Bush on July 23, 1992. Senator Joseph Biden, Chairman of the Senate Judiciary Committee, introduced S. 1289 as the Senate companion to H.R. 2363, and also joined in the effort to attach the amendment to the higher education bill.

The Ramstad Amendment requires institutions of higher education to develop and distribute a campus sexual assault policy. This policy must both describe the institution's sexual assault programs aimed at preventing sex offenses on campus, as well as outline the procedures to be followed once a sex offense has occurred.

To comply with the Ramstad Amendment, campus sexual assault prevention programs should promote awareness of rape, acquaintance rape, and other sex offenses. Additionally, the campus community should be informed of sanctions which may be imposed if an assailant is found guilty in a campus disciplinary proceeding.

When institutions hold disciplinary proceedings, the Ramstad Amendment requires that the accused and the accuser have the same opportunities to have others present during the hearing, and also that both parties be notified of the outcome of the proceeding.

The Ramstad Amendment requires that students be informed of

what they should do following a sex offense, addressing who should be contacted and the importance of preserving evidence. Students must also be informed of their options to report their assaults to both on-campus and local police, and be assisted by campus authorities in doing so.

Under the Ramstad Amendment, students must be notified of counseling, mental health or other services for sexual assault victims that exist on the campus or in the community.

Finally, the Ramstad Amendment requires that students be assisted in exercising their options to change academic and living situations following an assault, provided that such changes are reasonably available. Congressman Ramstad saw a need to legislate these procedures because historically many victims of campus sexual assault have been pressured to not report the assault, treated improperly, and misinformed of their rights by campus officials who were either misinformed or acting with the college's best interest in mind, rather than the victim's (see Appendix A).

Student Right to Know and Campus Security Act

Starting September 1, 1991, as a result of the federal Student Right to Know and Campus Security Act[3] (see Appendix B), colleges and universities must begin to collect data on campus crime and must publish their first report by September 1, 1992. Under Title II of the bill, colleges and universities are required to publish crime statistics every year so that prospective students and their families may learn about campus safety issues and make informed judgments in their choice of a campus. In addition, colleges are required to provide current students and employees with information about campus security policies at least once a year. Institutions must provide statistics concerning the occurrence on campus of the following crimes: murder, sex offenses (forcible or nonforcible), robbery, aggravated assault, burglary, and motor vehicle theft. In addition, institutions must provide statistics regarding the number of arrests involving liquor law violations, drug abuse violations, and weapons possession. See Appendix C for recommendations of the Association for Student Judicial Affairs regarding compliance with the Student Right to Know and Campus Security Act.

The bill also includes a provision that would permit colleges to disclose the results of campus disciplinary proceedings to victims of violent crimes. The Family Educational Rights and Privacy Act of

1974 (popularly know as the Buckley amendment) had been interpreted by many colleges as prohibiting them from making this information available to victims; this act will be discussed in greater
detail in the next section. Under the HEA, colleges must make this
information available to both the accused and the victim.

The Family Educational Rights and Privacy Act of 1974 (Buckley Amendment)

The Buckley amendment sets forth five provisions:

1. To require institutions of higher education to treat students
   in a fair and equitable manner.
2. To assure people of the existence of educational records and
   that the data is used properly.
3. To allow people to be knowledgeable of what information is
   recorded about them.
4. To allow people to effectively correct or amend incorrect information.
5. To assure people that those responsible for records take precautions to prevent misuse of data.

The act's intent is to provide privacy regarding the "official record"
of a student. This is usually interpreted to mean the academic record
of the student, not the criminal record. Many campus authorities,
however, feel that they are bound by the Buckley amendment to
maintain the confidentiality of accused students even after they have
been found guilty of violating the campus code of conduct. As a result, sexual assault victims who bring charges against their assailants
through the campus judicial process may never be informed of the
penalty imposed.

There have been challenges to the use of the Buckley amendment
to protect information of this nature. In fact, a decision by the circuit court in Missouri ruled that the Buckley amendment protection
only applied to personal demographics and admissions record materials, and that a student's disciplinary record was exempt.[4] The
case arose because the student newspaper of Southwest Missouri
State University published criminal records of students as a challenge to the Buckley amendment. U.S. District Court Judge Russell
Clark ruled that withholding crime reports was unconstitutional under the First and Fifth Amendments and that the state's open-

records law obliged the university to turn records over to the student newspaper.[5] Later that same year, the Arkansas state circuit court issued a similar ruling involving the campus paper at Southern Arkansas University.[6] Although these are fairly low-level decisions that do not have much precedential value (that is, very few courts are legally bound by them), they nevertheless serve as a useful guide; they also make intuitive sense. Several states have also passed "open campus" bills that require campus police to let the public look at their daily police logs and publish the information available there. The California and Massachusetts laws apply to both public and private institutions.[7]

Attorneys for the Department of Education, have contended that the Buckley amendment does apply to criminal records, requiring that fourteen universities that were releasing crime records because of the Southern Arkansas University and Southwestern Missouri State University decisions stop doing so or lose their federal funding. The Student Press Law Center of Washington, D.C., was successful in getting an injunction against the Department of Education. District Judge Stanley Harris granted the injunction based on the fact that the right to receive information and ideas is inherent in the rights to free speech and a free press explicitly guaranteed by the Constitution.[8] Therefore, this amendment no longer guarantees confidentiality to students regarding the felonies they commit on campus.

The Security on Campus organization advocates full disclosure of information regarding crime on campus. Its founders explain that

> the law enforcement exemption to Buckley should apply to any campus or security department that deals with crime on campus, not just those agencies that are formal law enforcement agencies that can make arrests and carry guns. Both the House and Senate intended all campus police and security departments to be included.
>
> It must be made clear that campus police or security officials can't avoid coming under this section simply by mixing their records. The Department of Education has contended that if the campus security department includes in its files about a criminal incident occurring on campus a report filed by a residence hall official who may have been the first person on the scene, that report and the entire file will be considered an educational record because the report was not created by the security department. Some schools would routinely get an RA or a dean to give a statement for the campus police file if they knew that as a result, they could avoid opening their crime reports to the public.[9]

Violence Against Women Act

A major piece of national legislation called the Violence Against Women Act (S 15, introduced during the 102nd Congress by Senator Joseph Biden of Delaware) was proposed to help victims of sexual assault on U.S. college campuses. Title IV of the Biden bill related to making college campuses safer for women. In addition to dealing with sexual assault on college campuses, the bill created new penalties for sex crimes, encouraged women to prosecute their attackers, targeted places most dangerous to women, created public transit and public parks, established a national commission on violent crime against women, protected women from abusive spouses and promoted arrests of the latter, provided more money for shelters, taught children about domestic violence, educated women about their rights, labeled sex crimes as bias or hate crimes, extended civil rights protection to all gender-motivated crimes, and educated state and federal judges about domestic violence, sexual assault, and gender bias.

Twenty million dollars would have been provided under this legislation for the neediest colleges to fund campus rape education and prevention programs and services. Colleges receiving any federal grant money would have been required to disclose to rape victims the outcome of the college disciplinary proceedings against their attackers. This legislation would have closed loopholes in campus crime reporting law by requiring that campuses report not only rape but also any other form of sexual assault. Finally, grantee colleges would have been required to state expressly in the campus code of conduct that sexual assault is a violation of their student disciplinary codes.

The sexual assault provisions of the Biden and Boxer bills were incorporated into the Higher Education Act (PL 102-325) in 1992 under Part D—Grants for Sexual Offenses Education. This section of the law provides funds to be used to:

- train campus security and college personnel, including campus disciplinary or judicial boards that address the issues of sexual offenses;
- develop, disseminate and implement campus security and student disciplinary policies to prevent and discipline sexual offense crimes;

- develop, enlarge or strengthen support services programs including medical or psychological counseling to assist victim's recovery from sexual offense crimes;
- create, disseminate, or otherwise provide assistance and information about victims' options on and off campus to bring disciplinary or other legal action;
- implement, operate, or improve other sexual offense education and prevention programs, including programs making use of peer-to-peer education.

No institution of higher education or consortium of such institutions shall be eligible for funds unless:

- their student code of conduct or other written policy governing student behavior explicitly prohibits all forms of sexual offenses;
- victims and offenders will both be notified of the outcome of any sexual assault hearing;
- they do not currently have a campus sexual assault education program

See Appendix D for complete information on this section of the law, as well as information on how to apply for these funds.

State Legislation

To date, four states (California, New York, Wisconsin, and Minnesota) have passed legislation relating to sexual assault education, prevention, policies, and reporting on college campuses. These laws were passed prior to the passage of the Student Right to Know and Campus Security Act and the Ramstad amendment to the Higher Education Act. Although the federal law is more comprehensive than the laws of some states, this is not the case with California. Table 9–1 summarizes the elements of the legislation from each state.

California

In 1987, California was the first state to address this issue legislatively when Representative Tom Hayden introduced Resolution 46, which required that campuses should establish clear policies and protocols to deal with sexual assault on campus. Many campuses, how-

TABLE 9–1

Elements of State Requirements Relating to Sexual Assault on College Campuses

State	California	New York	Wisconsin	Minnesota	Florida
Type of regulation					
Legislation	x	x	x	x	
Mandate by commissioner					x
Educational Component					
Acknowledges students as potential victims	x			x	x
Acknowledges faculty as potential victims	x			x	
Acknowledges staff as potential victims	x			x	
Individuals to be addressed not specified		x	x	x	
Residence life staff	x				
Public safety					
Counselors	x				x
Athletic programs	x				x
Fraternities and sororities	x				x
Provided at least once a year	x*				
Provided for new students	x				
Relationship to alcohol & drugs clear	x				x
Rape myths/risk factors included	x	x			x
Must include national & state statistics	x	x			
Law and penalties explained	x	x	x		x
Explanation of services available to victims	x	x			x
Prevention strategies				x	

	1	2	3	4	5
Reporting procedures explained	x				
Effective strategies must be employed	x				
Policy mandate					
Written policy					x
Written protocol					x
Must be made available to students		x*	x		?
Events off-campus may be handled					?
Reporting mandate					
Reporting procedures included					x
Who should be notified					x
Events must be reported to campus authority			x		
Written report must be made annually			x	x	
Incidence must be made available to students	x				x
Must have specifically trained officer	x				
Structure					
Peer education program required	x				x
Procedures for ongoing case management	x			x	x
Advisory committee must be in place					
Tied to financial aid				x	x
Type of institution affected					
Public	x		x	x	x
Private					x

* = every semester

ever, failed to do so; therefore, new legislation was approved in 1990 to require compliance. California Assembly Bill 3098, introduced by Representative Roybal-Allard, added provisions to the Donahoe Higher Education Act requiring that all private and state post secondary institutions develop written procedures or protocols to ensure that victims of sexual assault (committed upon the grounds or at off-campus grounds or facilities maintained by the institution) or affiliated student organizations receive treatment and information about their rights. According to the statute, specific elements in the policy should include who should be notified in the event of an assault, and the procedures for notification; legal reporting requirements and procedures for notification; legal reporting requirements and procedures for fulfilling these requirements; services and resources available to the victim; procedures for ongoing case management; and an explanation of options for the victim. No new funds are to be allocated to carry out these requirements.

In 1991, additional provisions were introduced by Representative Roybal-Allard[10] to amend the Donahoe Higher Education Act to require sexual assault education programs at all private and public post secondary institutions in California. Under these provisions, content of the sexual assault education programs must include that (1) college students are more vulnerable to rape than any other group; (2) the majority of reported victims and offenders are of college age; (3) many people have misconceptions about these crimes that enhance their vulnerability to victimization; (4) effective programs should be offered to faculty, staff, and students; (5) colleges need to emphasize to students the seriousness of sexual assault, the prevalence of rape and sexual assault, and the relationship between alcohol and drugs and these crimes; (6) materials on the college policy must be distributed in an effective way; (7) student organizations at high risk of involvement should be targeted; (8) residence life staff should receive training every semester; (9) programs should be provided in all new student orientation programs; (10) athletic teams should be targeted specifically; and (11) professional staff should also be trained regarding the needs of victims.

Assembly Bill 3739, which became law in September 1992, requires all institutions receiving public money for financial aid to release information to a student, employee, applicant, or member of the media upon request regarding campus crimes. This bill was introduced by Representative Pat Nolan.

New York

New York passed legislation introduced by Senator Kenneth LaValley in 1990 (S 7170, A 9624) that amends Section 6504 of the Education Law, which deals with sexual assault on college campuses. Beginning in 1991, the governing board of each college receiving public funds must provide incoming students with information on sexual assault laws, penalties, the procedure in place at the college to deal with these crimes, services available to victims, circumstances in which these crimes are likely to occur, and the methods the college employs to advise and update students about security procedures. Colleges are required to file a report annually to the state commissioner regarding compliance with these regulations.

The law applies to those colleges eligible to receive state aid. There must be an advisory committee on each campus consisting of six members (at least half of whom are women), of whom two are students, two are faculty members, and two are appointed by the president. The committee will review current campus policies and procedures for educating the campus about sexual assault, personal safety, and crime prevention; for reporting sexual assaults and dealing with victims during the investigation; for referring complaints to appropriate authorities; for counseling victims; and for responding to inquiries from concerned persons. This committee is to make a written report to the college's president annually.

Wisconsin

Wisconsin Act 177, passed in 1989, requires that sexual assault and sexual harassment information be included in orientation programs for the University of Wisconsin system and for vocational, technical, and adult education students. These programs must include the legal definition of sexual assault and harassment, and circumstances under which sexual behavior is illegal; national and state statistics on incidence of acquaintance sexual assault; rights of victims and services available at the institution and in the community; and prevention strategies. In addition, annually each institution must provide printed material on the legal definition of sexual assault and harassment, and a written report must be submitted to the state legislature regarding the college's efforts at compliance. Any employee of an institution who witnesses a sexual assault or receives information about an assault must report it to the dean of students. The dean of students must compile statistics regarding incidence on that campus; these statistics must be made available annually to the Wisconsin State Office of Justice Assistance.

Minnesota

Minnesota recently adopted Statute 135A 15, which reads as follows:

> The governing board of each public post secondary system (state university systems) and each public post secondary institution shall adopt a clear, understandable written policy on sexual harassment and sexual violence. The policy must apply to students and employees and must provide information about their rights and duties. It must include procedures for reporting incidents of sexual harassment and sexual violence and for disciplinary actions against violators. During student registration each public post secondary institution shall provide each student with information regarding its policy. Each private post secondary institution that enrolls students who receive state financial aid must adopt a policy that meets the requirements of this section. The higher education coordinating board shall coordinate the policy development of the systems and institutions and periodically provide for review and necessary changes in the policies.

The legislation went into effect on August 1, 1992 requiring every post-secondary private and public educational institution to develop plans for training programs for faculty, staff and students to prevent sexual harassment and violence on campus.

Each school must, after presenting its plan to its governing board, submit the plan to the higher education coordinating board (HECB) and attorney general for review by January 15, 1993. The HECB and attorney general must report their findings to the Minnesota legislature by March 15, 1993. Full implementation of the plans must be accomplished by the beginning of the 1994-1995 academic year. Each plan must address:

1. An evaluation of current security, education, and training programs that help protect people from sexual harassment and violence
2. A description of improvements that the school is prepared to make within the next three years
3. An implementation schedule and cost estimates
4. A statement that the plan has been reviewed by the school's governing board

Florida (Sexual Assault Education Mandate)

The chancellor of the Florida State University system has required those colleges to conduct acquaintance rape education programming. (This is not state legislation.) Based on the recommendations of the chancellor in June 1991, the board of regents for the state required the colleges in the state university system to do the following:

1. Establish and publish clearly worded codes prohibiting rape and other forms of sexual battery and imposition by students, faculty, and staff. The codes should detail consequences and enforcement methods.
2. Revise orientation programs for all incoming students to include a presentation of sexual assault, risk factors, and recovery services available.
3. Develop better coordination of law enforcement, housing, medical and counseling services (which should include round-the-clock availability of a therapist trained in sexual assault), and legal services to ensure appropriate intervention and follow-up.
4. Make every effort to hire a female police officer (or a male who has been appropriately trained and sensitized) into the rank of investigator, as this position tends to have the most contact with sexual assault victims.
5. Endeavor to investigate further the problems of sexual assault in the campus community, specifically the probable connection between alcohol consumption and sexual misconduct.
6. Assign appropriate officers on that campus to organize and facilitate a student volunteer group that will work to educate

student peers about sexual violence against women, with special efforts made with such all-male groups as fraternities and athletic teams.

These requirements only apply to colleges in the state university system. They do not even extend to colleges receiving other forms of other government aid, nor do they apply to private colleges.

Michigan (State Legislation Regarding Defamation of Character Suits While Criminal Charges Pending)

In 1990, the state of Michigan enacted legislation that made it impossible for a defendant to sue the victim of sexual assault in civil court as long as the criminal action with which he is charged is pending. This legislation is designed to respond to the situation in which the victim presses charges for sexual assault and the defendant responds by suing her for filing false charges, defamation, intentional infliction of emotional distress or other similar allegations. It was clearly a response to the cases in which this happened in Michigan; these cases are discussed in Chapter 8. The legislature undoubtedly thought that allowing these actions to be filed would have a chilling effect on the reporting of cases of sexual assault.

The ban under which the defendant cannot file a suit against the victim of the assault with which he is charged is not a permanent one; it lasts only as long as the criminal action has not been concluded. The legislation attempts to deal with the problem of suits that are filed for the purpose of harassment, not legitimate claims for the filing of patently false criminal charges. If the defendant is convicted, his claim that the charges are false or defamatory clearly has no merit. Even if there is no conviction, it would be more difficult to make claims of defamation as long as the trial showed that there was a reasonable basis on which the victim pressed charges against the defendant.

Conclusion and Recommendations

Federal legislators are beginning to recognize the seriousness of the problem of sexual assault on college campuses. The recent and pending pieces of federal legislation are long overdue. They are a step in the right direction, and they are extremely important because so few states have undertaken efforts to deal with these issues themselves. State legislation that is even more stringent than federal legislation already passed may clearly supplement the latter. The state of California has always been in the forefront regarding legislation about these issues; perhaps other states should look to California as a model for drafting legislation that will go beyond the intent of the current federal laws. With an increasing number of women in state and national government, it is possible that more legislation will be introduced and passed to help reduce the alarmingly high number of sexual assaults on college campuses.

Although the federal legislation now affects all states, only a handful of states addressed the issue of sexual assault prevention on their campuses before the passage of the federal laws. One state had addressed the issue through the office of the chancellor of higher education, so only schools in the state university system were affected. There were gaps in the requirements mandated for each state, although California has the most comprehensive legislation to date.

Sexual assault on campus is a serious issue that needs to be addressed, but until more members of state or federal legislatures introduce bills confronting these issues, many colleges will continue to ignore the threat their students face. A few legislators have begun to address this issue by introducing laws that will make our college campuses safer for potential victims, and places where defendants will feel as if they have been treated fairly. Even though legislation is in place, however, campuses may still violate the letter and spirit of the law. Careful monitoring of campuses and enforcement of the legislation is also crucial to accomplish the intent of these bills.

Solutions to the Problems of Campus Rape

We have shown in previous chapters the various ways in which campus sexual assault is a problem on the college campus. The problem lies both in the failure to take appropriate steps to prevent campus rape or sexual assault and in the mishandling of cases once they occur. This chapter will pull together all of the suggested solutions discussed in earlier chapters and will provide new insights for avoiding or dealing most effectively with this problem. The chapter culminates in a comprehensive list to help colleges handle this issue.

Before colleges and universities can solve the problem they must determine its extent on their campus through research. Education efforts must be put into place to inform men and women about acceptable forms of sexual interaction. This includes not only educating students, but also training for faculty and staff. The role of alcohol on a campus must be carefully and constantly examined, because, as the reader has seen, alcohol is so often a factor in acquaintance rapes.[1]

Administration Position Regarding Acquaintance Rape

Administrators need to acknowledge that acquaintance rapes and sexual assaults happen on their campuses. Only then can college policies address the issues regarding identification of exactly which behaviors constitute acquaintance rape and sexual assault, condemnation of these behaviors, and providing a plan for dealing with cases administratively. The policy and the programs should inform potential assailants that they may be liable through the campus judicial system, as well as civilly and/or criminally, for injuries resulting from acquaintance sexual assault. College personnel need to be trained regarding counseling strategies and protocols to deal with cases that they are likely to encounter. In addition, prevention programs as well as services for victims and assailants must be developed.

Once the administration has developed a policy regarding acquaintance rape, that policy should be disseminated to all students during new student orientation. Because not all students read all of the materials they are given or hear all of what is presented during orientation, the policy should be explained in both written materials and continuing presentations about acquaintance rape. It is not enough to provide students with this information only once during orientation week; they should be reminded on an ongoing basis throughout their college years.

Policies

Some administrators think sexual assault is not a problem on their campus. As a result, many institutions do not have appropriate policies against such behaviors.[2] Students are given the implicit message that acquaintance rape and sexual assault are tolerated on campuses, and that working with the criminal justice system will usually not result in a conviction.

Existing policies should be evaluated by those who understand the complexities of sexual assault cases on college campuses (judicial administrators, members of the campus sexual assault task force, and so on) to determine if they are sufficient to deal with any situation that may be reported. A provision of the policy should prevent any conflict of interest or its appearance in handling discipline cases.[3] The policy that is in place at the time of a rape is the policy that must be used to deal with it; many colleges are discovering too late that their existing policies and procedures are woefully inadequate to address the special problems that acquaintance sexual assault situations pose (such as the need for closed hearings, training the judicial board about rape myths, and disabusing the judicial board members of their beliefs in the sexual double standard). Ideally, campus policies should be prophylactic rather than remedial. Recommendations should address institutional concerns while providing some protection for both male and female students.

Policies and information should be delivered in both traditional and nontraditional formats so that they reach the maximum number of students. In addition to printed media (such as newspapers, pamphlets, flyers, and posters) information may be effectively directed to students through computer-accessible information systems and nonprinted media (films, songs, videos, television, and so forth). This option works best when the college has a well-developed department of telecommunications.

Each college should develop a policy regarding unacceptable sexual behavior that is similar to those for alcohol and drug use.[4] It should be stated clearly that the policy relates to all members of the campus community, including visitors. Such policies are often incomplete or are hidden in a section dealing with other behaviors, such as sexual harassment.[5] Sexual assault does not fit well in the sexual harassment section of college policy,[6] because sexual harassment usually covers situations dealing with an abuse of power in which one person (such as an employer, professor, or even a teaching assistant) has institutional power over the others. It involves different problems and behaviors and different adjustments on the part of the victim; see the first four chapters for a more detailed discussion of this issue. Most cases of acquaintance rape and sexual assault take place between students, however, and therefore do not fall within this category. Also, if the policy is under a section other than acquaintance rape or sexual assault, it is not easy to find within the table of contents or the index of the policy manual. Therefore, if a student wants to know what the policy is, he or she will have a difficult time locating the proper section.

In the codes we have reviewed, even if there are policies in place, they usually do not have minimum mandatory sentences indicated. The penalties for sexual assault should be listed in the campus code of conduct so that students understand the possible consequences of each type of behavior, and each behavior should have a minimum mandatory sentence associated with it. The penalties should be clear, and they should be enforced properly.

Schools with a sexual assault policy do not necessarily have higher reporting rates than those with no policy. Even if a policy exists, it may not be well publicized, and students may be unaware that it exists. If the policy is known to students but is not carried out in the event of a violation, victims may be less likely to report cases of acquaintance rape or sexual assault. On the other hand, if a policy has been in effect and serious sanctions have been carried out (such as expulsion, or fraternity charters being revoked), students learn that acquaintance rape and sexual assault behaviors will not be tolerated on campus. There is then likely to be a reduction in the rate of acquaintance rape and sexual assault, although so far few colleges have taken the necessary steps to achieve this reduction. Having a policy is necessary, but it alone will not account for high reporting rates.

Neither public or private institutions operate as a court of law; they simply find the accused guilty of violating the campus code of conduct. The campus code of conduct essentially becomes a contract between the institution and the student when the student enrolls; if the student violates this contract, he or she can be expelled. Therefore, the sections in the code of conduct (and other policies) related to sexual assault that are in place when a student enrolls at the institution are crucial to the way a sexual assault will be handled at that institution. Prospective students should inquire about the outcomes of recent sexual assault cases on a campus. Colleges that handle cases from an ethical or concerned approach (see Chapter 7) are the best for protecting the rights of both the victim and the defendant. The State Council of Higher Education for Virginia has developed "Campus Sexual Assault: A Guide for Administrators," detailing the types of things administrators should do to develop appropriate policies and procedures for reducing sexual assault and for dealing appropriately with those cases that do occur on campus (see Appendix E).

Terminology

Terminology is very important in policies and codes of conduct. The terms used in many codes are misleading, such as when *sexual harassment* is defined to cover sexual assault. In codes we have reviewed, moreover, terms such as *sexual abuse, sexual assault, acquaintance rape,* or *consent* are frequently used without being defined. Unless behaviors are specifically defined, many students, faculty, and staff will not understand which behaviors are prohibited.

For example, a policy may state, "Forcing a person to have sex without consent is considered sexual assault." The reader may assume that if a woman gets drunk and passes out, sex with her consent is not sexual assault, because she did not resist or say no. When a person passes out, he or she cannot give consent; therefore, sex under those circumstances is immoral. Many cases of sexual assault on college campus involve situations in which the victim is intoxicated to the point of not being able to give informed consent. We believe that the issue of consent is crucial and should be specifically included in campus judicial systems when determining the guilt of an assailant. The expectation of consent should be spelled out in the code of conduct, as should the role of intoxication in defining a behavior as sexual assault. These standards have already been adopted by many campuses. The importance of this issue is dealt with in greater detail in Chapter 5.

Protocol

Each college should establish a written protocol for dealing with sexual assault cases[7] that should include the following elements. First, the protocol should describe the college policy regarding which behaviors are defined as sexual assault offenses on campus. Second, information should be available regarding the specific personnel to notify and the notification procedures to follow, as well as those to whom reports should be made (with victim consent). Third, the specific legal reporting requirements and procedures for the college, county, and state are essential elements of the reporting protocol; the Student Right to Know and Campus Security Act mandates reporting of violent crimes to prospective students (see Chapter 9 for further clarification). Fourth, services that are available to victims, both on and off campus, should be listed. Fifth, the protocol should describe how cases are managed. The cases should be heard quickly and handled efficiently, not allowed to "slip through the cracks" until the case is forgotten or the assailant leaves the institution. Sixth, procedures for guaranteeing confidentiality for both the victim and the defendant should be included.

Cornell Advocates for Rape Education (CARE), an advisory committee to the vice president for human relations, has developed a pamphlet that presents information about what a victim needs to know and can expect if he or she reports the crime to the police. This pamphlet (see Appendix F) may be used as a model for colleges that are developing protocols.

Jurisdiction

As discussed in Chapter 5, colleges differ in the scope of their jurisdiction. Whereas some colleges can deal only with offenses that take place on the campus, others can also use the judicial hearing process for off-campus violations. We believe that the latter rule is more likely to provide protection for victims of sexual assault and to result in a campus where sexual assault is not tolerated. It is perfectly acceptable legally to have a broad jurisdiction of this type; however, it is very difficult to broaden jurisdiction once a college has determined its area of control.

What is most important is that colleges stick to the rules they have. Students should be made aware of the extent of their responsibility, and colleges should not attempt to prosecute cases that fall outside of their jurisdiction.

Recommendations Regarding Campus Judicial Action

It is best to keep legal requirements and practices out of campus hearings, while still maintaining the students' due process. The more the campus system attempts to mimic the criminal justice system, the greater the likelihood is of problems arising because campus officials are attempting to play "attorney" or "judge" without proper training. The two systems are intended to function differently and to serve different purposes, and therefore they should be approached differently. If the college insists on involving members of the legal community, however, we offer some suggestions in Chapter 5 to minimize the problems that are likely.

Hearing boards generally comprise three to seven members of the campus community, including students, staff, faculty, and/or administration. The exact composition of the judicial hearing board will differ from campus to campus, and possibly within a campus depending on the defendant or the nature of the case. On some campuses, there is a policy indicating that the majority of the members of the hearing board must be the same status (student, faculty, staff, or administration) as the defendant. The board members should be trained in understanding the definitions of unacceptable sexual behavior for their campus. Lack of consent, as defined by the college, should also be explained in detail during the judicial board member's training.

Those presenting a sexual assault case must be able to explain the inevitable inconsistencies and the perceived strange behavior of the victim. This may be done by explaining the effects of rape trauma syndrome and convincing the hearing board panel (in appropriate cases) that the victim has suffered from the syndrome as a result of her experience with the assailant. Evidence must also be offered about the great investment of time, energy, and emotional stamina on the part of the victim in going through the hearing. Asserting that a woman would put herself through the mental anguish and demoralization of a campus hearing just to be vindictive clearly indicates a lack of understanding of the traumatic effects of the entire judicial process on the victim.

Judicial board members must also be taught about the research available on acquaintance rape, so that they do not rely on their victim-blaming socialization to determine the outcome of the case. General training about sexual assault and the rape trauma syndrome, or an expert witness during the hearing, may serve the purposes satisfactorily. If this is not done, hearing board members may ask irrelevant or victim-blaming questions (such as "Do you always have sex on the first date?" or "Did you enjoy it when he performed oral sex on you?") that do not belong in the hearing.

In the criminal justice system, low reporting and conviction rates are generally characteristic of simple rapes (those with no other violence, a single attacker, and no other crime committed at the time).[8] Acquaintance rapes are usually simple rapes. Reporting and criminal conviction rates are much better in the case of aggravated rapes, but those are much less likely to take place, especially on a college campus. Because the rules of evidence are much more flexible on a college campus than in the criminal courts, a simple sexual assault is more likely to result in a guilty verdict in the campus system. Therefore, more assailants may be punished if acquaintance rape cases are heard by the college judicial board or officer rather than (or in addition to) the criminal courts, provided that the college system is well designed and administered.

Prehearing Considerations

Even before an official hearing, either the accused or the victim should be moved if both share a same residence hall and the accused appears to be an imminent threat to the victim. This has been done on college campuses in other matters concerning residence life; it must, however, also be clearly spelled out in the code of conduct. If the victim is in emotional distress and feels that she is in physical or emotional danger by remaining in the same residence hall as the accused, one of the two should be moved (at the victim's request) pending the outcome of the judicial board hearing. If such a move is denied and the victim is harmed, the college risks being sued.

Hearing Recommendations

There are very important considerations that should be included in campus judicial hearings that often result in different types of hearings than those in the criminal justice system. Cases should be dealt with as soon as possible after the event, and the hearing should be held in a setting that provides a safe and comfortable environment for both the victim and the accused.[9] Victims, defendants, and the entire campus community will benefit from the inclusion of these considerations.

VICTIMS' RIGHTS. The victim should have the option to be present during the hearing, in the same way that complainants are permitted to be present in civil cases. Her presence may be important, especially if the defendant did not make a statement before the hearing, so she can refute any false statements he may make during the hearing. The victim may choose not to be there, but if she is considered only a witness her evidence is likely to be critical. Without it, the case may not be able to be presented, so she is likely to be under pressure to be there if she has chosen to press charges. When campus judicial proceedings are modeled after a criminal proceeding, a witness is only permitted to be present when he or she testifies, unless she is also the complainant. Therefore, if the institution brings the charges against the defendant, the institution is the complainant and the victim is only a witness, and consequently she will only be permitted to be present during her testimony. Some systems expect the victim bear the sole responsibility of presenting her case, and even of gathering the evidence; she should not be required to bear that responsibility.

The victim should have the option of having a closed hearing. If hearings are closed (with only the board, the defendant, essential witnesses, and advisers present), the victim is more likely to be a cooperative witness. Without an adviser, the victim may not want to participate at all in the hearing; if the defendant is permitted to have one, she should also be permitted to have one. The victim should also have the option to have an adviser present for the hearing because she may need emotional support, and she may not be thinking clearly enough to make good decisions without advice.

As discussed in Chapter 5, the University of Rochester has adopted a procedure that allows the victim and alleged assailant, through the use of tape recorders, to be questioned and to testify without having to see each other. Cross-examination is also conducted through this method. This is a very cumbersome procedure, so it should only be applied in rare, suitable circumstances when the victim is fearful of seeing the defendant.

The names of any witnesses for either side should be made available to the opposing party two or three days prior to the hearing to give both sides enough time to prepare their cases adequately. Rape shield laws (which protect the victim by preventing irrelevant past sexual histories from being presented during a rape trial) or their equivalent should be incorporated into the rules of evidence for sexual assault cases heard on campus. The victim will probably be reluctant to file charges if she thinks that any aspect of her past sexual history may be brought up during the case. If her past sexual history is irrelevant, it should not be brought up during a hearing; previous sexual experiences with the assailant, however, are generally considered relevant. This principle should also apply with respect to the defendant.

Written and audio records should be kept of the hearing in the event of an appeal or a civil action against the college. In one case we know of, the audiotapes were defective and written records were not kept, so the defendant insisted on another hearing after being found guilty in the first. His request was granted.

DEFENDANTS' RIGHTS. When dealing with sexual assault cases, the college should not presume that the defendant is guilty. He may be extremely traumatized by the allegation and may need counseling himself. In many cases when the defendant believes that the victim is making a false accusation, this belief is because they have differing opinions of what occurred: he believes that she consented, and she believes that she did not. Although false accusations are extremely rare, they do happen. Therefore, the defendant may not be guilty and may feel that his life is being ruined by the allegation. In addition, some defendants may not believe that they are guilty, although they may have forced a woman to have sex. This may happen because men are often socialized to believe that women may say no or maybe but mean yes. The defendant may think that she really wanted sex even if she was saying no, and may therefore be incredulous that he has been charged with rape. In this situation the defendant may be guilty, but deny any wrongdoing.

In any event, the defendant must be treated with the same respect we are recommending for the victim. Either the defendant or the victim should have the right to insist that the hearing be closed. He should also have the right to have a support person in the hearing room with him. The hearing should take place as soon as possible after the assault (within a week, if possible), especially if an order of protection or suspension of the defendant has been ordered prior to the hearing. See Chapter 5 for a list of the rights that should be guaranteed in a code of conduct.

The defendant should also be able to know what the charges are against him and be able to challenge his accuser, either in person, on tape, or through a screen. A detailed discussion of the advantages and disadvantages of these different methods appears in Chapter 5.

Posthearing Recommendations

Once the board has determined a verdict, minimum recommended sentences are important. Historically, when hearing boards have found assailants guilty of rape, the defendants have been given very light sentences, such as community service and counseling. Some institutions are now requiring a minimum of expulsion for rape, and suspension for other forms of sexual assault.

Defendants should *not* be permitted to apply for continuances unless there are legitimate reasons for doing so. If a case has to be postponed, however, the accused student should not be permitted to register for subsequent semesters while charges are pending against him or until he has satisfied the condition of their penalties. Defendants may attempt to postpone the hearing indefinitely, or until after graduation. We have heard of many cases where this has happened; if they are successful, a guilty verdict may be relatively inconsequential. A clause in the campus policy stating that a student may not graduate while a charge is pending against him or her will eliminate this problem. There should also be an opportunity to put a statement of violation of the campus code of conduct on the defendant's permanent record in the case of serious convictions (such as sexual assault). Unfortunately, many college judicial hearings drag on for months or years, and even when the assailant is found guilty, the penalty is inappropriately lenient.

In our experience, campus disciplinary hearings often do not deal adequately and fairly with allegations of sexual assault. Campus judicial boards have been known to wait until the case is heard in criminal court before they will pass judgment; this process may take years. The function and process are different in criminal courts, civil courts, and campus judicial hearings. There are legitimate reasons for holding campus hearings quickly after the incident, and also for postponing the campus hearing until the criminal case has been tried. These issues are discussed in greater depth in Chapters 5 and 8. Even after conviction in criminal courts, campus judicial boards sometimes find the assailant innocent of any wrongdoing.

If colleges handle cases poorly, giving more latitude to either the victim or the defendant, the chances of a civil suit increase. In the event of civil suits against the college, the institution should be insured for third-party liability suits.[10]

Penalty Enforcement

Often college personnel do not take sufficient steps to prevent unwanted contact or proximity between victims and their assailants. In addition to the housing order discussed in the section on prehearing recommendations, another penalty often imposed is preventing assailants from going into the victim's residence hall, by way of an order of protection or a no-contact order. These orders may be handed down either between a charge and the hearing or after a guilty verdict. In our experience, however, these penalties are often not enforced. The residence hall staff may not have even been informed of such a restriction or shown photographs of the assailant, so they cannot enforce it. Intimidation and threats to witnesses should be prohibited in the student code.[11]

In one case, the assailant went into the victim's dorm (after he was forbidden from doing so) and wrote a threatening note on her message board. When this was brought to the attention of the dean of students he said that he could do nothing about it, because he had not ordered the restriction in writing. Restrictions should be very clear, and they should be put in writing. There is really no reason why this administrator could not have disciplined the assailant for violating the conditions of his sentence.

Another assailant caught in the victim's residence hall after being prohibited from being there said he was only there because he was doing his laundry. In another case, an assailant who was suspended from the college was permitted back on campus to take exams. Yet another assailant admitted to harassing his victim repeatedly after the rape charge by making up to one hundred menacing phone calls to her over several months following the rape. Victims in these situations are terrified of having to interact with or see their assailant. Few campuses have been able to provide the victims with peace of mind and a harassment-free environment unless they suspend or expel the assailant after he is found guilty. Even if the defendant is prevented from harassing the victim, his friends may do so on his behalf.

Administrative Procedures

If a rape does occur, there are many steps the administration can take to deal with the situation more effectively and to serve as a deterrent to future acquaintance rapes. First, the administration must take a tough stand with assailants. In the event that a rape occurs within an organization (such as a brother committing an acquaintance rape at a fraternity house) or is condoned by an organization (such as a pledge having sex with a particular person while she was passed out, as a condition of pledging), members of that organization should be punished, or the organization should be removed from campus. In fact, some national headquarters of fraternities (Zeta Beta Tau, for example) are eliminating pledging completely because of the alcohol and violence often associated with it.[12]Because fraternities are often implicated in acquaintance or gang rapes,[13] the administration should carefully examine the fraternity system and structure, and should revise or eliminate it if necessary. The first violation of the campus code of conduct should be dealt with swiftly and harshly. Whether or not the case results in a criminal conviction, a student who violates the college code of conduct should be punished appropriately through the campus judicial system.

Personnel Recommendations

It is important to have a coordinated policy where all members of the campus community, especially the helping professionals, know what is expected to happen following a sexual assault. Each campus should establish a position for a sexual assault services coordinator and to train judicial board members, safety officers, counselors, and medical personnel; confer with university counsel; monitor all cases; and provide support for victims and alleged assailants. Unless one person is responsible for all of these functions, they are likely to be carried out in an uncoordinated fashion. The consequence may be that some necessary functions may remain undone, whereas others may be duplicated by several individuals who do not know what the others are doing. Ideally, a team should be available; however, on small campuses one person is responsible for carrying out many of these functions, and that person is often unreasonably burdened and stressed.

There should be a rapid response team in place to become mobilized in the event of a rape. A victim should have to make only one phone call, and the team member should contact all other members. The team should include representatives from public safety, the counseling office, the medical staff, the dean of students' office, victim advocacy, and the local rape crisis center. The team, or a representative of it, should go to the victim to prevent her from having to seek out each member and tell her story repeatedly, but the decision about when and how to tell her story should be up to the victim. The University of Northern Illinois and the University of Connecticut have such teams in place, and have found them to be very successful.

A sexual assault task force or coalition should be created to oversee the acquaintance rape–related efforts on a campus, and to provide guidance to the sexual assault services coordinator and the administration. Representation should be varied, drawing from groups such as the dean of students' office, residence life, campus police, the health center (including members from the health education department, psychological services, the sexuality counseling department, and the medical services), religious organizations on campus, the intrafraternity or pan-Hellenic Council, representatives from underrepresented groups (such as minorities) and international students offices, and the office of equal opportunity. Academic faculty should also be represented. Those faculty groups with a professional interest in this subject include women's studies, political science, nursing, psychology, sociology, human development and family studies, philosophy, criminal justice, law, social work, human service studies, medicine, physical education, and health education. Members of community agencies with a vested interest in acquaintance rape, such as the local rape crisis center, and the battered women's task force should also be included. Finally, it is important to include students on the task force, particularly those who are members of such organizations as fraternities, sororities, or sports teams.

Public Safety Recommendations

Because some campus rapes are reported to off-campus police, efforts should be coordinated with local police agencies regarding reporting and evidence collection. It should always be the responsibility of a police agency (usually campus safety), rather than the victim to collect evidence. It should also be clear to the victim and all others involved whose obligation it is to collect evidence. The victim should never be expected to gather evidence, regardless of which agency has jurisdiction over the crime investigation. Each of the two departments (campus safety and the local police) should be aware of the role and discoveries made by the other. They should work in a well-coordinated way to keep each other informed of the progress of the investigation and judicial processes; Chapter 6 discusses the importance of establishing and maintaining these relationships. The college should develop and implement an anonymous third-party reporting system to document the nature and scope of sexual assault crimes that are not formally reported to campus security.[14]

There should also be some mechanism in place to collect and disseminate accurate statistics regarding the incidence of acquaintance rapes on campus and the disposition of those cases. This is now required by federal legislation (the Student Right to Know legislation); as discussed in Chapter 9, some states have additional requirements in this regard as well. It is impossible to determine if education and prevention efforts have been successful in a campus community without knowing what has happened in the past, and what the needs of the campus community are. In addition, the more that is known about acquaintance rape patterns on campus, the greater the likelihood is of developing programs to meet the specific needs of a particular campus community.

Security measures are absolutely necessary on college campuses. Currently, some campuses still have insufficient security procedures in place. Measures should be implemented to reduce the likelihood of acquaintance rape and sexual assault victimization. These measures are different than those needed for stranger rape, but current campus crime prevention strategies primarily provide resources to deal only with the latter. Specific prevention strategies related to acquaintance rape include informing all students of the fact that sexual assault can and does happen between people who know each other on that campus. All students should be educated regarding their rights and the law; safety officers can provide this information during their lectures on rape prevention.

Safety programs can make the campus less dangerous for students. Although these programs are probably most useful in stranger rape prevention, they may also help prevent acquaintance rape. Direct "blue light" phones to the campus police throughout the campus would allow a woman who was being harassed by her date to call for help. An escort service and/or special free buses after dark (with stops at the police phones) would provide a student transportation home in the event that she was feeling uncomfortable and did not want to rely on her date for a ride. If a woman and a male acquaintance are walking home from the library at night, and he begins to assault her sexually, the direct phones to the campus police may be helpful in preventing a rape.

Certified "safe houses" with occupants carefully screened and trained in crisis intervention, emergency measures, and self-defense would provide a woman with refuge in the event that she was feeling threatened while away from her apartment or residence hall. This is especially important if there is a high crime rate on the campus, or if a large percentage of the students live off campus. These safe houses could be located in buildings on campus or in the surrounding community. In either case, if a woman was walking alone (at night on her way home from the library, for example) and believed that she was in danger, she could seek short-term refuge in the safe house while waiting for the campus or local police to come to her aid (depending on the jurisdiction she was in at the time). These safe houses should be visibly marked so they can be identified from a distance, and there should be enough of them so they will cover all the necessary territory and still be fairly close together.

Services for Victims

The services for victims should be comprehensive, including counseling, medical services, and victim advocacy. Services should be available for transporting the victim to the hospital, police, and counseling. Counseling referrals should be made to therapists trained in acquaintance rape issues, and this counseling should be free of charge.[15] Most campuses provide limited counseling services; however, support groups may also be helpful in meeting the counseling needs of victims. It is very important that any of the individuals representing the institution avoid victim-blaming statements or behaviors during any interactions with the victim.[16]

Counseling for acquaintance rape victims may be provided either on a one-to-one basis, or in a group setting. Also, support groups should be available for individuals close to the victim. Medical personnel should be readily available to provide medical care as well as counseling, especially if the victim is uncomfortable seeking help from psychological services personnel.

An institution should provide victim support, but it should not pressure the victim to pursue any particular course of action. It should help her if she wants to press charges in criminal court, but respect her wishes if she does not want to do so. A trained victim advocate should be able to help the victim make sense of her options in both the criminal justice and campus judicial systems, to keep her informed about the progress in the case, and to help her deal with any problems she is having with the college. In addition, an effort should be made to hire more female campus police officers with specialized sexual assault training to respond to these cases. The victim should be consulted and informed in all matters that affect her in the institution's handling of the incident, and her wishes should be respected if at all possible.[17]

In some cases, college representatives have attempted to handle the case quietly and expeditiously, and in doing so have acted in irresponsible ways that have increased their risk of liability and caused additional emotional harm to the victim. One incident involved a freshman victim, an upperclass assailant, and large quantities of alcohol. The victim was talked into signing a legal document by a campus representative stating that she would not file a complaint with the criminal justice system or insist on a hearing within the campus judicial system if the assailant would be moved from her residence hall. In this case, the victim felt pressured into signing the document, and in addition did so because she did not understand all her options. Colleges must explain all the options to a victim and support her in whatever choice she makes, if they are interested in her mental health and in avoiding civil litigation.

Alcohol-Related Efforts

One of the greatest contributing factors to acquaintance rape is the use and abuse of alcohol by college students.[18] Seventy-five percent of men and 50 percent of women involved in these cases had been drinking at the time of the assault.[19] Enforcing a prohibition of alcohol on campus is crucial to reducing the incidence of acquaintance rape. The college should make alcohol policies more stringent (or enforce the current policies, if they are adequate) for many reasons, the least of which is that if the victim is under twenty-one, she could sue the college in civil court for not providing a safe, alcohol-free environment, especially in the residence hall. Campuses may be civilly liable in this situation for not enforcing their own codes. The drinking age is twenty-one, and most victims who are raped while drunk are underage. Many campuses state that underage drinking is a violation of the campus code of conduct, but underage students often drink alcohol behind closed residence hall doors if they are not disturbing others. Most colleges do not conduct random room checks, and often do not stop this behavior because they do not want to violate the student's right to privacy.

One way to decrease the probability of acquaintance rape is to limit the amount of alcohol available to students. If the college sponsors effective and appropriate nonalcoholic events, students may discover that they can have fun in an alcohol-free environment. The consumption of alcohol by students should be discouraged not only because alcohol is illegal for most students, but also because it creates an environment in which acquaintance rapes are more likely to occur. There is a tendency for college personnel to take a tough stand with public drinking and to be much more lenient with drinking that takes place in residence hall rooms. Consequently, students choose to drink in their residence halls—especially hard liquor, which is often easier to conceal than beer. These private places, unfortunately, are where acquaintance rapes are more likely to occur. Campus policies regarding alcohol therefore must be stringent and enforced rigorously in all locations; the selective enforcement that currently exists may be creating a more serious problem than existed prior to the introduction of the twenty-one-year-old drinking age.

There have been a number of policies and recommendations implemented at various colleges and universities that may help reduce the alcohol problem on college campuses. Brown University in Providence, Rhode Island, has a dean of substance abuse who identifies high-risk students, and works with them on a one-to-one basis. At some institutions, any student brought up on charges when alcohol has been consumed must attend a mandatory education program about alcohol; for a second offense in which alcohol was involved, the offender must participate in a drug and alcohol treatment program.[20]

Some campus authorities are taking action for drug and alcohol offenses occurring beyond campus limits. If an assailant is drunk at the time of any violation of the campus code, whether on campus or off, he or she may be subject to future involuntary drug testing. If offenders are caught using drugs and alcohol while committing a violation, there should be counseling available and support groups available for them.

Alcohol plays a major role in the commission of crimes on college campuses. Those at highest risk for crime victimization while in college are most likely to be fraternity or sorority members, juniors or seniors living off campus, and alcohol and drug users.[21] Therefore, both victims and perpetrators are at increased risk if they drink alcohol. Those who commit acquaintance rapes often have low self-esteem and are particularly susceptible to peer pressure, which may be why they joined a group such as a fraternity or sports team. Students from high-income households, as compared to those from lower-income households, are more likely both to victimize and to be victimized through the ploy of getting another intoxicated to gain sexual favors.[22] Because many college students come from high-income families, this is a serious potential danger in the college community.

Educational Programs

Educational programs should be an important part of any college's rape prevention services. Effective sexual assault education and prevention may reduce the incidence of rape on campus, may reduce the likelihood of a successful lawsuit against a college, and may provide a better atmosphere in which students respect one another.

A comprehensive and effective education program should provide information to students, faculty, and staff about which behaviors constitute sexual assault and what to expect if it happens. In the absence of programs and policies, whatever "education" students receive is from the often uninformed and sensational media and/or gossip on campus. The best way to ensure that educational efforts are reaching the groups in need and having the desired effect is to conduct research to determine the needs of the campus. Administrative funds must be allocated not only for research, but also to fund the other important efforts suggested in this book.

Educational programs should be addressed to men as well as women, because rape will not stop until men stop raping. Telling women how to avoid rape is insufficient to stop the problem. Unfortunately, the approach taken by most educators is to place the responsibility for avoiding rape primarily on the potential victims (for example, don't go to a man's apartment, don't stay at a fraternity party after two in the morning, don't get drunk). This kind of advice not only blames the victim, it also gives women a false sense of security ("If I don't do these risky things, then I can't be raped"). Unfortunately, there is nothing a woman can do to guarantee that she will not be victimized; this is the reality of rape. Information about every sexual assault committed on or near campus should be disseminated in a timely fashion to the members of the campus community so that students can take appropriate measures to protect themselves.[23]

Because a disproportionate number of acquaintance and gang rapes happen in fraternity houses, or are committed by fraternity members or athletes,[24] and because sorority women are likely to socialize with these men, fraternities, sororities, and sports teams should be involved in the planning and implementation of programs. By getting input from these groups, the programs designed for them are more likely to meet their needs and to speak to the issues of importance to them. Sororities and fraternities may want to combine for a coeducational program; these may be particularly effective because they allow for a dialogue between the men and women.

If acquaintance rape prevention programs are developed, run, and sponsored by students (as opposed to faculty and staff), they are more likely to attract larger audiences and to have greater impact. Students should be involved in every stage of the project: planning, implementation, evaluation, and funding procurement. Programs that include male student leaders such as fraternity presidents and sports team captains are likely to garner even greater support from the student body. New student orientation programs about acquaintance rape should also be made available.

Programs Specifically for Men

Because many acquaintance and gang rapes occur in all-male living units (such as fraternities[25]) programs should be tailored for and presented to all male groups which perpetuate this type of behavior, including athletes and fraternity men. Another group that may become involved in acquaintance rape is male foreign students, who do not understand the social norms of this culture. Sometimes, foreign students come to the United States thinking that all American women are "loose" and always ready for sex; forced sex in this circumstance may be a matter of true misunderstanding. It would be helpful to provide an orientation session designed specifically for international students which addresses issues such as appropriate and inappropriate behavior in sexual situations.

Programs Specifically for Women

Usually in rape education programs for women, the implicit or explicit message is that women should make themselves safe by changing their own behavior and monitoring that of the men they date. This implies that it is a woman's responsibility to stop or avoid rape, and that she is responsible not only for her own behavior, but for the behavior of men. This is morally and legally wrong. Therefore, we advocate programs for mixed-sex groups in which a dialogue can be started to get men and women talking with each other about how to prevent rape. Until this is a perfect world, women will not be safe by simply telling men to stop raping. So, until that time, women will be able to decrease their vulnerability to rape by attempting to assess and control their environment, but they should never be expected to stop rape by themselves.

We believe that it is inappropriate, in general, to provide specific programs for women on rape prevention. There are, however, several exceptions to this rule. Women's self-defense programs may physically empower women, especially if they have been victims of sexual assault and are afraid of being in the same room as men. In addition, research has linked training in self-defense and assertiveness with avoidance of rape if a woman is already in a threatening situation.[26] Programs for cohesive female groups, such as female sports teams, may also be effective if they address the specific norms and concerns of the group. It is important, though, that no victim-blaming elements (whether subtle or blatant) are presented in the program.

Programs for Coeducational Groups

If young people hold some stereotypic sex-role attitudes, they are at risk for acquaintance rape involvement. Training can teach students of both sexes to interact with their sexual partners in a more respectful and responsible way. Programs should be designed to empower participants to avoid acquaintance rape by helping them understand the dysfunctional aspects of peer pressure, gender-stereotypic behaviors, and drug and alcohol use, and by giving them realistic alternative means of interacting with others.

Improvisational, interactive theater works well in presenting the message in an interesting and realistic manner. Live actors, if they present the material well, are much more effective at making a point and making the issue seem real; it is hard to forget the image of a person appearing to be raped a few feet from you. If live actors present the program, they can personalize it to reflect the issues of the students in the group. This type of personalization is usually not possible if a tape or packaged program is used.

Programs for Faculty and Staff

Public safety officers and members of the medical and psychological services communities should be trained in how to deal with the special needs of campus sexual assault victims. In addition, anyone who is likely to be the first person to see the victim after the assault, such as a resident adviser or residence hall director, should also receive specialized training on how to identify and respond to sexual assault victims on campus.

Dissemination of Information

One possible way to decrease the incidence of acquaintance rape is to publicize data regarding acquaintance rapes that have occurred on campus, as well as the resulting penalties, through the campus newspaper and radio and television stations. These media may also be used to make public service announcements on rape awareness or prevention. One way to reach almost all students is to take out an ad in the student newspaper with information about what acquaintance rape and sexual assault are, what related campus policies are regarding sexual assault, and where to go if it happens to the student or someone he or she knows.

A formal brochure should be developed specifically for each campus and made available to all students. It should identify rape myths and explain what behaviors constitute acquaintance rape, how to avoid it, what to do if it happens, and what types of feelings the victim is likely to have. In addition, a list of resources and educational programs relating to acquaintance rape should be provided to counselors and health professionals so that they can make appropriate referrals and recommendations.

Cornell University has developed a brochure to provide victims, potential victims, and friends of victims with information regarding what reactions a victim is likely to have and where she can go for help. This brochure is called "Helping a Friend Who Has Been Raped or Sexually Assaulted" in the belief that more people will pick it up if it does not imply that they themselves have been sexually assaulted. This brochure, which can be used as a model for other campuses to develop appropriate information and materials, appears in Appendix G.

Conclusion

Although educational programs will not guarantee that acquaintance rape and sexual assault will stop, they may help in reducing the number of sexual assaults on a campus. In addition, if a college is making an effort to prevent rape through educational and other programs, it is less likely to be sued successfully in civil court.

The best way to deal with sexual assault on campus is to prevent it, so colleges should make sure that they have comprehensive rape prevention programs available to all of their students; programs for men are of special importance. In addition, any member of the campus professional or student community who is likely to interact with victims and assailants should have training in how to deal with these issues (for example, medical personnel, residence life staff, and campus police). No matter how good the rape prevention efforts are on campus, however, it is unlikely that rape will be eliminated completely. Therefore, effective policies and procedures must be in place to deal with rapes that do occur. If a case is reported, the victim must receive support, and if the allegations are proven, the assailant should be dealt with to the fullest extent that campus policy permits. This will give the message to others who would commit a similar act that such behavior is not acceptable.

Victims are not likely even to report a rape to the campus police if the judicial process on campus is poorly run. Most victims of acquaintance rape and sexual assault do not attempt to have the assailant arrested; they would like him to know that what he did was wrong, however, so that he will not repeat that type of behavior with others. Even more importantly, victims want and need emotional help so that they can put the assault behind them and get on with their lives. For some victims, going to the police adds to their emotional trauma rather than reducing it, so they often choose to talk to someone at the counseling center (or a sympathetic friend) rather than to the police.

If the college institutes the suggestions offered in this book, more women will probably come forward as victims, not only to press charges but to utilize the counseling services available to them. Fewer men will consider it acceptable to take advantage of women sexually. Colleges will be better places for students to study, learn, and develop into well-rounded adults. Once an effective rape prevention program is implemented and campus policies and procedures are tightened up, the reporting rate of rape will probably increase in the short run. Once the word is out to students that rape will not be tolerated on campus (and offenders are separated from campus), however, the rate of rape should decrease. Of course, because defendants are considered innocent until proven guilty, colleges must be careful to protect their rights as well. Unfortunately, though, colleges have historically been much better at providing the defendant with his rights than the victim with hers.

It is possible to change the way acquaintance rapes are handled on college campuses. Although policy recommendations are the most important first step, there are many other avenues administrators can pursue to make campuses safer. All members of the college community will benefit from decreasing the number of acquaintance rapes on campus. Funds should be allocated to carry out all of the policy, procedural, and educational recommendations contained in this book. In addition, research should be funded to determine the acquaintance rape patterns on campus—where it happens, how often, and under what circumstances. Prevention efforts are most effective if they are aimed at the specified patterns and problems on a given campus. This money will be well spent; it will save the college from spending money defending lawsuits, and from losing contributions or applicants as a result of bad publicity about mismanaged cases.

Implementation and enforcement of effective policies are probably the most important element in reducing the incidence of sexual assault on campus. Once students realize that they will not be able to get away with committing sexual assault on campus, they are likely to stop. Publicity about suspensions and expulsions for that type of offense will serve as a deterrent for others. Educational programs are also necessary so that all students, faculty, and staff know what acquaintance rape is, that it will not be tolerated on campus, how to proceed if it occurs, and what they can expect if acquaintance rape does occur. Judicial policies and procedures that condemn acquaintance rape and carry harsh sanctions are important to send a message to all potential rapists that they will be severely punished if they are found guilty of committing an acquaintance rape on campus. The summary of recommendations that follows provides specific suggestions to carry out these aims.

Summary of Recommendations to Create a Campus Free of Acquaintance Rape

I. Administrative policies and procedures
  A. Administrative response
      1. Administration must take a tough stand with assailants
      2. Eliminate or reevaluate the role of organizations that commit or support gang or acquaintance rape
      3. Carefully examine the fraternity system and structure, and revise if necessary
      4. The first violation of the policy should be dealt with swiftly and harshly; even if the case does not result in a criminal conviction the college policy should be carried out
      5. Establish a position on campus for someone to train safety officers and counselors, confer with university counsel, monitor these cases, and support those involved in such cases
      6. Create a rapid response team to be mobilized in the event of a reported rape
      7. Provide proactive and preventive (rather than reactive) media coverage
      8. Conduct research to determine the extent of the problem on your campus, and develop programs and interventions to reflect its needs
      9. Develop and implement a third-party reporting mechanism
  B. Personnel recommendations
      1. Coordination with local police agencies
      2. Some mechanism to collect and disseminate accurate statistics
      3. Implementation of security measures to reduce the likelihood of acquaintance sexual assault victimization

4. Organize a task force or coalition representing the following:
    a. Dean of students' office
    b. Residence life
    c. Public safety
    d. Health center
        (1) Health education department
        (2) Psychological services
        (3) Sex counselor
        (4) Medical personnel
    e. Academic faculty
        (1) Women's studies
        (2) Psychology
        (3) Sociology
        (4) Human development and family studies
        (5) Nursing
        (6) Political science
        (7) Philosophy
        (8) Criminal justice
        (9) Law
        (10) Social work
        (11) Human service studies
        (12) Medicine
        (13) Physical education
        (14) Health education
    f. Local rape crisis center
    g. Religious organizations on campus
    h. Office of equal opportunity
    i. Students
    j. Intrafraternity council
    k. Pan-Hellenic council
    l. International students office
C. Personnel safety recommendations
    1. Public safety
        a. "Blue light" direct phones to public safety throughout campus
        b. Special free buses after dark with stops at "blue light" phones

      c. Escort service at night

      d. Special training for safety officers

    2. Safe houses

  D. Financial

    1. Allocate funds for prevention of sexual assault

    2. Support research to determine the extent of the problem on your campus

  E. Policy

    1. Develop a college policy regarding acceptable sexual behavior (similar to those for alcohol and drugs); the policy should clearly outline penalties that will follow specific behaviors

    2. Establish a written protocol for dealing with sexual assault cases (available in a sexual assault intervention handbook), including the following:

      a. College policy regarding sexual assault on campus

      b. Notification procedures and designated personnel to be notified (with victim consent)

      c. Legal reporting requirements and procedures

      d. Services available for victims

      e. On- and off-campus resources available

      f. Procedures for ongoing case management

      g. Procedures for guaranteeing confidentiality

      h. Minimum mandatory sentences

      i. Prohibiting graduation while charges are pending against the accused

      j. Preventing registration for future semesters until the condition of the sentence has been satisfied

      k. The accused may be moved from his residence hall at the discretion of the victim

    3. Judicial code recommendations

      a. Visitors to campus who are sexually assaulted on campus should be covered under the policy

      b. Sanctions may be applied against organizations that condone rape or sexual assault

      c. Terms such as *lack of consent*, *rape* and *sexual assault* should be clearly defined in the campus code of conduct

4. Hearing recommendations
   a. Closed hearings should always be provided as an option
   b. Rape shield laws should apply
   c. Witnesses should be made known to both sides seventy-two hours before the hearing
   d. Allow the victim's testimony to be videotaped in appropriate circumstances
   e. Develop a written agreement with the District Attorney at a campus hearing that will not violate the defendant's Fifth Amendment rights
   f. Accord defendants and victims the same rights
5. Defendant's rights
   a. To be treated as innocent until proven guilty
   b. A rapid hearing, if possible
   c. Respect
   d. To minimize as much as possible the length of time he is suspended prior to the hearing
   e. To be informed, in writing, of the charges against him
   f. To be given written notice of the hearing at least two days in advance
   g. To receive a list of witnesses who will appear in support of the charges
   h. Veto power over any judicial board members
   i. To bring an advisor
   j. To remain silent
   k. To examine witnesses and documentary evidence, and to provide an explanation and argument on his behalf
   l. To receive, upon request, a written transcript or tape of the proceedings
   m. To appeal the decision
6. Victim's rights
   a. To decide whether to press charges
   b. To have an advisor present at the hearing
   c. To have living arrangements modified, if necessary
   d. To be present at the hearing

    e. Not to have sexual history discussed during the hearing

    f. To be notified immediately of the outcome of the hearing

    g. To be separated from the defendant during the hearing, by a screen, closed circuit TV, or by means of tape recordings.

    h. To be present during the hearing

    i. To have counsel or adviser available during the hearing

F. Services for victims

  1. Provide the victim with as much support as she needs, but do not pressure her to pursue a course of action with which she is uncomfortable; if she wants to press charges, help her with that process, but respect her wishes if she does not want to pursue legal recourse.

  2. Establish a comprehensive program for assisting victims

  3. Referral to free therapists trained in acquaintance rape

  4. Availability of a trained victim advocate

  5. Counseling

    a. Individual counseling

    b. Acquaintance rape victim support groups

    c. Support groups for significant others

    d. Victim's assistance advocates

  6. Trained medical personnel available to provide care for the victim and to collect evidence if necessary

II. Educational efforts

A. Training for faculty and staff

  1. Train support staff (residence life, counselors, public safety, etc.) to deal with this problem

  2. Train medical personnel to examine and provide services to acquaintance rape victims

  3. Encourage faculty to discuss this issue in their classes

B. Provide programs for all students on acquaintance rape and strategies

  1. Discuss acquaintance rape in orientation programs for new students

  2. Provide programs in single-sex living units, such as residence halls, fraternities, and sororities

3. Make women's self-defense classes available
4. Offer assertiveness training for males and females
5. Provide self-esteem programs for males and females
6. Offer programs on the dysfunction of sex-role stereo-typing
7. Develop programs for all-male groups prone to this type of behavior
8. Hold a special orientation session each semester with international students to describe appropriate behavior towards women on campus
9. Make the sexual assault policy known to all students during new student orientation in an oral and written presentation
10. Contact parents before and while their children are your students

C. Programs should reflect administration philosophy regarding acquaintance rape issues
1. Address these programs to men as well as women
2. Inform students that they may be civilly as well as legally liable for psychological and physical injuries resulting from harassment or acquaintance rape
3. Involve fraternities and sororities in the planning and implementation of programs
4. Involve the student government in funding, sponsorship, and/or implementation of rape education programs
5. Appeal directly to male campus leaders, fraternity presidents, and sports team captains to get involved; they may be able to influence others
6. Ensure that there is a mechanism to coordinate all these prevention efforts

D. Written materials should be developed and disseminated
1. Develop and provide an informal brochure for all students explaining what victims should do
2. Admissions literature should address the problem and state that the campus administration is committed to preventing and prosecuting acquaintance rape

E. Information should be delivered in a variety of traditional and nontraditional ways
1. Utilize alternate information and delivery programs

      a. Printed media

      b. Computer-accessible information

      c. Nonprinted media

  2. Create a speakers bureau of interested faculty, students, and staff and train them appropriately; provide presenters with an honorarium

  3. Organize a campus wide "speak out" to sensitize the campus community

  4. Offer a program of a "mock trial" of an acquaintance rape

  5. Have representatives from the local women's center provide programs or assistance in planning programs

  6. Post announcements of programs in male living quarters, locker rooms, etc.

  7. Males should cofacilitate programs on acquaintance rape

  8. Develop a master list of all resources and programs available relating to acquaintance rape programs (for the use of counselors, health professionals, students, and researchers)

  9. Publicize incidence date regarding acquaintance rapes and penalties in the campus newspaper

10. Use campus radio and TV to make public service announcements

11. Exposure to this information should be repetitive and varied in presentation

12. The terms *sexual assault, acquaintance rape, date rape,* etc., should not be in the title; those terms will scare away those who need to hear the message the most

13. Use theater (both improvisational and plays) to raise consciousness on campus

14. Hold a "take back the night" march

15. Have a "rape education" week

16. Cancel classes one day and hold rape awareness events

17. Publicize a "myth of the month" in the school paper or on bookmarks

F. Alcohol-related efforts

  1. Provide interesting nonalcoholic events for students

  2. Discourage the consumption of alcohol by students

3. Enforce the college's alcohol policy; do not permit drinking in rooms if students are underage
4. The first time a student violates the campus code while drinking, mandate participation in an alcohol program and impose probation
5. Realize that campus sexual assaults are almost always alcohol related

Appendix A

Ramstad Amendment to the Higher Education Act

(2) POLICY DEVELOPMENT.—Section 485(f) of the Act is amended by adding at the end the following new paragrah:

"(7)(A) Each institution of higher education participating in any program under this title shall develop and distribute as part of the report described in paragraph (1) a statement of policy regarding—

"(i) such institution's campus sexual assault programs, which shall be aimed at prevention of sex offenses; and

"(ii) the procedures followed once a sex offense has occurred.

"(B) The policy described in subparagraph (A) shall address the following areas:

"(i) Education programs to promote the awareness of rape, acquaintance rape, and other sex offenses.

"(ii) Possible sanctions to be imposed following the final determination of an on-campus disciplinary procedure regarding rape, acquaintance rape, or other sex offenses, forcible or nonforcible.

"(iii) Procedures students should follow if a sex offense occurs, including who should be contacted, the importance of preserving evidence as may be necessary to the proof of criminal sexual assault, and to whom the alleged offense should be reported.

"(iv) Procedures for on-campus disciplinary action in cases of alleged sexual assault, which shall include a clear statement that—

"(I) the accuser and the accused are entitled to the same opportunities to have others present during a campus disciplinary proceeding; and

"(II) both the accuser and the accused shall be informed of the outcome of any campus disciplinary proceeding brought alleging a sexual assault.

"(v) Informing students of their options to notify proper law enforcement authorities, including on-campus and local police, and the option to be assisted by campus authorities in notifying such authorities, if the student so chooses.

"(vi) Notification of students of existing counseling, mental health or student services for victims of sexual assault, both on campus and in the community.

"(vii) Notification of students of options for, and available assistance in, changing academic and living situations after an alleged sexual assault incident, if so requested by the victim and if such changes are reasonably available.

"(C) Nothing in this paragraph shall be construed to confer a private right of action upon any person to enforce the provisions of this paragraph."

Appendix B

Student Right to Know and Campus Security Act

TITLE I—STUDENT RIGHT-TO-KNOW

SEC. 101. SHORT TITLE.

This title may be cited as the "Student Right-To-Know Act".

SEC. 102. FINDINGS.

The Congress finds that—

(1) education is fundamental to the development of individual citizens and the progress of the Nation as a whole;

(2) there is increasing concern among citizens, educators, and public officials regarding the academic performance of students at institutions of higher education;

(3) a recent study by the National Institute of Independent Colleges and Universities found that just 43 percent of students attending 4-year public colleges and universities and 54 percent of students entering private institutions graduated within 6 years of enrolling;

(4) the academic performance of student athletes, especially student athletes receiving football and basketball scholarships, has been a source of great concern in recent years;

(5) more than 10,000 athletic scholarships are provided annually by institutions of higher education;

(6) prospective students and prospective student athletes should be aware of the educational commitments of an institution of higher education; and

(7) knowledge of graduation rates would help prospective students and prospective student athletes make an informed judgment about the educational benefits available at a given institution of higher education.

SEC. 103. ADDITIONAL GENERAL DISCLOSURE REQUIREMENTS RELATING TO COMPLETION OR GRADUATION.

(a) DISCLOSURE OF COMPLETION OR GRADUATION RATES.—Section 485(a)(1) of the Higher Education Act of 1965 (20 U.S.C. 1092(a)(1)) (in this Act referred to as the "Act") is amended—

(1) by striking "and" at the end of subparagraph (J);

(2) by striking the period at the end of subparagraph (K) and inserting "; and"; and

(3) by adding at the end thereof the following new subparagraph:

"(L) the completion or graduation rate of certificate- or degree-seeking, full-time students entering such institutions.".

(b) CONSTRUCTION OF DISCLOSURE REQUIREMENTS.—Section 485(a) of such Act (42 U.S.C. 1092(a)) is further amended by inserting after paragraph (2) the following new paragraph:

"(3) In calculating the completion or graduation rate under subparagraph (L) of paragraph (1) of this subsection or under subsection (e), a student shall be counted as a completion or graduation if, within 150 percent of the normal time for completion of or graduation from the program, the student has completed or graduated from the program, or enrolled in any program of an eligible institution for which the prior program provides substantial preparation. The information required to be disclosed under such subparagraph—

"(A) shall be available beginning on July 1, 1993, and each year thereafter to current and prospective students prior to enrolling or entering into any financial obligation;

"(B) shall cover the one-year period ending on June 30 of the preceding year; and

"(C) shall be updated not less than biennially.

"(4) For purposes of this section, institutions may exclude from the information disclosed in accordance with subparagraph (L) of paragraph (1) the completion or graduation rates of students who leave school to serve in the armed services, on official church missions, or with a recognized foreign aid service of the Federal Government.".

(c) ANALYSIS OF POTENTIAL INSTITUTIONAL OUTCOMES.—(1) In conjunction with representatives of institutions of higher education, the Secretary shall analyze the feasibility and desirability of making available to students and potential students—

(A) the completion or graduation rate of individuals at an institution broken down by program or field of study;

(B) the completion or graduation rate of an institution reported by individual schools or academic divisions within the institution;

(C) the rate at which individuals who complete or graduate from the program of an institution pass applicable licensure or certification examinations required for employment in a particular vocation, trade, or professional field;

(D) the rate at which individuals who complete or graduate from an occupationally specific program and who enter the labor market following completion of or graduation from such a program obtain employment in the occupation for which they are trained; and

(E) other institutional outcomes that may be appropriate.

(2) In calculating the completion or graduation rate under paragraph (1), a student shall be counted as a completion or graduation if, within 150 percent of the normal time for completion of or graduation from the program, the student has completed or graduated from the program, or enrolled in any program of an eligible institution for which the prior program provides substantial preparation.

(d) REPORT.—The Secretary shall submit a report to the appropriate committees of Congress before August 1, 1991 on the analysis conducted pursuant to subsection (c).

SEC. 104. REPORTING REQUIREMENTS FOR INSTITUTIONS OF HIGHER EDUCATION.

(a) AMENDMENT.—Section 485 of the Act (20 U.S.C. 1092) (as amended by section 103) is further amended by adding at the end thereof the following new subsection:

"(e) DISCLOSURES REQUIRED WITH RESPECT TO ATHLETICALLY RELATED STUDENT AID.—(1) Each institution of higher education which participates in any program under this title and is attended by students receiving athletically related student aid shall annually submit a report to the Secretary which contains—

"(A) the number of students at the institution of higher education who received athletically related student aid broken down by race and sex in the following sports: basketball, football, baseball, cross country/track, and all other sports combined;

"(B) the number of students at the institution of higher education, broken down by race and sex;

"(C) the completion or graduation rate for students at the institution of higher education who received athletically related student aid broken down by race and sex in the following sports: basketball, football, baseball, cross country/track and all other sports combined;

"(D) the completion or graduation rate for students at the institution of higher education, broken down by race and sex;

"(E) the average completion or graduation rate for the 4 most recent completing or graduating classes of students at the institution of higher education who received athletically related student aid broken down by race and sex in the following categories: basketball, football, baseball, cross country/track, and all other sports combined; and

"(F) the average completion or graduation rate for the 4 most recent completing or graduating classes of students at the institution of higher education broken down by race and sex.

"(2) When an institution described in paragraph (1) of this subsection offers a potential student athlete athletically related student aid, such institution shall provide to the student and his parents, his guidance counselor, and coach the information contained in the report submitted by such institution pursuant to paragraph (1).

"(3) For purposes of this subsection, institutions may exclude from the reporting requirements under paragraphs (1) and (2) the completion or graduation rates of students and student athletes who leave school to serve in the armed services, on official church missions, or with a recognized foreign aid service of the Federal Government.

"(4) Each institution of higher education described in paragraph (1) may provide supplemental information to students and the Secretary showing the completion or graduation rate when such completion or graduation rate includes students transferring into and out of such institution.

"(5) The Secretary, using the reports submitted under this subsection, shall compile and publish a report containing the information required under paragraph (1) broken down by—

"(A) individual institutions of higher education; and

"(B) athletic conferences recognized by the National Collegiate Athletic Association and the National Association of Intercollegiate Athletics.

"(6) The Secretary shall waive the requirements of this subsection for any institution of higher education that is a member of an athletic association or athletic conference that has voluntarily published completion or graduation rate data or has agreed to publish data that, in the opinion of the Secretary, is substantially comparable to the information required under this subsection.

"(7) The Secretary, in conjunction with the National Junior College Athletic Association, shall develop and obtain data on completion or graduation rates from two-year colleges that award athletically related student aid. Such data shall, to the extent practicable, be consistent with the reporting requirements set forth in this section.

"(8) For purposes of this subsection, the term 'athletically related student aid' means any scholarship, grant, or other form of financial assistance the terms of which require the recipient to participate in a program of intercollegiate athletics at an institution of higher education in order to be eligible to receive such assistance.".

(b) EFFECTIVE DATE.—The amendments made by this section shall take effect July 1, 1992, except that the first report to the Secretary of Education shall be due on July 1, 1993.

SEC. 105. ANALYSIS OF ATHLETIC ACTIVITY REVENUES.

(a) IN GENERAL.—The Secretary, in conjunction with institutions of higher education and collegiate athletic associations, shall analyze the feasibility of and make recommendations regarding a requirement that institutions of higher education compile and report on the revenues derived and expenditures made (per sport) by such institutions' athletic department and intercollegiate athletic activities.

(b) REPORTS.—The Secretary shall prepare a report on the activities described in subsection (a) and transmit such report to the appropriate committees of Congress before April 1, 1991.

TITLE II—CRIME AWARENESS AND CAMPUS SECURITY

SEC. 201. SHORT TITLE.

This title may be cited as the "Crime Awareness and Campus Security Act of 1990".

SEC. 202. FINDINGS.

The Congress finds that—
(1) the reported incidence of crime, particularly violent crime, on some college campuses has steadily risen in recent years;
(2) although annual "National Campus Violence Surveys" indicate that roughly 80 percent of campus crimes are committed by a student upon another student and that approximately 95 percent of the campus crimes that are violent are alcohol- or drug-related, there are currently no comprehensive data on campus crimes;
(3) out of 8,000 postsecondary institutions participating in Federal student aid programs, only 352 colleges and universities voluntarily provide crime statistics directly through the Uniform Crime Report of the Federal Bureau of Investigation, and other institutions report data indirectly, through local police

agencies or States, in a manner that does not permit campus statistics to be separated;

(4) several State legislatures have adopted or are considering legislation to require reporting of campus crime statistics and dissemination of security practices and procedures, but the bills are not uniform in their requirements and standards;

(5) students and employees of institutions of higher education should be aware of the incidence of crime on campus and policies and procedures to prevent crime or to report occurrences of crime;

(6) applicants for enrollment at a college or university, and their parents, should have access to information about the crime statistics of that institution and its security policies and procedures; and

(7) while many institutions have established crime preventive measures to increase the safety of campuses, there is a clear need—

(A) to encourage the development on all campuses of security policies and procedures;

(B) for uniformity and consistency in the reporting of crimes on campus; and

(C) to encourage the development of policies and procedures to address sexual assaults and racial violence on college campuses.

SEC. 203. DISCLOSURE OF DISCIPLINARY PROCEEDING OUTCOMES TO CRIME VICTIMS.

Section 438(b) of the General Education Provisions Act (20 U.S.C. 1232g(b)) is amended by adding at the end thereof the following new paragraph:

"(6) Nothing in this section shall be construed to prohibit an institution of postsecondary education from disclosing, to an alleged victim of any crime of violence (as that term is defined in section 16 of title 18, United States Code), the results of any disciplinary proceeding conducted by such institution against the alleged perpetrator of such crime with respect to such crime."

SEC. 204. DISCLOSURE OF CAMPUS SECURITY POLICY AND CAMPUS CRIME STATISTICS.

(a) DISCLOSURE REQUIREMENTS.—Section 485 of the Act (20 U.S.C. 1092) (as amended by sections 103 and 104) is further amended by adding at the end thereof the following new subsection:

"(f) DISCLOSURE OF CAMPUS SECURITY POLICY AND CAMPUS CRIME STATISTICS.—(1) Each eligible institution participating in any program under this title shall on September 1, 1991, begin to collect the following information with respect to campus crime statistics and campus security policies of that institution, and beginning September 1, 1992, and each year thereafter, prepare, publish, and distribute, through appropriate publications or mailings, to all current students and employees, and to any applicant for enrollment or employment upon request, an annual security report containing at least the following information with respect to the campus security policies and campus crime statistics of that institution:

"(A) A statement of current campus policies regarding procedures and facilities for students and others to report criminal actions or other emergencies occurring on campus and policies concerning the institution's response to such reports.

"(B) A statement of current policies concerning security and access to campus facilities, including campus residences, and security considerations used in the maintenance of campus facilities.

"(C) A statement of current policies concerning campus law enforcement, including—

"(i) the enforcement authority of security personnel, including their working relationship with State and local police agencies; and

"(ii) policies which encourage accurate and prompt reporting of all crimes to the campus police and the appropriate police agencies.

"(D) A description of the type and frequency of programs designed to inform students and employees about campus security procedures and practices and to encourage students and employees to be responsible for their own security and the security of others.

"(E) A description of programs designed to inform students and employees about the prevention of crimes.

"(F) Statistics concerning the occurrence on campus, during the most recent school year, and during the 2 preceding school years for which data are available, of the following criminal offenses reported to campus security authorities or local police agencies—

"(i) murder;

"(ii) rape;

"(iii) robbery;

"(iv) aggravated assault;

"(v) burglary; and

"(vi) motor vehicle theft.

"(G) A statement of policy concerning the monitoring and recording through local police agencies of criminal activity at off-campus student organizations which are recognized by the institution and that are engaged in by students attending the institution, including those student organizations with off-campus housing facilities.

"(H) Statistics concerning the number of arrests for the following crimes occurring on campus:

"(i) liquor law violations;

"(ii) drug abuse violations; and

"(iii) weapons possessions.

"(I) A statement of policy regarding the possession, use, and sale of alcoholic beverages and enforcement of State underage drinking laws and a statement of policy regarding the possession, use, and sale of illegal drugs and enforcement of Federal and State drug laws and a description of any drug or alcohol abuse education programs as required under section 1213 of this Act.

"(2) Nothing in this subsection shall be construed to authorize the Secretary to require particular policies, procedures, or practices by institutions of higher education with respect to campus crimes or campus security.

"(3) Each institution participating in any program under this title shall make timely reports to the campus community on crimes considered to be a threat to other students and employees described in paragraph (1)(F) that are reported to campus security or local law police agencies. Such reports shall be provided to students and employees in a manner that is timely and that will aid in the prevention of similar occurrences.

"(4) Upon the request of the Secretary, each institution participating in any program under this title shall submit to the Secretary a copy of the statistics required to be made available under paragraphs (1)(F) and (1)(H). The Secretary shall—

"(A) review such statistics and report to the Committee on Education and Labor of the House of Representatives and the Committee on Labor and Human Resources of the Senate on campus crime statistics by September 1, 1995; and

"(B) in coordination with representatives of institutions of higher education, identify exemplary campus security policies, procedures, and practices and disseminate information concerning those policies, procedures, and practices that have proven effective in the reduction of campus crime.

"(5)(A) For purposes of this subsection, the term 'campus' includes—

"(i) any building or property owned or controlled by the institution of higher education within the same reasonably contiguous geographic area and used by the institution in direct support of, or related to its educational purposes; or

"(ii) any building or property owned or controlled by student organizations recognized by the institution.

"(B) In cases where branch campuses of an institution of higher education, schools within an institution of higher education, or administrative divisions within an institution are not within a reasonably contiguous geographic area, such entities shall be considered separate campuses for purposes of the reporting requirements of this section.

"(6) The statistics described in paragraphs (1)(F) and (1)(H) shall be compiled in accordance with the definitions used in the uniform crime reporting system of the Department of Justice, Federal Bureau of Investigation, and the modifications in such definitions as implemented pursuant to the Hate Crime Statistics Act."

(c) EFFECTIVE DATES.—The amendments made by this section shall take effect on September 1, 1991, except that the requirement of section 485(f)(1) (F) and (H) of the Higher Education Act of 1965 (as added by this section) shall be applied to require statistics with respect to school years preceding the date of enactment of this Act only to the extent that data concerning such years is reasonably available.

SEC. 205. PROGRAM PARTICIPATION AGREEMENT REQUIREMENTS.

Section 487(a) of the Act (20 U.S.C. 1094(a)) is amended by adding at the end thereof the following new paragraph:

"(12) The institution certifies that—

"(A) the institution has established a campus security policy; and

"(B) the institution has complied with the disclosure requirements of section 485(f)."

TITLE III—CALCULATION OF DEFAULT RATES

SEC. 301. CALCULATION OF DEFAULT RATES.

Section 435 of the Act (20 U.S.C. 1085) is amended—

(1) in subsection (l), by striking out "The term" and inserting in lieu thereof "Except as provided in subsection (m), the term"; and

(2) in subsection (m), by inserting immediately after the first sentence the following: "In determining the number of students who default before the end of such fiscal year, the Secretary shall include only loans for which the Secretary or a guaranty agency has paid claims for insurance, and, in calculating the cohort default rate, exclude any loans which, due to improper servicing or collection, would result in an inaccurate or incomplete calculation of the cohort default rate.".

TITLE IV—CONFORMING REGULATIONS

SEC. 401. CONFORMING REGULATIONS.

(a) IN GENERAL.—The Secretary is authorized to issue regulations to carry out the provisions of this Act.

(b) SUSPENSION.—Subparagraphs (c) through (f) of section 668.44 of title 34, Code of Federal Regulations, are suspended.

Approved November 8, 1990.

LEGISLATIVE HISTORY—S. 580 (H.R. 1454):

HOUSE REPORTS: No. 101-518 accompanying H.R. 1454. (Comm. on Education and Labor) and No. 101-883 (Comm. on Conference).
SENATE REPORTS: No. 101-209 (Comm. on Labor and Human Resources).
CONGRESSIONAL RECORD, Vol. 136 (1990):
    Feb. 22, considered and passed Senate.
    June 5, H.R. 1454 considered and passed House; S. 580, amended, passed in lieu.
    Sept. 13, Senate concurred in House amendment with an amendment.
    Oct. 22, House agreed to conference report.
    Oct. 24, Senate agreed to conference report.

Appendix C

Association for Student Judicial Affairs Policy Recommendations

Regarding the Student Right to Know and Campus Security Act

1. It is recommended that every institution designate one official prior to August 1, 1991 or as soon after as possible to administer the institution's response to the Act.
2. Develop a campus wide committee to review security policies, emergency response procedures, and procedures for reporting. Headed by a senior administrator, the team should include representatives from campus safety and security, student affairs admissions, legal counsel, university relations, public information, personnel, academic affairs and student government.
3. Every institution should have in place a comprehensive crime prevention and public safety education program.
4. Institutions not already having an effective reporting system should develop by August 1, 1991, incident/offense report forms, a record keeping system and a process for reporting statistics to the appropriate persons and agencies. Also, a mutual assistance procedure should be established between the institution and state and local law enforcement for the sharing of reports and data.
5. Each institution should develop a comprehensive drug and alcohol education program aimed at all students and employees.
6. The campus wide committee should determine appropriate methods to make "timely" notifications to all students and employees of crimes that pose a threat to them (flyers, newsletters, campus paper, notification to resident students, etc.)
7. Careful evaluation and definition of all property "controlled" by the institution which may include off campus property owned or controlled by the institution or its recognized organizations. This may include fraternity houses, rented property for social activities, or private residence halls built on university land.
8. Although one person may take the responsibility of compiling the report, others on the committee should review and consult on the information compiled.
9. Different formats should be considered for the report, brochure, etc.

Source: Gifford, D., Fitzgerald, T., & Diekow, D. (1992).

Grants for Sexual Offenses Education

SEC. 1541. GRANTS FOR CAMPUS SEXUAL OFFENSES EDUCATION.

(a) GRANTS AUTHORIZED.—

(1) IN GENERAL.—The Secretary of Education (hereafter in this part referred to as the "Secretary") is authorized to make grants to or enter into contracts with institutions of higher education or consortia of such institutions to enable such institution to carry out sexual offenses education and prevention programs under this section.

(2) AWARD BASIS.—The Secretary shall award grants and contracts under this section on a competitive basis.

(3) EQUITABLE PARTICIPATION.—The Secretary shall make every effort to ensure the equitable participation of private and public institutions of higher education and to ensure the equitable geographic participation of such institutions in the activities assisted under this part.

(4) PRIORITY.—In the award of grants and contracts under this section, the Secretary shall give priority to institutions of higher education or consortia of such institutions that show the greatest need for the sums requested.

(b) GENERAL SEXUAL OFFENSES PREVENTION AND EDUCATION GRANTS.— Funds provided under this part may be used for the following purposes:

(1) To provide training for campus security and college personnel, including campus disciplinary or judicial boards, that address the issues of sexual offenses.

(2) To develop, disseminate, or implement campus security and student disciplinary policies to prevent and discipline sexual offense crimes.

(3) The develop, enlarge, or strengthen support services programs including medical or psychological counseling to assit victims' recovery from sexual offense crimes.

(4) To create, disseminate, or otherwise provide assistance and information about victims' options on and off campus to bring disciplinary or other legal action.

(5) To implement, operate, or improve sexual offense education and prevention programs, including programs making use of peer-to-peer education.

(c) MODEL GRANTS.—Not less than 25 percent of the funds appropriated for this section in any fiscal year shall be available for grants or contracts for model demonstration programs which will be coordinated with local rape crisis centers for the development and implementation of quality rape prevention and education curricula and for local programs to provide services to student sexual offense victims.

(d) ELIGIBILITY.—No institution of higher education or consortium of such institutions shall be eligible to be awarded a grant or contract under this section unless—

(1) its student code of conduct, or other written policy governing student behavior explicitly prohibits all forms of sexual offenses;

(2) it has in effect and implements a written policy requiring the disclosure to the victim of any sexual offense of the outcome of any investigation by campus police or campus disciplinary proceedings brought pursuant to the victim's complaint against the alleged perpetrator of the sexual offense, except that nothing in this section shall be interpreted to authorize disclosure to any person other than the victim; and

(3) the Secretary shall give priority to those applicants who do not have an established campus education program regarding sexual offenses.

(e) APPLICATIONS.—

(1) IN GENERAL.—In order to be eligible to be awarded a grant or contract under this section for any fiscal year, an institution of higher education or consortium of such institutions shall submit an application to the Secretary at such time and in such manner as the Secretary shall prescribe.

(2) CONTENTS.—Each application submitted under paragraph (1) shall—

(A) set forth the activities and programs to be carried out with funds granted under this part;

(B) contain an estimate of the cost for the establishment and operation of such programs;

(C) explain how the program intends to address the issue of sexual offenses;

(D) provide assurances that the Federal funds made available under this section shall be used to supplement and, to the extent practical, to increase the level of funds that would, in the absence of such Federal funds, be made available by the applicant for the purpose described in this part, and in no case to supplant such funds; and

(E) include such other information and assurances as the Secretary reasonably determines to be necessary.

(f) GRANTEE REPORTING.—Upon completion of the grant or contract period under this section, the grantee institution or consortium of such institutions shall file a performance report with the Secretary explaining the activities carried out together with an assessment of the effectiveness of those activities in achieving the purposes of this section. The Secretary shall suspend funding for an approved application if an applicant fails to submit an annual performance report.

(g) DEFINITIONS.—For purposes of this part, the term "sexual offenses educational and prevention" includes programs that provide education seminars, peer-to-peer counseling, operation of hotlines, self-defense courses, the preparation of informational materials, and any other effort to increase campus awareness of the facts about, or to help prevent, sexual offenses.

(h) GENERAL TERMS AND CONDITIONS.—

(1) REGULATIONS.—Not later than 90 days after the date of enactment of this section, the Secretary shall publish proposed regulations implementing this section. Not later than 150 days after such date, the Secretary shall publish final regulations implementing this section.

(2) REPORTS TO CONGRESS.—Not later than 180 days after the end of each fiscal year for which grants or contracts are awarded under this section, the Secretary shall submit to the committees of the House of Representatives and the Senate responsible for issues relating to higher education and to crime, a report that includes—

(A) the amount of grants or contracts awarded under this section;

(B) a summary of the purposes for which those grants or contracts were awarded and an evaluation of their progress; and

(C) a copy of each grantee report filed pursuant to subsection (f) of this section.

(i) AUTHORIZATION OF APPROPRIATIONS.—For the purpose of carrying out this part, there are authorized to be appropriated $10,000,000 for the fiscal year 1993 and such sums as may be necessary for each of the 4 succeeding fiscal years.

Appendix E

CAMPUS SEXUAL ASSAULT

A GUIDE FOR ADMINISTRATORS

August 1992

State Council of Higher Education for Virginia

Adapted by Vicki Mistr from A Guide for College Presidents and Governing Boards: Strategies for Eliminating Alcohol and Other Drug Abuse on Campuses (1990), by M. Lee Upcraft, Assistant Vice President for Counseling and Health Services, Pennsylvania State University and John D. Welty, President, California State University, Fresno. Used with permission.

A Checklist on Policy

Ask these questions	YES	NO
1. Does the campus have a comprehensive sexual assault and rape policy?	☐	☐
a. Does the policy clearly and concisely define the institution's expectations, rules and sanctions?	☐	☐
b. Is the policy consistent with state and local laws?	☐	☐
c. Does it address behavior of all students, faculty, and staff?	☐	☐
d. Does it address behavior of individuals and of groups, such as fraternities, sororities, athletic groups, military organizations?	☐	☐
e. Does it address the rights of the victim and of the accused?	☐	☐
2. Were students, faculty, and staff involved in developing the policy?	☐	☐
3. Is the policy distributed to all individuals and groups that are affected?	☐	☐
4. Does the president speak out frequently on the institution's sexual assault and rape policy?	☐	☐
5. Is the policy reviewed by the president and trustees to consider changing knowledge, campus experience, legislation, and legal precedents?	☐	☐

Double check these indicators	YES	NO
Is the policy stated in official documents for		
a. students?	☐	☐
b. faculty?	☐	☐
c. staff?	☐	☐
Is the policy mailed with student admissions materials?	☐	☐
Is the policy distributed at		
a. student orientation?	☐	☐
b. faculty orientation?	☐	☐
c. staff orientation?	☐	☐
Are the victim's rights stated in the policy?	☐	☐
Are the rights of the accused stated in the policy?	☐	☐
Are there presidential speeches and written statements?	☐	☐
Is there an annual review, with dates set on the official calendar?	☐	☐

1

A Checklist on Enforcement

Ask these questions	YES	NO
1. Is the campus sexual assault and rape policy enforced with consistency and timeliness?	☐	☐
2. Is there a written protocol for receiving reports of sexual assault and rape violations?	☐	☐
3. Is reporting encouraged?	☐	☐
4. Is the policy enforced for all persons on campus?	☐	☐
5. Are appropriate sanctions applied to violators?	☐	☐
6. Is the policy enforced off-campus?	☐	☐
7. Is confidentiality maintained?	☐	☐
8. Is there a protocol for dealing with the media?	☐	☐
9. Do students view enforcement policies as fair and equitably applied?	☐	☐

Double check these indicators	YES	NO
Are there records of violations by		
a. students?	☐	☐
b. faculty?	☐	☐
c. staff?	☐	☐
Are inconsistencies revealed in enforcement practices and records of violations?	☐	☐
Is the protocol in publications for		
a. students?	☐	☐
b. faculty?	☐	☐
c. staff?	☐	☐
Are there incentives to encourage reporting?	☐	☐
a. Is a third-party reporting procedure in place?	☐	☐
b. Are there confidential records of sexual-assault investigations?	☐	☐
Is the media protocol published in the handbook?	☐	☐
Have the students been surveyed about their perception of policy enforcement?	☐	☐

2

A Checklist on Education and Prevention

Ask these questions	YES	NO		Double check these indicators	YES	NO
1. Is funding adequate for education and prevention programs?	☐	☐				
2. Is a specific office responsible for education and prevention programs?	☐	☐	→	Does the office have the resources, time, appropriately trained staff, space, etc. to fulfill its responsibilities?	☐	☐
3. Is educational programming coordinated?	☐	☐		Is there a document that lists existing programs and sponsoring units?	☐	☐
4. Are education and prevention programs offered to	☐	☐		Does one person have responsibility for coordination?	☐	☐
a. students?	☐	☐				
b. faculty?	☐	☐				
c. staff?	☐	☐				
5. Are education and prevention programs offered	☐	☐	→	Is there printed information available about each program?	☐	☐
a. at orientation?	☐	☐		a. at orientation?	☐	☐
b. in residence halls?	☐	☐		b. in residence halls?	☐	☐
c. in the student union?	☐	☐		c. in the student union?	☐	☐
d. in classrooms?	☐	☐		b. in classrooms?	☐	☐
e. in academic courses?	☐	☐		e. in academic courses?	☐	☐
f. for student organizations?	☐	☐		f. for student organizations?	☐	☐
g. at faculty and staff meetings?	☐	☐		g. at faculty and staff meetings?	☐	☐
6. Are peers involved in educational programs?	☐	☐	→	Have peers been selected?	☐	☐
				trained?	☐	☐
				supervised?	☐	☐
7. Are campus student organizations included in educational programming?	☐	☐	→	Is printed information available about campus organizations involved in education and prevention efforts?	☐	☐
8. Is the community involved in educational programs?	☐	☐	→	Has the local rape crisis center been asked to assist?	☐	☐
				Does the center have the resources to do so?	☐	☐
9. Are educational programs evaluated?	☐	☐	→	Are evaluation reports available for review?	☐	☐

3

A Checklist on Treatment and Support

Ask these questions	YES	NO
1. Are programs about crisis intervention, treatment and support available to	☐	☐
a. students?	☐	☐
b. faculty?	☐	☐
c. staff?	☐	☐
2. Are treatment services available to	☐	☐
a. students?	☐	☐
b. faculty?	☐	☐
c. staff?	☐	☐
3. Are members of the campus community trained to respond to disclosures of sexual assault or rape?	☐	☐
4. Are students and employees encouraged to seek treatment?	☐	☐

Double check these indicators	YES	NO
Is printed information available about programs for each group?	☐	☐
a. students?	☐	☐
b. faculty?	☐	☐
c. staff?	☐	☐
Is printed information about treatment available for each group?	☐	☐
a. students?	☐	☐
b. faculty?	☐	☐
c. staff?	☐	☐
Is a training program in place?	☐	☐
Are there written protocols for faculty and staff?	☐	☐
Is treatment available		
a. on campus?	☐	☐
b. through community resources?	☐	☐

4

A Checklist on Assessment

Ask these questions	YES	NO
Are assessment mechanisms in place to examine the effectiveness of		
a. policy development?	☐	☐
b. policy enforcement?	☐	☐
c. programming?	☐	☐
d. treatment and support?	☐	☐

Double check these indicators	YES	NO
Does the assessment include		
a. qualitative evaluation?	☐	☐
b. quantitative evaluation?	☐	☐
Is there a written assessment of the institution's sexual -assault policy development, programming, and treatment and support services?	☐	☐

5

Appendix F:

Should You Take Legal Action
After an Assault?

If You Have Been Sexually Assaulted:

In addition to coping with what has happened to you, you may be wondering whether or not you should report the incident to law enforcement authorities. In order to make that decision, you need to know what is likely to happen if you report the incident. This document focuses on information about the criminal court process as well as issues regarding confidentiality and support.

In addition, there is some information about the Cornell Judicial Administrator's office. Questions about violations of the Campus Code of Conduct can best be answered by the Judicial Administrator. Appointments can be made by calling 255-4680. The meetings are private and completely confidential.

Medical Care After an Assault:

If you have not done so, you should seek medical care from Gannett Health Center, the hospital or a private physician; Gannett staff or Public Safety will provide transportation to students, staff and faculty who require medical care after an assault has occurred. You will benefit from being examined for physical injury and disease. You will also have the opportunity to discuss options for counseling available on campus (or downtown) and for pregnancy prevention. Post–sexual assault and rape services provided by Gannett are free to students at Cornell. Gannett staff are bound by confidentiality and will not notify anyone including other staff, faculty or students without your permission.

The kind of evidence that supports a legal case against an assailant should be collected within 72 hours of an assault. The special examination to collect evidence can also be conducted at the time you seek medical care. It is your right to decide whether you want to go through the evidence collection exam, and you may ask the doctor, nurse or clinician to stop at any time. Many women find this examination invasive, but the evidence collection is extremely important should you decide to pursue criminal charges.

Reporting the Assault:

The decision to report the crime is yours. You do have the option to simply report the incident for police or public safety records without pressing charges. There will be no investigation unless a formal complaint is filed.

Filing a complaint may make you feel better. Some women find taking legal action therapeutic. The process of providing facts concerning the rape can relieve a sense of helplessness. Some women feel that contributing to the prosecution of the assailant may prevent someone else from being victimized.

However, the wheels of justice turn slowly and it could take a year for your case to reach a conclusion. Deciding whether to file a complaint or not is a difficult choice. You should know that:

- Once an assault is reported to law enforcement agencies and charges are filed, the police initiate an investigation. The police decide whether a woman's complaint is evidence for an arrest. Only "founded" complaints are forwarded to the District Attorney for prosecution. The District Attorney's office will then determine whether there is enough evidence to prosecute.
- One study reported that of the "founded" cases, only 1/3 of the cases involving stranger rape and 7% of those involving acquaintances led to indictments (an assailant was arrested and charged with a crime). If an arrest is made, conviction is still not guaranteed. Some studies estimated that of those cases in which arrests were made, only between 20% and 32% resulted in convictions (Estrich, 1987) [seee p.5].

If You Choose to Report, to Whom Should You Report the Crime?

Where the crime occurred determines which police department will be responsible for the investigation. Members of the Cornell community may find it most efficient to call Public Safety (255-1111) regardless of whether the incident occurred on or off campus. Although Public Safety's jurisdiction is limited to the Cornell campus, they will contact the appropriate departments for you.

The police are responsible for determining whether or not a crime has been committed. During the course of the investigation, they will need to ask very graphic questions about what happened. This is routine for the officers, but you may feel more comfortable if you have someone with you during questioning. You may also request that a female officer take your statement, although the availability of a female officer cannot be guaranteed.

Can You Get an Order of Protection?

An Order of Protection is available through the criminal court and/or the Judicial Administrator's office. The order can prohibit the accused from trying to contact you or from approaching your home, classes or where you work. Information about an Order of Protection is available from the police and from the Judicial Administrator's office (223 Day Hall).

Will Anyone Contact Your Parents Without Your Permission?

If you are eighteen years or over no law enforcement agencies, University offices or crisis intervention agencies will contact your parents. However, if you are not eighteen, some departments of the university have a legal obligation to contact your parents or guardians. In either case, your parents may be notified if you are hospitalized for serious physical injuries resulting from the assault.

Will Your Peers Find Out What Happened?

University and law enforcement personnel will do their best to maintain your privacy. If a victim over eighteen requests complete confidentiality (no notifications), Public Safety will honor the request. They can help you identify other people on campus who may offer support (such as people at CURW [Cornell United Religious Works], ISSO [International Students and Scholars Office], Dean of Students, or COSEP).

Once a case goes to the prosecutor, confidentiality cannot be assured. Friends,

Residence Life staff and others may be questioned during an investigation. Law enforcement personnel will need to visit the scene of the crime to search for evidence.

Will Your Name Appear in the Media?

Most newspapers and television stations in New York State choose not to report the name of a survivor of a sexual assault or rape who has gone to the authorities; however, sometimes the survivor's name is publicized if the perpetrator is acquitted after a trial. The choice as to whether or not to print a survivor's name is entirely at the editor's discretion and confidentiality cannot be assured once charges are filed.

Will the University Take Any Action Against the Assailant?

Cornell University will not take action unless a complaint is filed with the Judicial Administrator (J.A.). The university has a Campus Code of Conduct (Code) that applies to students, faculty and staff. This Code addresses behavior that occurs on campus, in a University-related residential organization (Co-ops, Fraternities, Sororities) or in an educational facility. It is a violation of the Code to harass, threaten, abuse, assault or rape another person. The Judicial Administrator or the University Hearing Board can take administrative action against a Cornell member who is found guilty of violating the Code. The range of penalties include community service hours, counseling, a no-contact order, suspension or expulsion from the university.

What Is the Role of the Judicial Administrator?

The J.A. receives complaints concerning alleged violations of the Code, investigates those complaints, charges accused with violations when there is sufficient evidence, and attempts to resolve cases. Cases can be resolved either by the J.A. or by going to a hearing. If a case goes to a hearing the J.A. presents the case to the University Hearing Board. To learn more about the campus judicial process call 255-4680 to set up an appointment or stop by 223 Day Hall. Meetings with the J.A. are confidential.

What is the Role of the District Attorney's Office?

Once a case is brought to the District Attorney's Office, it is an Assistant District Attorney (ADA) who decides whether to press charges and continue to prosecute the case. If the case goes to criminal trial, it is not you, but the State of New York that is pressing charges against the assailant. While the ADA must work closely with you because you will probably be the principal witness, the ADA represents the people of New York and is not acting as your lawyer.

In addition, keep in mind that neither you nor the Assistant District Attorney has control over whether the defendant pleads guilty to the charge, or to a lesser charge that may be offered by the ADA.

What is Your Role If Criminal Charges Are Filed?

Your job is to provide the police (and eventually the ADA) with the details of what happened and all relevant evidence. You will be asked questions that must be answered completely and honestly. More details may come back to you as you recover from the assault, and should be reported to the police and/or the ADA as you remember them.

The ADA may need to ask questions that seem irrelevant to your case, including details about your past sexual history. The ADA has an obligation to explain to you the relevance of his/her questions and how the information may be important to your case. You will probably be asked to describe what happened during the assault many times: at a preliminary hearing, before the Grand Jury, at a pre-trial hearing and at the trial.

What Happens After the Defendant is Arrested?

After a defendant has been arrested, he/she is arraigned in the court of jurisdiction. The purposes of the arraignment are to furnish the defendant with a copy of the charge(s), to assure the defendant has legal counsel and to review the amount of bail. If the judge sets bail at the arraignment, a preliminary hearing will be scheduled within 5–6 days. If there is no bail, the ADA may present the case to the Grand Jury without a preliminary hearing.

What is a Preliminary Hearing?

A preliminary hearing takes the form of a mini trial in which testimony is taken under oath. The judge, defendant, defendant's attorney, the prosecutor and any victims or witnesses subpoenaed are present. At the preliminary hearing the D.A.'s Office has to establish: (1) that a felony has been committed in Tompkins County, and (2) probable cause exists to believe that the defendant committed the felony. During this usually brief proceeding, the defendant's attorney may cross examine the state's witnesses and produce any evidence he or she wishes. In some cases, the defendant may waive the preliminary hearing and the case will be sent directly to Grand Jury.

What is the Grand Jury's Role?

In order to get an indictment for a felony charge (e.g. rape or sexual assault), evidence must be presented to the Grand Jury which consists of 16–23 citizens. The ADA must establish that there is reasonable cause to believe that the defendant committed the crime charged. The ADA calls witnesses to testify, and only the ADA asks questions. There is no cross-examination and no judge present. The defendant may exercise his right to testify before the Grand Jury as well.

If the Case Goes to Trial, What is the Usual Process?

The ADA presents the case for the state and has the burden of proving beyond a reasonable doubt that the defendant did commit the alleged crime. The defendant may present evidence, although he has no obligation to do so. Furthermore, the defendant may not be compelled to testify. The trial may be before a judge alone, or before a judge and jury. The defendant has the right to request a jury trial. During the trial, the ADA will ask you to take the witness stand and, under oath, answer questions about who you are and what you know about the case. The attorney for the defendant will cross-examine you.

Do You Have to Testify/Face the Person Who Committed the Crime?

If you are called in to testify, you will have to face the accused. It is a constitutional right of defendants to be able to face their accusers.

Will You Be Notified About the Status of the Case?

You will be notified when the trial date approaches or if the case has been plea-bargained. Because of an overloaded judicial system, there are likely to be unpredictable delays.

What If Your Case Is Plea Bargained?

In a plea bargain, the accused either pleads guilty to the charge or to a lesser charge. If the defendant pleads guilty to a lesser charge, *this does not mean no one believes you,* but that the ADA has decided that a reduced charge is preferable. Many factors are involved in the ADA's decision. For example, the ADA may be unable to prove the case beyond a reasonable doubt: you may be unwilling or unable to participate in further prosecution: further delay of the case may be undesirable. If there is a plea bargain, you will not have to appear in court.

Can You Appeal if the Defendant is Found Not Guilty?

The right to appeal is a decision reserved for the defendant. Neither you nor the State of New York may appeal the jury's or judge's decision.

If the Defendant is Found Guilty, Then What Happens?

Once found guilty, the defendant is sentenced by the judge. The judge considers many factors: the guidelines provided in the penal law; the defendant's prior criminal record; the recomendation of the ADA, etc. The defendant may be sentenced to jail, probation, restitution for medical expenses or damaged property, or perhaps a combination of the above. You may want to request the opportunity to speak at the sentencing.

Is it Worth it to File a Complaint?

There are no easy answers as to whether you should report to law enforcement. It is a personal and individual decision. It is in your best interests to have someone close to you who can support you through the decision-making process. People who go through the long process of a trial need to believe in themselves and develop a strong support system. The process could take six months to a year or more, which might interfere with your academic work or other plans.

If you choose to file the complaint, the defense attorney will manipulate any tools legally available to make your complaint less credible. It is essential to trust yourself, and when in doubt reach out for support. Take your time and don't go through it alone.

Who Can Aid You With the Process?

Friends, family and professional counselors are among those who may be able to offer appropriate and consistent personal support. Ithaca Rape Crisis has had extensive experience with the legal system and can offer significant support to victims of sexual assault. The services are free and confidential. Some victims hire their own lawyers to advise and inform them about the intricacies of legal procedures (though the lawyer has no legal standing in a criminal case).

In addition to criminal prosecution, you have the option of hiring an attorney to initiate a civil complaint against the assailant. In a civil case, the victim sues the defendant for damages for the harm they have done to you. Monetary compensation may be sought.

We hope this information is useful to you as you decide the best course of action and begin the healing process.

FOR MORE INFORMATION

For medical care:
Gannet Health Center
CGSS (Contraception, Gynecology & Sexuality Services)   255-3978
Emergencies   255-5155

For support:
Sex Counselor   255-3978
Ithaca Rape Crisis (24 hrs.)   277-5000
Suicide Prevention and Crisis Service (24 hrs.)   272-1616

To discuss your options:
Judicial Administrator   255-4680
Public Safety   255-1111
District Attorney   274-5461
Ithaca Rape Crisis (24 hrs.)   277-5000

TO LEARN MORE

Braswell, Linda (1990) *Quest for Respect: A Healing Guide for Survivors of Rape,* Pathfinder Publishing, CA.

Estrich, Susan (1987) *Real Rape,* Harvard University Press, MA.

Johnson, Kathryn. (1985) *If You Are Raped: What Every Woman Needs to Know.* Learning Publications, FL.

Ledray, Linda. (1986) *Recovering from Rape.* Holt and Company, NY.

McEvoy, Alan and Brookings, Jeff (1991) *If She Is Raped: A Guidebook for Husbands, Fathers and Male Friends.* Learning Publications, FL.

These books are available in the Alternatives Library, Anabel Taylor or the Health Education Office, Gannet Health Center.

This information has been compiled by the CARE (Cornell Advocates for Rape Education) Committee. Thanks is owed to Laura Barnhill, Tompkins County ADA and Marjorie Hodges, Cornell Judicial Administrator, for their suggestion for this handout. Although every effort has been made to ensure its accuracy, this is not a legal document.

Additional copies are available from Gannett Health Center.

Appendix G

Helping a Friend Who Has Been Raped or Sexually Assaulted

Acquaintance rape and sexual assault are a growing concern on college campuses across the nation. You may find yourself in a situation in which someone you know is raped or sexually assaulted. Would you know what to do?

This brochure exposes common myths about rape, offers specific suggestions about what to do and what not to do when someone is assaulted, and lists resources available on campus and in the Ithaca community.

We hope that as you think about the problem of acquaintance rape and sexual assault, you will want to help ensure that the Cornell community reflects the fundamental values of civilized behavior and respect for the dignity of every individual.

Cornell Advocates for Rape Education (CARE)

This brochure is published by Cornell Advocates for Rape Education (CARE). Although every effort has been made to ensure its accuracy, this brochure is not a legal document.

WHAT'S THE TRUTH ABOUT RAPE?

Believing myths won't help the victim or you. Perhaps you have heard
some of these:

Myth	Fact
Victims are to blame in some way for the assault.	The rapist is always responsible for having committed rape. Regardless of the victim's appearance, behavior, judgment, or previous actions, the victim is not responsible for the rape. Rapists are responsible for rape.
Rape is an expression of sexual desire.	Rape is an expression of hostility and aggression with sex as the vehicle. Rape is a violent abuse of power in which one person acts without regard for the pain and trauma inflicted on another.
It won't happen to me.	One study found that one in four college women have been victims of rape or sexual assault. About 10 percent of sexual assault victims are men.
Men can't stop themselves when they are sexually aroused.	Men are capable of, and responsible for, controlling both their minds and their bodies, just as women are.
Rape is usually committed by strangers.	College women are in far greater danger of being raped by a friend or a fellow student than by a stranger. Almost 90 percent of college women who were raped knew their assailants.
It's no big deal if a woman is forced to have sex with someone she knows (for example, a friend, date, boyfriend, or spouse)—and it isn't really rape.	Sexual intercourse forced by an acquaintance is rape. In some ways it is more traumatic than stranger rape because the victim's trust in others and in her own judgment can be seriously damaged.
Men are never victims of sexual assault.	Both men and women may be perpetrators or victims of sexual assault. Unfortunately male victims rarely seek help, due to embarrassment and the fear that they will not be taken seriously.
Sexual violence does not occur between lesbians or between gay men.	Sexual violence does occur in same-sex relationships. Fear of homophobic responses may prevent victims from seeking help.
If the victim was drunk or drugged, he or she was asking for it.	Inability to give consent is not "asking for it." In New York State, forcing sexual contact on a woman or man without consent is against the law.

How You Can Help: DOs and DON'Ts

Do believe your friend. People rarely lie about rape or assault.

Do listen to your friend and concentrate on understanding her or his feelings.

Do allow your friend to be silent; you don't have to talk every time he or she stops talking.

Do let your friend know that you understand her or his feelings. For example, you might say, "You must have been very frightened."

Do ask how you can help.

Do offer to accompany your friend in seeking medical attention or counseling or in going to police.

Do help your friend regain a sense of control. Support him or her in making decisions about whom to tell and how to proceed.

Do remind your friend that rape is the rapist's fault, not the victim's.

Do offer shelter or companionship so that your friend doesn't have to be alone.

Do help your friend learn about, recognize, and seek treatment for signs of rape trauma syndrome (see next page).

Don't ask questions that imply that the rape was your friend's fault, such as "Why did you go to his room?" "Why didn't you scream?" "Why didn't you run away?"

Don't touch or hug your friend unless you're sure your friend is comfortable with physical contact.

Don't act in ways that are upsetting to your friend. Be wary of phrases like "If I could find the creep, I'd kill him." Although you may be trying to be supportive, that type of comment might upset your friend even more.

Don't tell anyone about the assault without your friend's permission.

Don't tell your friend what to do; rather, help her or him explore the options. Among the complex decisions your friend will have to make are whether to report the assault to the police and whether to press charges. Rape crisis counselors and the judicial administrator can be helpful in discussing the options.

WHAT TO DO WHEN SOMEONE IS RAPED

Immediately after a rape, you and your friend should consider taking these steps:

1. **Call the Ithaca Rape Crisis Center (277-5000).** They can provide an advocate who is knowledgeable about the needs of rape victims and who will offer to accompany you and your friend through the other two steps:

2. **Get medical attention.** Your friend will benefit from being examined for physical injury and disease and discussing options for pregnancy prevention. At this time your friend may choose to have physical and medical evidence of assault recorded for legal purposes. Should your friend decide later to press charges, such evidence will significantly increase the possibility of successful prosecution. Medical services are available at Gannett Health Center and at the Tompkins Community Hospital Emergency Room.

3. **Notify the police.** An informational report does not obligate your friend to press charges and is very helpful to police.

RAPE TRAUMA SYNDROME

Even though the actual assault is over, your friend may suffer from rape trauma syndrome, a variety of difficulties commonly experienced after a sexual assault. People respond to sexual assault in many different ways, ranging from extreme calm to extreme agitation. Your friend might experience any or all of the following reactions: emotional shock, denial, nightmares, sleeplessness, intrusive memories or thoughts about the assault, inability to work or make decisions, impaired relationships, and feelings of guilt, despair, depression, fear, anxiety, self-blame, or anger.

Some of these reactions may be short-lived; others can be troubling for months or years. In either case, it is important to know that information and help are available. Contact the Ithaca Rape Crisis Center or Gannett Health Center (Psychological Service or the sex counselor).

You Can't Do Everything

Despite your best intentions, you need to realize that there are limits to what a friend can do to help. At times your friend may not want to deal with the rape and, as a result, may even avoid you. If you need to express feelings your friend doesn't want to hear, find a trustworthy confidant or counselor. There will also be times when you need time off from helping, when you should help your friend find other support. No matter how much support you are able to give your friend, a counselor with expertise in treating victims of rape and sexual assault can play a very important role in your friend's recovery.

Important Legal Information

Forcing or coercing someone to have sexual intercourse or engage in other sexual contact is against the law. Specifically, in New York State if a woman is forced to have sexual intercourse or if she is unable to consent, the behavior of the perpetrator is considered rape. The force necessary can be any amount or threat of physical force that places the woman in fear of injury or in fear for her life. The perpetrator does not need to use a weapon or beat her to make her fearful of injury or in fear for her life.

The courts have ruled that a woman is unable to consent if she is mentally incapacitated or is physically helpless due to drug or alcohol consumption, is asleep, or is less than seventeen years of age. If a woman has intercourse without her consent, it is rape.

Forcing or coercing a man or a woman to engage in any sexual contact other than sexual intercourse under the circumstances mentioned above is considered sexual abuse or sodomy.

What We Can Do

By understanding the issues and taking action as individuals, we can begin to work toward changes that will prevent rape and sexual assault.

- Learn the facts by reading the following books:

  Against Our Will, by Susan Brownmiller

  Coping with Date Rape and Acquaintance Rape, by Andrea Parrot

  I Never Called It Rape, by Robin Warshaw

  Men on Rape, by Tim Beneke

  No Fairy Godmothers, No magic Wands: The Healing Process After Rape, by Judy H. Katz

  Recovering from Rape, by Linda Ledray

- Take a course in self-defense.

- Attend campus and community rape-awareness presentations.

- Think about and learn to recognize the connections between rape and other manifestations of inequality such as sexual harassment, racism, and violence against gays and lesbians.

- Work with others who share your concerns regarding rape and sexual assault, through community groups such as the Ithaca Rape Crisis Center, the Ithaca Men's Network, and Planned Parenthood and campus groups such as Peer Sexuality Educators; Cornell Advocates for Rape Education; the Greek Task Force on Peer Relationships; the Gay, Lesbian, and Bisexual Coalition; and the Cornell Women's Center.

- Respect yourself and develop relationships based on mutual respect.

RESOURCES

For immediate assistance following a rape or a sexual assault, you can make confidential inquiries at the following places:

Ithaca Rape Crisis Center   277-5000

Department of Public Safety   255-1111

Dean of Students Office   255-6839

Gannett Health Center

   Contraception, Gynecology, and Sexuality Service (CGSS)   255-3978

   Sex Counselor   255-6936

   Psychological Service   255-5208

   Overnight Observation Unit   255-5155

Your residence hall director (RHD) or resident adviser (RA)

Other helpful resources:

Office of the Judicial Administrator   255-4680

Cornell United Religious Work   255-4214

Empathy, Assistance, and Referral Service (EARS)   255-3277

Planned Parenthood of Tompkins County   273-1513

Suicide Prevention and Crisis Service of Ithaca   272-1616

Notes

Chapter 1

1. Koss, M. P., Gidicz, C. A., & Wisniewski, N. (1987). "The Scope of Rape: Incidence and Prevalence of Sexual Aggression and Victimization in a National Sample of Higher Education Students." *Journal of Consulting and Clinical Psychology*, 55(2):162–170.
2. Parrot A., Cummings, N. Marchell, T., & Hother, J. (1993). "A Rape Awareness Prevention Model for Athletes." *Jouranl of American College Health*.
3. Kirkpatrick, C., & Kanin, E. J. (1957). "Male Sexual Aggression on a University Campus." *American Sociological Review*, 22:52–58.
4. Barrett, K. (1982, September) "Date Rape: A Campus Epidemic." *Ms., 11,* 48–52.
5. See, for example, Koss, M., & Oros, C. (1982). "Sexual Experience Survey: A Research Instrument Investigating Sexual Aggression and Victimization." *Journal of Counseling Psychology*, 50(3):455–457; Parrot, A. (1985). "Comparison of Acquaintance Rape Patterns Among College Students in a Large Coed University and a Small Women's College." Paper presented at the annual meeting of the *Society for the Scientific Study of Sex*, San Diego, CA; Koss, Gidicz, & Wisniewski, (1987).
6. Parrot (1985).
7. Struckman-Johnson, C. (1991). "Male Victims of Acquaintance Rape," in A. Parrot & L. Bechhofer (eds.), *Acquaintance Rape: The Hidden Crime.* New York: John Wiley & Sons, 192–214; Muehlenhard, C. & Falcon, P. (1991). "Men's Heterosocial Skills and Attitudes Toward Women as Predictors of Verbal Coercion and Forceful Rape." *Sex Roles 23* (5/6) 241–259.
8. Hannan, K. E., & Burkhart, B. (in press). "The Typogrlaphy of Violence in College Men: Frequency, and Comorbidity of Sexual and Physical Aggression." *Journal of College Student Psychotherapy.*
9. Hauserman, N. & Lansing, P. (1981–1982). "Rape on Campus." *Journal of College and University Law*, 8(2): 182–202.
10. Parrot, A. (1991). "Recommendations for college policies and procedures to deal with acquaintance rape," in A. Parrot & L. Bechhofer (eds.), *Acquaintance Rape: The Hidden Crime.* New York: John Wiley and Sons, p. 368.
11. *Student Leader Press Service*, weekly edition, October 22, 1990, p. 3.
12. Sanday, Peggy (1990). *Fraternity Gang Rape.* New York: New York University Press, p. xxiv.

13. Parrot (1991).
14. Personal conversation with Katie Koestner, October 10, 1992.
15. Sanday (1990), p. xxiv.
16. "Date Rape and a List at Brown." *New York Times*, November 18, 1990, p. 26.
17. Personal conversation with Toby Simon, associate dean of student life, Brown University, October 2, 1992.
18. Swanson, C. R., Chamelin, N. C., & Territo, L. (1981). *Criminal Investigation.* (2nd ed.) New York: Random House.
19. Bohmer, C. & Blumberg, A. (1975). "Twice Traumatized: The Rape Victim and the Legal Process." *Judicature.* 58(8). pp. 390–399.

Chapter 2

1. Koss, M. P., Gidicz, C. A., & Wisniewski, N. (1987). "The Scope of Rape: Incidence and Prevalence of Sexual Aggression and Victimization in a National Sample of Higher Education Students." *Journal of Consulting and Clinical Psychology, 55*(2): 162–170.
2. Burkhart, B. R., & Stanton, A. L. (1985). "Sexual Aggression in Acquaintance Relationships," in G. Russel (ed.), *Violence in Intimate Relationships.* Spectrum Press. Englewood Cliffs, N.J.
3. Polonko, K., Parcell, S., & Techman, J. (1986). "A Methodological Note on Sexual Aggression." Paper presented at the national convention of the Society for the Scientific Study of Sex, St. Louis.
4. Koss et al. (1987).
5. Collison, M. (1992, February 26). "A Berkeley Scholar Clashes with Feminists over Validity of Their Research on Date Rape." *Chronicle of Higher Education.*
6. Burkhart, B. (1983, December). "Acquaintance Rape Statistics and Prevention." Paper presented at the Acquaintance Rape and Prevention on Campus Conference, Louisville, KY, Parrot, A. (1992). "A Comparison of Male and Female Sexual Assault Victimization Experiences Involving Alcohol." Paper presented at the annual meeting of the Society of the Scientific Study of Sex, San Diego, CA.
7. Koss et al. (1987); Hannan, K. E., & Burkhart, B. (in press). "The Typography of Violence in College Men: Frequency, and Comorbidity of Sexual Aggression and Physical Aggression." *Journal of College Student Psychotherapy*; Koss, M. (1992, October). "Alcohol, Athletics, and the Fraternity Rape Connection." Paper presented at the second International Conference on Sexual Assault on Campus, Orlando, FL.
8. Garrett-Gooding, J. & Senter, R. (1987). "Attitudes and Acts of Sexual Aggression on a University Campus." *Sociological Inquiry*, 59: 348–371.
9. Hoffman, E. (1986, March 17). "Rape and the College Athlete: Part One." *Philadelphia Daily News*, p. 104.
10. Koss, M. (1991, October). Keynote address presented at the first International

Conference on Sexual Assault on Campus, Orlando, FL; Bird, L. (1991). "Psycho-Social and Environmental Predictors of Sexually Assaultive Attitudes and Behaviors among American College Men." Ph.D. dissertation at the University of Arizona.

11. Sanday, P. (1990). *Fraternity Gang Rape.* New York: New York University Press.

12. Walters, J., McKellar, A., Lipton, M., & Karme, L. (1981). "What Are the Pros and Cons of Co-Ed Dorms?" *Medical Aspects of Human Sexuality, 15*(8): 48–56.

13. Rapaport, K. R., & Posey, D. (1991) "Sexually Coercive College Males," in A. Parrot & L. Bechhofer (eds.) *Acquaintance Rape: The Hidden Crime.* New York: John Wiley & Sons; Malamuth, N., & Dean, C. (1991) "Attraction to Sexual Aggression," in A. Parrot & L. Bechhofer (eds.), *Acquaintance Rape: The Hidden Crime.* New York: John Wiley & Sons.

14. Personal communication, Dean Cooper, dean of students, Clarkson College, October, 15, 1992.

15. Parrot, A., & Bechhofer, L. (eds.). (1991). *Acquaintance Rape: The Hidden Crime.* New York: John Wiley & Sons.

16. Koss et al. (1987).

17. Parrot, A. (1985). "Comparison of Acquaintance Rape Patterns Among College Students in a Large Co-Ed University and a Small Women's College." Paper presented at the annual meeting of the Society for the Scientific Study of Sex, San Diego, CA.; Parrot, A., & Lynk, R. (1983). "Acquaintance Rape in a College Population." Paper presented at the eastern regional meeting of the Society for the Scientific Study of Sex, Philadelphia.

18. O'Sullivan, C. (1991). "Acquaintance Gang Rape on Campus," in A. Parrot & L. Bechhofer (eds.), *Acquaintance Rape: The Hidden Crime.* New York: John Wiley & Sons, 140–156.

19. Tierney (1984).

20. Groth & Birnbaum (1979).

21. O'Sullivan (1991).

22. Sanday, (1990).

23. Sanday, (1990).

24. Judge Lois Forer, personal communication, March 18, 1991.

25. Parrot, A. (1993). *Coping with date rape and acquaintance rape.* (2nd ed.) New York: Rosen Publishing Group.

26. Biden (1991).

27. Warshaw, R. (1988) *I Never Called It Rape: The Ms. Report on Recognizing, Fighting, and Surviving Date and Acquaintance Rape.* New York: Harper and Row.

28. Burt, M. (1991). "Rape Myths and Acquaintance Rape," in A. Parrot & L. Bechhofer (eds.), *Acquaintance Rape: The Hidden Crime.* New York: John Wiley and Sons, 26–40.

29. Brownmiller, S. (1975). *Against Our Will: Men, Women and Rape.* New York: Simon and Schuster.

30. Estrich, S. (1987). *Real Rape: How the Legal System Victimizes Women Who Say No.* Cambridge, MA: Harvard University Press.
31. The same psychological condition suffered by returning Vietnam veterans, as classified in the diagnostic and statistical manual used by psychologists and psychiatrists to diagnose psychiatric illness.
32. Burgess (1991).
33. Estrich (1987).
34. Harry O'Reilly, seminar, "Investigating Sex Crimes," 1991, Ithaca, NY.
35. Muehlenhard. C.L., Friedman, D.E., & Thomas, C.M. (1985). "Is Date Rape Justifiable? The Effects of Dating Activity, Who Initiated, Who Paid, and Man's Attitudes Toward Women." *Psychology of Women Quarterly,* 9(3): 297–310.
36. Johnson, K.M. (1985) *If you are raped.* Holmes Beach, FL: Learning Publications.; Burt, M. (1980). "Cultural Myths and supports for rape." *Journal of Personality and Social Psychology.* 38, 217–230.

Chapter 3

1. Elkind, D. (1967). "Egocentrism in Adolescence." *Child Development,* 38:1025–1034.
2. In one study undertaken by Jacquelyn White and John Humphrey at the University of North Carolina at Greensboro, women ran twice the risk of rape or attempted rape in their first year of college if they had been sexually assaulted as adolescents, although family violence or sexual victimization in childhood seemed not to affect the risk of rape in the first year of college. Paper presented at the annual meeting of the American Psychological Association, reported in the *Palm Beach Post,* August 17, 1992, p. 3A.

Chapter 4

1. *Wooster Voice,* vol. 108:20, February 28, 1992, p. 1.
2. Personal communication with Natasha Roit, attorney for the plaintiff, September 2, 1992.
3. Merry, S. E., & Silbey, S. S. (1984). "What Do Plaintiffs Want? Reexamining the Concept of Dispute." *Justice System Journal* 2: 151–178, at p. 153.
4. Interview with Carla Kjellberg, attorney for the plaintiffs, August 26, 1991.
5. Felstiner, W. L. F. (1974). "Influences of Social Organization on Dispute Processing." *Law and Society Review,* 9:63–94.
6. Holmstrom, L. L. & Burgess, A. W. (1978). *The Victim of Rape: Institutional Reactions.* New York: John Wiley & Sons.
7. Ford, D. A. (1991). "Prosecution as a Victim Power Resource: A Note on Empowering Women in Violent Conjugal Relationships." *Law and Society Review,* 25(2):313–334.
8. Bohmer, C., & Blumberg, A. (1975). "Twice Traumatized: The Rape Victim and the Legal Process." *Judicature,* 58(8):390–399.

9. Some lawyers are trying to use the assailant's family's homeowners insurance policy as a source of funds to pay any damages awarded. We know of one case (*Coverdale*) where that has succeeded.

10. For details, see Chapter 8.

11. Bumiller, K. (1988). *The Civil Rights Society*. Baltimore: Johns Hopkins University Press.

Chapter 5

1. See Edward N. Stoner II & Kathy L. Cerminara (1990). "Harnessing the 'Spirit of Insubordination': A Model Student Disciplinary Code." *Journal of College and University Law* 17 (2):89–121, at 92.

2. Georgetown University Student Code of Conduct, 1991, p. 11.

3. Bard College Student Handbook, 1991–1992, p. 75.

4. Brown University Student Handbook, 1991–1992. Offenses III, p. 100.

5. Amendment to the Undergraduate Judicial Code, Duke University, effective 1/7/91. The actual clauses read as follows:
   SEXUAL ASSAULT I. By stranger or acquaintance, rape, forcible sexual penetration, however slight, of another person's anal or genital opening with any object. These acts must be committed by force threat, intimidation or through the use of the victim's mental or physical helplessness of which the accused was aware or should have been aware.
   SEXUAL ASSAULT II. By stranger or acquaintance, the touching of an unwilling person's intimate parts (defined as genitalia, groin, breast, or buttocks, or clothing covering them) or forcing an unwilling person to touch another's intimate parts. The clause ends with an identical sentence about force, etc., as in the first clause.

6. Stanford University Student Conduct Policies, 1990, p. 4.

7. As will be discussed later in this chapter, Stanford is unlikely to have a problem with the courts, as the university has such a high standard of proof that it is very difficult to obtain a conviction.

8. 418 F2d 163 (7th Cir. 1969).

9. UCLA Student Conduct Code, 1983, p. 14.

10. St. Norbert's College Student Handbook 1990–91, p. 55.

11. A Partial Proposed Revision of the Antioch College Sexual Offense Policy, February 1992.

12. Luther College Student Handbook, 1991–2, s.6.1.2., p. 23.

13. SMU, *The Peruna Express*, 1991–92. Student Code of Conduct H 3.d., p. 84.

14. Lawrence University, Appleton, Wisconsin. Supplement entitled "Sexual Harassment Policy and Procedures", dated September 1991, p. 1.

15. Brown University Student Handbook 1991–92, p. 100.

16. William and Mary Student Handbook 1991–92, p. 110.

17. Carleton College Student Handbook, 1990–91, p. 58.

18. Bulletin of Duke University, 1990–91, p. 42.

19. Carleton College Student Handbook, pp. 53–54. It is this clause that got Carleton into trouble recently when it tried to prosecute a student for behavior off campus. See the section on jurisdiction in Chapter 6.
20. William and Mary Student Handbook, p. 96.
21. St. Norbert's College Student Handbook, p. 70.
22. Bulletin of Duke University, p. 42.
23. Lawrence University Student Handbook, 1991–1992. p. 65.
24. St. Lawrence University Judicial System Constitution, Clause X, Section 4, revised August 15, 1989.
25. SUNY-Brockport, Codes of Student Social Conduct, pp. 11–12.
26. SMU, *The Peruna Express*, p. 84.
27. For example, the College of William and Mary grants to both victim and accuser the right not to have his or her unrelated past sexual history discussed in the hearing (Student Handbook, 1991–92, p. 119).
28. William and Mary Student Handbook, p. 119.
29. *Goss* v. *Lopez*, 419 U.S. 565. (1975).
30. James M. Picozzi (1987). "University Disciplinary Process: What's Fair, What's Due, and What You Don't Get." Yale Law Journal, 96: 2132–2161, at 2134.
31. For a discussion of this issue, see Kaplin, W. A. (1985). *The Law of Higher Education*. (2nd ed.) San Francisco, CA: Jossey Bass, 312–314.
32. For a discussion of the whole issue, see *Tedesci* v. *Wagner College*, 49 N.Y. 2d 652, 404 N.E. 2d 1302, 1304–06 (1980).
33. Lisa L. Swem (1987). "Due Process Rights in Student Disciplinary Matters." *Journal of College and University Law*, 14(2):359–382, at 361.
34. See, for example, the case of *Board of Curators of the University of Missouri* v. *Horowitz* 435 U.S. 78 (1978), in which the court said that teachers are education experts and therefore a court should not replace a teacher's academic judgment.
35. The Supreme Court, in the case of *Matthews* v. *Eldridge*, 424 U.S. 319 (1976), established three criteria to decide how much process is due. They balanced (1) the private interest affected by the official action, (2) the risk of an erroneous deprivation of that interest, and (3) the public interest.
36. 292 F. 2d 150 (5th Cir.) cert. denied U.S. 930 (1961).
37. Id. at 159.
38. 419 U.S. 565. (1975).
39. *Alpha Tau Omega Fraternity, Tau Chapter, Undergraduate Students* v. *University of Pennsylvania and George S. Koval*. 10 Phila 149 (1984).
40. From personal communication, Judge Lois Forer, retired judge of the Court of Common Pleas, Philadelphia, March 18, 1991.
41. Bradley Student Handbook, 1991–1992. p. 30.
42. For example, Brown University forbids lawyers to be present except at what would be a "capital/life offense" under Rhode Island law. When they are allowed, it is only for the purpose of safeguarding the student's rights and not to affect the outcome of the case (*Brown Student Handbook*, p. 90). Bard College is even more unwilling to have lawyers. Its code reads, "In no case shall legal

counsel be permitted to attend or participate in a hearing of the SJB" (Bard College Student Handbook, 1991–1992, p. 91).

43. Personal interview with Joan Carbone, dean of students, Rutgers University, July 8, 1992.
44. See, for example, *Greenhill* v. *Bailey,* 519 F. 2d.5 (8th Cir. 1975).
45. 582 F. 2d 100 (1st Cir. 1978), at 104.
46. See Swem (1987), p. 374.
47. *Picozzi* v. *Sandalow,* 623 F. Supp. 1571 (E.D. Mich. 1986).
48. For cases on this issue, see Swem (1987), pp. 378–379.
49. Interview with Tom McCormick, then judicial adviser at Cornell, May 9, 1991.
50. The Georgetown Student Code of Conduct states: "Formal rules of evidence do not apply in hearings. The chairperson of the Board can admit as evidence whatever reasonable persons would accept as having some relevance to the case" (p. 21). Cornell University also makes clear that the "strict rules of evidence do not apply" (Cornell University Campus Code of Conduct, 1990, p. 20).
51. The case is *Watts* v. *Old Dominion University,* filed in the Circuit Court for the City of Norfolk, in Chancery, Docket No. C92-792. Personal communication from Pat Kelly, general counsel for Old Dominion University, October 22, 1992.
52. SMU, *The Peruna Express,* p. 126. Cornell, which is a lawyer-dominated system, has a similar rule; Cornell University Campus Code of Conudct, p. 20.
53. For example, SMU's code of conduct both defines and explains the standard of proof "by the greater weight of credible evidence that it is more likely than not that the accused violated the Student Code of Conduct" (*The Peruna Express,* 1991–92, p. 126).
54. Cornell University's code reads that "the complainant's burden of persuasion is met when a violation has been proven by clear and convincing evidence." Cornell University Campus Code of Conduct, 1990, p. 20.
55. See, for example, Brown University Student Handbook, p. 90.
56. Carleton College Student Handbook, p. 55.
57. See Swem (1987), pp. 369–371 for details of cases on this point.
58. Picozzi (1987), pp. 2147–2148.
59. See Swem (1987), pp. 380–381.
60. *Leonardi* v. *Sanders,* Circuit Ct. 10th Judicial District, Motion No. 91L651, filed Nov. 14, 1991.
61. *Diamondback* (University of Maryland student newspaper), January 21, 1992, p. 1.
62. For an extensive, albeit anti-university view of the inherent bias in judicial hearings, see Picozzi (1987).
63. Swem (1987), p. 371.
64. In *Soglin* v. *Kauffman,* 418 F.2d 163 (7th Cir. 1969), the court stated that the University of Wisconsin could not charge a student with misconduct when it had not specifically defined what constituted "misconduct."
65. Stoner & Cerminara (1990), p. 91.

66. Kaplin (1985).
67. *Gross* v. *Carleton College*, Rice County Minn. Third Judicial District, Temporary Restraining Order dated April 3, 1992.
68. 278 Cal. Rptr. 918 (Cal. App. 1 Dist. 1991).
69. "University Bans Overnight Guests of Opposite Sex." *New York Times*, February 2, 1992, p. 44.
70. Houghton College Student Guide, 1990–1993, p. 13.
71. St. Lawrence University Judicial System Constitution, effective August 15, 1989, pp. 2–3.
72. Stanford University Student Conduct Policies, 1990, pp. 29–32.
73. Readers are referred also to two articles that present model student codes: Stoner & Cerminara, (1990); and Pavela, G. (1979–1980). "Limiting the 'Pursuit of Perfect Justice' on Campus: A Proposed Code of Student Conduct." *Journal of College and University Law*, 6(2): 137–160. This latter code is less helpful for our purposes, since it does not refer specifically to sexual assault. Such are the changes that have taken place that this would be impossible today.
74. Adapted from University of Delaware Code of Conduct, University of Delaware Student Handbook, 1991–92, p. 24.
75. Brown University Student Handbook, 1991–1992, p. 100.
76. Duke University, Amendment to the Undergraduate Judicial Code, effective 1/7/91.
77. Adapted from bulletin of Duke University, 1990–91, p. 42.
78. Adapted from Georgetown University Code of Conduct, 1991, p. 9.
79. Adapted from William and Mary Student Handbook, 1991–92, p. 110.
80. This clause is adapted from William and Mary Student Handbook, 1991–92, p. 92.
81. Adapted from St. Norbert College Student Handbook, 1990–91, p. 70.
82. SMU, *The Peruna Express*, 1991–92, p. 123.
83. This section is drawn from several codes, including Texas A & M University, University Regulations 1991–92, pp. 33–34; SUNY-Brockport Codes of Student Social Conduct, pp. 11–12.; Lawrence University Student Handbook 1991–1992, p. 65.
84. Adapted from SMU, *The Peruna Express*, 1991–92, pp. 84–85.
85. Adapted from a proposed amendment to the Cornell University Campus Code of Conduct, passed by the Codes and Judicial Committee in the spring of 1992, but not yet approved by the Senate.

Chapter 6

1. See, for example, Smith, M. C. (1989, January–February). "Cops or Watchmen? Policy Considerations in the Role of Campus Security." in *Campus Law Enforcement Journal*, Jan.–Feb. 38–39.
2. Nichols, D. (1985, September–October). "A Study: The Role-Perception Conflict of Campus Public Safety Departments." *Campus Law Enforcement Journal*, 4–7.

3. *Martin* v. *USC* information obtained from a personal interview with Martin's lawyer, Natasha Roit, September 2, 1992.

4. McBride, R. B., Davis, J., & McCarron-Burns, A. (1992). "Prevailing Campus Police Selection Models in Public University Systems." *Campus Law Enforcement Journal*, Mar–Apr. 30–31.

5. Personal conversation with Michael Czerepuszko, February 6, 1991.

6. Personal communication from Randall H. Hausner, accreditation manager, Cornell Public Safety Department, July 7, 1992.

7. Personal interview with Kim Brosdahl, associate director of housing and security, Moorhead State University, Moorhead, Minnesota.

8. Personal interview with Scott Wargin, supervisor for safety and security, Johnson County Community College, Overland Park, Kansas.

9. Personal communication from Randall H. Hausner, June 7, 1992.

10. Lecture by Leslie Scoville of Rutgers Campus Security, "Sexual Assault and Prevention: Views of Campus Law Enforcement," First International Conference on Sexual Assault on the Campus, Orlando, FL, October 3, 1991.

11. Letter from Dan Fite, director of public safety, Santa Clara University, February 25, 1992.

12. Personal Communication with Harvey Kessleman, vice president for student services, Stockton State College, February 6, 1992.

13. See Nichols (1985), p. 4.

14. For detailed information on this issue, see chapter 9.

15. Texas A & M University gives the vice president for student services the task of determining whether, as a result of an off-campus offense, the "continued presence of the student is likely to interfere with the educational process and the orderly operation of the University." Texas A & M University Regulations, 1991–92, p. 31.

16. Personal interview with Harvey Kesselman, vice president for student services, Stockton State College, Febuary 6, 1992.

17. State of New York, Court of Claims, Claim No. 82740, DOL No. 91127497, filed June 17, 1991.

18. For a detailed analysis of this issue, see a recent opinion of the Attorney General of Maryland. 74 *Opinions of the Attorney General* (1989) (Opinion No. 89-002 (January 23, 1989)).

19. For example, *Kusner* v. *Leach*, 439 A. 2d 223 (1982).

20. For example, *Wallace* v. *Florida A & M University*, 433 So 2d 600 (Fla. App. 1983).

21. *Gross* v. *Carleton College*, Rice County Minn. Third Judicial District, Temporary Restraining Order dated April 3, 1992.

22. *Watts* v. *Old Dominion University*, Circuit Court for the City of Norfolk, In Chancery, Docket No. C-92-792.

23. Personal communication from William G. Boice, commander of major investigations, Cornell Department of Public Safety, July 7, 1992.

24. In the case of *Stoneking* v. *Bradford Area School District*, 882 F. 2d 720 (3d Cir., 1989), the court held that state officials are liable for "adopting and main-

taining a practice custom or policy of reckless indifference" to suspected sexual assault of students, and "discouraging student complaints about such conduct."

25. Personal communication from Jeffrey B. Brookings, Wittenberg University, October 4, 1991.
26. Public Law 101-542, signed into law November 8, 1990.

Chapter 7

1. Permission to release the text of the complaint granted by individual complainant.
2. Personal communication with Dean Michael Cooper, January 15, 1993.
3. Collison, M. (1992, February 26). "A Berkeley Scholar Clashes with Feminists over Validity of Their Research on Date Rape." *Chronicle of Higher Education.*
4. Parrot, A. (1987). "Using Improvisational Theater Effectively in Acquaintance Rape Prevention Programs on College Campuses." Paper presented at the annual meeting of the Society for the Scientific Study of Sex, Atlanta.
5. Rothman, J. (1974). *Planning and Organizing for Change.* New York: Columbia University Press; Scales, P. (1980). "Barriers to Sex Education." *Journal of School Health*, 337–341; Olmosk, K. E. (1972). *1972 Annual Handbook for Group Facilitators.* Washington, DC: National Training Laboratories, National Education Association; Havelock, R. G., & Havelock, M. C. (1973). *Training for Change Agents: A Guide to the Design of Training Programs in Education and Other Fields.* Ann Arbor: Institute for Social Research, University of Michigan; Brager, G., & Holloway, S. (1978). *Changing Human Service Organizations: Politics and Practice.* New York: Free Press.

Chapter 8

1. External Review Committee, *An Evaluation of the University of Southern California's Sexual Assault Policies, Procedures and Programs*, June 3, 1992.
2. Information obtained from an interview with Natasha Roit, attorney for the two plaintiffs, September 2, 1992; an interview with Valerie Paton, former assistant dean of students at USC, October 29, 1992; and an article, "University, Blamed in Rape, Is Told to Pay Victim," *New York Times*, March 29, 1992, p. 18.
3. *Hegel* v. *Langsam*, 29 Ohio Misc. 147, 148 (1971).
4. W. Page Keeton (ed.), *Prosser and Keeton on the Law of Torts*, 5th ed. (St Paul, Minnesota: West Publishing Co., 1984), p. 164.
5. *Relyea* v. *Florida* 385 So 2d, 1378 (Fla. Dist. Ct. App. 1980).
6. 65 N.C. ALpp. 579, 309 S.E. 2d 701 (1983).
7. Id., at 583, 309 S.E. 2d at 703.
8. *Cutler* v. *Board of Regents*, 459 So. 2d 413, 414–415 (Fla. Dist. Ct. App. 1984)
9. 62 N.Y. 2d 506, 467 N.E. 2d 493, 478 N.Y.S. 2d 829 (1984).
10. Id. at 509, 467 N.E. 2d at 494, 478 N.Y.S. 2d at 830.
11. 389 Mass. 47, 449 N.E. 2d 331. (1983).

12. Id. at 52, 449 N.E. 2d at 336.
13. Filed in the Circuit Court, 10th Judicial Circuit, Peoria County, Ill., Gen. No. 91 L 65.
14. *Newark Star Ledger*, January 11, 1992.
15. Interview with Kimberley Sorrentino, Ms. Coverdale's attorney, August 14, 1992.
16. Filed in the District Court, 4th Judicial District, No. 91–12999.
17. Personal interview with Daniel Manning, attorney for the plaintiff, June 30, 1992.
18. 123 Cal. App. 3d 275 (1981).
19. 278 Cal. Rptr. 918 (Cal. App. 1 Dist. 1991).
20. U.S. District Court, Northern District of New York, Civ. action No. 89-643.
21. *Doe v. George Mason University*, filed November 24, 1992, in Fairfax County District Court. *Broadside* (George Mason University student newspaper), December 7, 1992.
22. 36 Cal. 3d 799, 685 P. 2d 1193, 205 Cal. Rptr. 842 (1984).
23. 685 P. 2d 1193, at 1201.
24. This case was settled in October 1991. Filed in the District Court, Third Judicial District, Minnesota, No. C8-91-435.
25. *New York Times*, March 29, 1992, p. 18.
26. This language is drawn from a case in which a high school student was sexually assaulted by her teacher. The principal was aware of this as well as other allegations against the teacher and did nothing about it. The court held that such behavior was a policy of reckless indifference to the civil rights of the student, and therefore it would fit under a 1983 claim. *Stoneking v. Bradford Area School District*, 882 F. 2d 720 (3d Cir. 1989).
27. It has been raised as one of several bases for the suit in the case of *Doe v. George Mason University*.
28. Personal interview with John Murray, plaintiff's father, November 23, 1991.
29. Personal communication with Pamela Liapakis, attorney for Ms. Davis.
30. These statutes, which have been passed in the last ten to fifteen years, very from state to state. Generally, they exclude testimony of the victim's prior sexual behavior with people other than the defendant unless the defense can prove to the judge that it is relevant.
31. For an extensive discussion of the role of fraternities in campus sexual assault, especially gang rape, see Sanday, P. (1990). *Fraternity Gang Rape*. New York: New York University Press.
32. *Steadman v. University of New Hampshire*, 90-E-229, Strafford County Superior Court, filed Feb. 13, 1991. Further information was obtained from a personal conversation with Mr. Steadman's attorney, Mr. John Lyons, July 6, 1992.
33. No. 87-34091-CZ (Washtenaw County Cir. Ct. Mich. Filed Oct. 20, 1987. On app. No.1114.12 Mich. Ct. App. Sept. 1989).
34. Personal communication from Julie Steiner, Sexual Assault Prevention and Awareness Center, University of Michigan, October 6, 1991.

35. It would seem that Mr. Steadman filed this suit as part of his strategy against the University of New Hampshire. That case seems to be fraught with political and racial overtones. Personal interview with John Lyons, attorney for the plaintiff, July 6, 1992.

36. Cooperstein, E. T. (1989). "Protecting Rape Victims from Civil Suits by Their Attackers." *Law and Inequality*, 8: 279–308.

37. *Alpha Tau Omega Fraternity, Tau Chapter, Undergraduate Students v. University of Pennsylvania and George S. Koval* 10 Phila 149 (1984).

38. For some information on this, see Kaplin (1985), pp. 56–57.

39. *Relyea v. State of Florida*, 385 So. 2d 1378 (Ct. of Appl. 1990)

40. *Cutler v. Board of Regents of the State of Florida*, 459 So. 2d 413 (1984).

41. Docket No. 99-1702 and L-12175-89, Superior Court of New Jersey Middlesex County, plaintiff's brief in opposition to Rutgers' motion for summary judgment and in support of plaintiff's cross-motion for partial summary judgment.

42. Court of Claims Act, s. 8, ch. 860. (1939).

43. See *Mason v. Southern New England Conference Association of Seventh day Adventists*, 692 F2d 135 (1982).

44. Interview with Jody Asbury, Alena Johnson, and Brook Gordon-Hare, of the dean of students' office, University of Rochester, July 23, 1991.

Chapter 9

1. Starting in September 1991, colleges and universities are required to publish crime statistics every year so that students and their families may make informed judgments about campus safety. In addition, colleges are required to provide students and employees with information about campus security policies at least once a year.

2. Passed in 1992. An earlier version of this legislation was called the Sexual Assault Victims' Bill of Rights, which sought to guarantee victims of sexual assault the right to have sexual assaults investigated by civil and criminal authorities; be free from pressure to not report these crimes, or to report them as lesser offenses; have the same representation, and ability to have others present, in campus proceedings as campus authorities permit the accused; have cooperation in obtaining medical evidence; be informed of any federal or state rights to test sexual assault suspects for communicable diseases; have access to existing campus mental health and victim support services; be provided housing that guarantees no unwanted contact with alleged sexual assault assailants; live in a campus free of sexually intimidating circumstances, with the option to move out of such circumstances.

3. See Appendix B.

4. *Bauer v. Kincaid*, 759 F. Supp. 575 (1991)k.

5. ZZweifel, D. (1992, April). "The Courts Say Campus Papers Can Report on Crime." *ASNE Bulletin*, p. 40.

6. *Jones v. Southern Arkansas*, CIV-90-88 (Columbia County Circuit Court, May 10, 1991).

7. Personal communication with Michael Easton, Student Press Law Center, December 21, 1992.
8. Zweifel (1992).
9. Personal communication with Howard and Connie Clery, April 30, 1992.
10. Assembly Bill No. 3098, Chapter 423.

Chapter 10

1. Polonko, K., Parcell, S., & Teachman, J. (1986). "A Methodological Note on Sexual Aggression." Paper presented at the national convention of the Society for the Scientific Study of Sex, St. Louis; Bausell, C., & Maloy, C. E. (1990, January). "The Links Among Drugs, Alcohol, and Campus Crime: A Research report." Paper presented at the fourth National Conference on Campus Violence.
2. Parrot, A. (1989). "Acquaintance Rape Patterns and College Response in New York State." Paper presented at the New York State Conference on Acquaintance Rape on College Campuses, Albany.
3. Report of the USC External Review Committee (1992).
4. Hughes, J. O., & Sandler, B. R. (1987, April) *"Friends" Raping Friends: Could It Happen to You?* Washington, DC: Association of American Colleges.
5. Parrot, A. (1992). "A Comparison of Male and Female Sexual Assault Victimization Experiences Involving Alcohol." Paper presented at the annual meeting of the Society of the Scientific Study of Sex, San Diego; Parrot (1989).
6. Hughes & Sandler (1988).
7. Adams, A., & Abarbanel, G. (1988). *Sexual Assault on Campus: What Colleges Can Do.* Santa Monica, CA: Santa Monica Rape Treatment Center.
8. Estrich, S. (1987). *Real Rape: How the Legal System Victimizes Women Who Say No.* Cambridge, MA: Harvard University Press.
9. USC External Review Committee (1992).
10. Ehrhart, J. K., & Sandler, B. R. (1985). *Campus Gang Rape: Party Games?* Washington, DC: Association of American Colleges.
11. USC External Review Committee (1992).
12. Taylor, R. J. (1992). "Fraternities, Sororities, and Campus Security." Paper presented at the Sixth National Towson State Conference on Campus Violence, Baltimore.
13. Ehrhart & Sandler (1985).
14. USC External Review Committee (1992).
15. Ehrhart & Sandler (1985).
16. Ehrhart & Sandler (1985).
17. Ehrhart & Sandler (1985).
18. Polonko, Parcell, & Teachman (1986).
19. Warshaw, R. (1988) *I Never Called It Rape: The Ms. Report on Recognizing, Fighting, and Surviving Date and Acquaintance Rape.* New York: Harper and Row.
20. Bausell & Maloy (1990).

21. Bausell & Maloy (1990).

22. Lane, K. E., & Gwartney-Gibbs, P. A. (1985). "Violence in the Context of Dating and Sex." *Journal of Family Issues, 6,* 45–49.

23. USC External Review Committee (1992).

24. Warshaw (1988); Hughes & Sandler (1987).

25. Ehrhart & Sandler (1985); Warshaw (1988).

26. Bart, P., & O'Brien, P. H. (1985). *Stopping Rape: Successful Survival Strategies.* New York: Pergamon Press.

References

Adams, A., & Abarbanel, G. (1988). *Sexual Assault on Campus: What Colleges Can Do*. Santa Monica, CA: Santa Monica Rape Treatment Center

Assembly Bill 3739 State of California. 1992

Assembly Concurrent Resolution No. 46—Relative to Rape on University or College Campuses (1987). Sate of California

Barrett, K. (1982, September). "Date rape: A Campus Epidemic." *Ms.*, 11, 48-52.

Bart, P., & O'Brien, P. H. (1985). *Stopping Rape: Successful Survival Strategies*. New York: Pergamon Press.

Bausell, C., & Maloy, C. E. (1990, January). "The Links Among Drugs, Alcohol, and Campus Crime: A Research Report." Paper presented at the fourth National Conference on Campus Violence.

Berger, V. (1979). "Man's Trial, Woman's Tribulation: Rape Cases in the Courtroom." *Columbia University Law Review*, 77: 1-103.

Biden, J. (1991) *Violence Against Women: The Increase in Rape in 1990*. Washington, DC: Committee on the Judiciary, United States Senate.

Bird, L. (1991). "Psycho-Social and Environmental Predictors of Sexually Assaultive Attitudes and Behaviors Among American College Men.: Ph.D. dissertation at the University of Arizona.

Bohmer, C., & Blumberg, A. (1975) "Twice Traumatized: The Rape Victim and the Legal Process." *Judicature*, 58(8):390-399.

Bohmer, C. (1991). "Acquaintance Rape and the Law," in A. Parrot & L. Bechhofer (eds.), *Acquaintance rape: The hidden crime*. New York: John Wiley and Sons, 317–333.

Brager, G., & Holloway, S. (1978). *Changing Human Service Organizations: Politics and Practice*. New York: Free Press.

Brownmiller, S. (1975). *Against Our Will: Men, Women and Rape*. New York: Simon and Schuster.

Bumiller, K. (1988). *The Civil Rights Society*. Baltimore: Johns Hopkins University Press.

Burkhart, B. (1992, October). "A New Mythology of Manhood." Paper presented at the second International Conference on Sexual Assault on Campus, Orlando, FL.

Burkhart, B. R., & Stanton, A. L. (1985). "Sexual Aggression in Acquaintance Relationships," in G. Russel (ed.), *Violence in Intimate Relationships*. Spectrum Press.

Burkhart, B. (1983, December). "Acquaintance Rape Statistics and Prevention." Paper presented at the Acquaintance Rape and Prevention on Campus Conference in Louisville, KY.

Burt, M. (1980). "Cultural Myths and Supports for Rape." *Journal of Personality and Social Psychology*, 38: 217-230.

Burt, M. (1991). "Rape Myths and Acquaintance Rape," in A. Parrot & L. Bechhofer (eds.), *Acquaintance Rape: The Hidden Crime*. New York: John Wiley and Sons, 26–40.

California Assembly Bill 365 (1991). State of California.

California Assembly Bill 3098, Chapter 423 (1990). State of California.

Campus Sexual Assault Victims' Bill of Rights (1992). United States Congress.

Collison, M. (1992, February 26). "A Berkeley Scholar Clashes with Feminists over Validity of Their Research on Date Rape." *Chronicle of Higher Education*.

[Comment.] (1990). "Civil Compensation for the Victim of Rape." *Cooley Law Review* 7: 193–211.

Cooperstein, E. T. (1989). "Protecting Rape Victims from Civil Suits by Their Attackers." *Law and Inequality*, 8: 279–308.

Education Law Section 6450 (1990). State of New York.

Elkind, D. (1967). "Egocentrism in Adolescence." *Child Development*, 38: 1025–1034.

Eskenazi, G. (1991, February). "Male Athletes and Sexual Assault." *Cosmopolitan*, 220-223

Estrich, S. (1987). *Real Rape: How the Legal System Victimizes Women Who Say No*. Cambridge, MA: Harvard University Press.

External Review Committee. (1992, June 3). "An Evaluation of the University of Southern California's Sexual Assault Policies, Procedures and Programs." Los Angeles, CA: USC.

Family Education and Rights of Privacy Act (1974). United States Congress.

Felstiner, W. L. F. (1974). "Influences of Social Organization on Dispute Processing." *Law and Society Review*, 9: 63–94.

Fernstermaker, S. (1988). "Acquaintance Rape on Campus: Attribution of Responsibility and Crime," in M. Pirog-Good & J. Stets, *Violence in Dating*. New York: Praeger.

Food, D. A. (1991). "Prosecution as a Victim Power Resource: A Note on Empowering Women in Violent Conjugal Relationships." *Law and Society Review*, 25 (2): 313–334.

Frankel, V. (1991, May). "Life After Rape." *Mademoiselle*, 199, 244.

Garrett-Gooding, J. & Senter, R. (1987). "Attitudes and acts of sexual aggression on a university campus." Sociological Inquiry, 59: 348–371.

Giarrusso, R., Johnson, P. B., Goodchilds, J. D., & Zellman, G. (1979, April). *Adolescent cues and signals: Sex and assault*. Paper presented at the meeting of the Western Psychological Association, San Diego.

Gibbs, N. (1991, June 3). "When Is It Rape." *Time*, 48–55.

Gifford, D., Fitzgerald, T., Diekow, D. (1992, February). The Student Right to

Know and Campus Security Act: Issues and Concerns. A paper presented at the Conference of the Association of Student Judicial Affairs.

Goodchilds, J. D., Zellman, G., Johnson, P. B., & Giarusso, R. (1979, April). *Adolescent perceptions of responsibility for dating outcomes.* Paper presented at the meeting of the Eastern Psychological Association, Philadelphia, PA.

Goodchilds, J. D., Zellman, G., Johnson, P. B., & Giarrusso, R. (1988). Adolescents and their perceptions of sexual interaction outcomes. In A. W. Burgess (Ed.), *Sexual assault*, (Vol. II, pp. 245-270). New York: Garland. (Original work published in 1979.)

Gray, M. D., Lesser, D., & Bounds, C. (1990, January). "The Effectiveness of Personalizing Acquaintance Rape Prevention Programs on Perception of Vulnerability and Risk Taking Behavior." Paper presented at the fourth National Conference on Campus Violence, Towson, MD.

Groth, N. & Birnbaum, H. J. (1979). *Men Who Rape.* New York: Plenum

H. R. 5960 Sexual Assault Prevention Act. (1992). United States Congress.

Hannan, K. E., & Burkhart, B. (in press). "The Typography of Violence in College Men: Frequency, and Comorbidity of Sexual and Physical Aggression." *Journal of College Student Psychotherapy.*

Havelock, R. G., & Havelock, M. C. (1973). *Training for Change Agents: A Guide to the Design of Training Programs in Education and Other Fields.* Ann Arbor: Institute for Social Research, University of Michigan.

Hauserman, N., & Lansing, P. (1981–1982). "Rape on Campus." *Journal of College and University Law,* 8(2): 182–202.

Hilberman, E. (1976). *The Rape Victim.* New York: Basic Books.

Hirsch, K. (1990, September/October). "Fraternities of Fear: Gang Rape, Male Bonding, and the Silencing of Women." *Ms.,* 52–56.

Hoffman, R. (1986, March 17). "Rape and the College Athlete: Part One." *Philadelphia Daily News,* p. 104.

Holmstrom, L. L., & Burgess, A. W. (1978). *The Victim of Rape: Institutional Reactions.* New York: John Wiley & Sons.

Hughes, J. O., & Sandler, B. R. (1987, April). *"Friends" Raping Friends: Could It Happen to You?* Washington, DC: Association of American Colleges.

Hughes, J. O., & Sandler, B. R. (1988, September). *Peer Harassment: Hassles for Women on Campus.* Washington, DC: Association of American Colleges.

Johnson, K. M. (1985) *If You are Raped.* Holmes Beach, FL: Learning Publications.

Kaplin, W. A. (1985). *The Law of Higher Education* (2nd ed.) San Francisco, CA: Jossey Bass.

Kesselman, H. (1992, October), "A Model Campus Code for Addressing Sexual Assault." A paper presented at the second International Conference on Sexual Assault on Campus, Orlando, FL.

Kirpatrick, C., & Kanin E. J. (1957). "Male Sexual Aggression on a University Campus." *American Sociological Review,* 22: 52-58.

Koss, M. (1992, October). Keynote address presented at the first International Conference on Sexual Assault on Campus, Orlando, FL.

Koss, M., & Harvey, M. (1991). *The Rape Victim: Clinical and Community Approaches to Treatment*. (2nd ed.) Lexington, MA: Stephen Greene Press.

Koss, M. P., Gidicz, C. A., & Wisniewski, N. (1987). "The Scope of Rape: Incidence and Prevalence of Sexual Aggression and Victimization in a National Sample of Higher Education Students." *Journal of Consulting and Clinical Psychology*, 55(2): 162–170.

Koss, M., & Oros, C. (1982). "Sexual Experience Survey: A Research Instrument Investigating Sexual Aggression and Victimization." *Journal of Counseling Psychology*, 50(3): 455–457.

Lafree, G. D. (1989). *Rape and Criminal Justice*. Belmont, CA: Wadsworth.

Lane, K. E., & Gwartney-Gibbs, P. A. (1985). "Violence in the Context of Dating and Sex." *Journal of Family Issues*, 6: 45–49.

Long, N. T. (1985). "The Standard of Proof in Student Disciplinary Cases." *Journal of College and University Law*, 12(1): 71–178.

Merry, S. E., & Silbey, S. (1984). "What Do Plaintiffs Want? Reexamining the Concept of Dispute." *Justice System Journal*, 9(2); 151–178.

McBride, R. B., Davis, J. & McCarron-Burns, A. (1992, March–April). "Prevailing Campus Police Section Models in Public University Systems." *Campus Law Enforcement Journal*, 30–31.

Michigan Statutes, S. 1902, Amendment to Act 236 of the Public Acts of Michigan, 1961 (1991). State of Michigan.

Miller, B., & Marshall, J. C. (1987). "Coercive Sex on the University Campus." *Journal of College Student Personnel*, 28: 38–46.

Minnesota Statute 363.01, Subd. 41 (1990). Sexual Harassment. State of Minnesota.

Minnesota Statute 135A 15 (1990). Sexual Harassment/Sexual Violence Policies. State of Minnesota.

Minutes of the Board of Regents (1991, June 27). State of Florida.

Muehlenhard, C. L., & Falcon, R. L. (1990). "Men's Heterosocial Skills and Attitudes Toward Women as Predictors of Verbal Coercion and Forceful Rape." *Sex Roles*. 23(5/6) 241-259.

Muelenhard, C. L., Friedman, D. E., & Thomas, C. M. (1985). "Is Date Rape Justifiable? The Effects of Dating Activity, Who Initiated, Who Paid, and Man's Attitudes Toward Women." *Psychology of Women Quarterly*, 9(3): 297–310.

Muehelenhard, C., & Hollabaugh, L. C. (1988). "Do Women Sometimes Say No When They Mean Yes? The Prevalence and Correlates of Women's Token Resistance to Sex." *Journal of Personality and Social Psychology*, 54(5): 872–879.

Netmark, J. (1991, May). "Out of Bounds: The Truth About Athletes and Rape." *Mademoiselle*, 196–199, 244.

Nichols, D. (1985, September–October). "A Study: The Role-Perception Conflict of Campus Public Safety Departments." *Campus Law Enforcement Journal*, 4–7.

Nicholson, G., Rapp, J. A., & Carrington, F. (1987). "Campus Safety: A Legal Imperative." *Education Law Reporter*, 33: 981–998.

[Note] (1983, Spring). "Recourse for Rape Victims: Third Party Liability." *Harvard Women's Law Journal*, 4:105–160.

[Note.] (1989). "The Liability and Responsibility of Institutions of Higher Education for the On-Campus Victimization of Students. *Journal of College and University Law*, 16(1): 119–135.

[Note.] (1989). "Pennsylvania's College and University Security Information Act: The Effect of Campus Security Legislation on University Liability for Campus Crime." *Dickinson Law Review*, 94: 179–197.

Olmosk, K. E. (1972). *1972 Annual Handbook for Group Facilitators*. Washington, DC: National Training Laboratories, National Education Association.

O'Sullivan, C. (1991). "Acquaintance Gang Rape on Campus," in A. Parrot & L. Bechhofer (eds.), *Acquaintance rape: The hidden crime*. New York: John Wiley and Sons, 140–156.

Parrot, A. (1981). "Effects of Teacher Training on Sexuality Education." Doctoral dissertation, Cornell University, Ithaca, New York.

Parrot, A. (1985). "Comparison of Acquaintance Rape Patterns Among College Students in a Large Co-Ed University and a Small Women's College." Paper presented at the annual meeting of the Society for the Scientific Study of Sex, San Diego, CA.

Parrot, A. (1987). "Using Improvisational Theater Effectively in Acquaintance Rape Prevention Programs on College Campuses." A paper presented at the annual meeting of the Society for the Scientific Study of Sex, Atlanta.

Parrot, A. (1988). "University Policies and Procedures Regarding Acquaintance Rape." Paper presented at the twenty-first annual meeting of the American Association of Sex Educators, Counselors, and Therapists, San Francisco.

Parrot, A. (1989). "Acquaintance Rape Patterns and College Response in New York State." Paper presented at the New York State Conference on Acquaintance Rape on College Campuses, Albany.

Parrot, A. (1991). *Acquaintance Rape and Sexual Assault Training Manual*. 5th ed. Holmes Beach, FL: Learning Publications.

Parrot, A. (1992). "A Comparison of Male and Female Sexual Assault Victimization Experiences Involving Alcohol." Paper presented at the annual meeting of the Society for the Scientific Study of Sex, San Diego, CA.

Parrot, A. (1993). *Coping with Date Rape and Acquaintance Rape*. (2nd ed.) New York: Rosen Publishing Group.

Parrot, A., & Bechhofer, L. (eds.). (1991). *Acquaintance Rape: The Hidden Crime*. New York: John Wiley & Sons.

Parrot, A., Cummings, N., Marchell, T., & Hofher, J. (1993). "A Rape Awareness Prevention Model for Athletes." *Journal of American College Health*.

Parrot, A., & Lynk, R. (1983). "Acquaintance Rape in a College Population." Paper presented at the eastern regional meeting of the Society for the Scientific Study of Sex, Philadelphia, PA.

Pavela, Gary (1979–1980). "Limiting the 'Pursuit of Perfect Justice' on Campus: A Proposed Code of Student Conduct." *Journal of College and University Law*, 6(2): 137–160.

Picozzi, J. M., (1987). "University Disciplinary Process: What's Fair, What's Due, and What You Don't Get." *Yale Law Journal*, 96: 2132–2161.

Pineau, L. (1989). "Date Rape: A Feminist Analysis." *Journal of Law and Philosophy*, 8: 217–243.

Polonko, K., Parcell, S., & Teachman, J. (1986). "A Methodological Note on Sexual Aggression." Paper presented at the national convention of the Society for the Scientific Study of Sex, St. Louis.

Public Law 102-325. The Higher Education Amendment Act. (1992). United States Congress.

Richmond, D. R. (1989). "Students' Right to Counsel in University Disciplinary Proceedings." *Journal of College and University Law*, 15(3): 289–312.

Rothman, J. (1974). *Planning and Organizing for Change.* New York: Columbia University Press.

Rowland, J. (1985). *The Ultimate Violation.* New York: Doubleday and Company.

Sanday, P. (1990). *Fraternity Gang Rape.* New York: New York University Press.

Sandberg, G., Jackson, T., & Petretic-Jackson, P. (1987). "College Students' Attitudes Regarding Sexual Coercion and Aggression: Developing Educational and Preventive Strategies." *Journal of College Student Personnel*, 28: 302–311.

Sandler, B., & Ehrhart, J. K. (1985). *Campus Gang Rape: Party Games?* Washington, DC: Project on the Status and Education of Women, American Association of Colleges.

Sanford, L. (1985). *Women and Self-Esteem.* New York: Penguin.

Scales, P. (1980). "Barriers to Sex Education." *Journal of School Health*, 337–341.

"Silent No More." (1990, December 17). *People*, 94–99.

Smith, M. C. (1988). *Coping with Crime on Campus.* New York: Macmillan.

Smith, M. C. (1989, January–February). "Cops or Watchmen? Policy Considerations in the Role of Campus Security." *Campus Law Enforcement Journal.* 38–39.

Steinberg, T. N. (1991). "Rape on College Campuses: Reform Through Title IX." *Journal of College and University Law*, 18(1): 39–71.

Stoner E. N., II, & Cerminara, K. L. (1990). "Harnessing the 'Spirit of Insubordination': A Model Student Disciplinary Code." *Journal of College and University Law*, 17(2): 89–121.

Struckman-Johnson, C. (1991). "Male Victims of Acquaintance Rape," in A. Parrot & L. Bechhofer, *Acquaintance Rape: The Hidden Crime.* New York: John Wiley & Sons, 192–214.

Student Right to Know and Campus Security Act, Public Law 101-542 (1990). United States Congress.

Swanson, C. R., Chamelin, N. C., & Territo, L. (1981). *Criminal Investigation,* (2nd ed.) New York: Random House.

Sweet, E. (1985, October). "Date Rape: The Story of an Epidemic and Those Who Deny It." *Ms.*, 14: 56–59.

Swem, L. L. (1987). "Due Process Rights in Student Disciplinary Matters." *Journal of College and University Law*, 14(2): 359–382.

Taylor, R. J. (1992). "Fraternities, Sororities, and Campus Security." Paper presented at the sixth National Towson State Conference on Campus Violence, Baltimore.

Territo, L. (1983, September). "Campus Rape: Determining Liability." *Trial*, 100–103, 122.

Tierney, B. (1984). "Gang Rape on College Campuses." *Response to Violence in the Family and Sexual Assault*, 7(2): 1–2.

Walters, J., McKellar, A., Lyston, M., & Karme, L. (1981) What Are the Pros and Cons of Co-Ed Dorms? *Medical Aspects of Human Sexuality*, 15(8): 48–56.

Warshaw, R. (1988) *I Never Called It Rape: The Ms. Report on Recognizing, Fighting, and Surviving Date and Acquaintance Rape*. New York: Harper and Row.

Wisconsin Act 177 (1989). State of Wisconsin

Zweifel, D. (1992, April). "The Courts Say Campus Papers Can Report on Crime." *ASNE Bulletin*, p. 40.

Acknowledgments

We are fortunate to have had the assistance of many people in many fields in the preparation of this book. They have provided us with information and helped us to make our presentation more accurate and balanced. Some, including Steve Allen, Nina Cummings, Ned Lebow, Chris Tangen, Michael Cooper, and Congressman James Ramstad, deserve special thanks for the guidance and encouragement they provided. In addition we would like to thank (in no particular order) the many people who shared information with us and gave us technical assistance.

We thank the following lawyers and judges who gave generously of their time to provide crucial information: the late Frank Carrington, Lois Forer, Margie Hodges, Aileen Adams, Norman Pearlman, Carla Kjellberg, Richard Kaspari, Becky Palmer, Sheldon Steinbach, Jeffrey Newman, J. Michael Dady, Stephanie Lampert, Daniel Manning, George Lindner, Kimberley Sorrentino, Robert Wirth, John Lyons, Greg Miller, Eileen Wagner, Dean Leboeuf, Sylvia Clute, Tom Powell, Patrick Kelly, Natasha Roit, and Tom McCormick.

We would also like to thank the following people at all levels of campus administration for their insights: Harvey Kesselman, Michael Cooper, Richard Rankin, Carolyn McPherson, Toby Simon, Valerie Paton, Joan Carbone, Jodie Asbury, Brooke Gordon-Hare, and Jane Jervis.

We thank the following members of campus security forces for their considerable assistance: Randy Hausner, William Boyce, Ann Glavin, Dan Fite, Alena Johnson, and Bruce McBride.

We also thank some other people whose help has been very important to us: Chauquita Bailor, Clover Nicholas, Katie Koestner, Julie Steiner, Chip Tangen, Cathy Leonardi, David Clarke, Elizabeth Van Duyne, John Murray, Pat Hawley, Connie and Howard Clery,

Bernice Sandler, Claudette McShane, Victoria Nourse and the Student Press Law Center.

Our greatest thanks go to all those victims of campus sexual assault and their families, who, despite their pain, frustration, and anger, were nevertheless willing to share their stories and insights with us to help improve the problem of campus sexual assault.

Index